THE BIOLOGY OF AGING

John W. Brookbank

Professor Emeritus, Microbiology and Cell Science
Institute of Food and Agricultural Sciences
University of Florida
Gainesville

HARPER & ROW, PUBLISHERS, New York
Grand Rapids, Philadelphia, St. Louis, San Francisco,
London, Singapore, Sydney, Tokyo

1817

Sponsoring Editor: Glyn Davies
Project Editor: David Nickol
Art Direction/Cover Coordinator: Heather A. Ziegler
Cover Design: Wanda Lubelska Design
Production: Kewal K. Sharma

THE BIOLOGY OF AGING

Library of Congress Cataloging-in-Publication Data

Brookbank, John W.
    The biology of aging / John W. Brookbank.
        p.   cm.
    Includes bibliographical references.
    ISBN 0-06-041019-1
    1. Aging—Physiological aspects.   2. Aging.   I. Title.
    [DNLM: 1. Aging—physiology.   WT 104 B871b]
    QP86.B68   1990
    574.3'72—dc20
    DNLM/DLC
    for Library of Congress   89-26737
                                                          CIP

89   90   91   92   9 8 7 6 5 4 3 2 1

Contents

CHAPTER 4:   GENETICS AND THEORIES OF AGING 62

CHAPTER 5:   AGING AT THE CELLULAR LEVEL 89

CHAPTER 6:   CANCER, GENETIC DISEASE, AND CELLULAR AGING 109

Preface

The study of aging is a multidisciplinary one. In terms of the sciences, it involves biology at the base, followed in ascending order by medical sciences, psychology, and sociology. Other areas of study are also involved. For one, architects are concerned with the design of dwellings suited to aging people and the design of public facilities such that the elderly population has easy access. The umbrella term for all these areas of study is *gerontology*. In medicine, the speciality branch concerned with treatment of older patients is called *geriatrics*.

A text describing the biology of aging should include information on aging and senescence in all life forms. It would seem reasonable that mortality among living things might have a universal cause, it being a basic property of most, but not all, living organisms. As humans, we want the answer to the question of mortality to satisfy our curiosity about the nature of life and death and, perhaps more, to raise the question of our potential for immortality. Why do we grow old and die? Is there an alternative? Is molecular genetics powerful enough to alter our evolutionary destiny?

While these are all questions of the most basic sort, the answers, if and when they are found, may raise problems of their own. What is the price of extended longevity? Like many technological advances, extension of the human life span will certainly raise ethical and moral questions along with biological ones. We have seen what controversies fetal transplants, in vitro fertilization, and surrogate motherhood—to name a few—have brought. This isn't to say that humans cannot cope with these kinds of problems; we seem to adapt to scientific advances. But, along with technological progress, science should be aware of the resulting societal impacts.

Ideally, science and society should talk to each other to avoid surprises. In actuality, things seem to be a little more haphazard.

Meanwhile, the extension of human life span is some way off. The biology of aging is in the descriptive phase—the beginnings of understanding. There are no universal laws of aging and senescence as there are in molecular genetics. This level of understanding awaits more complete descriptive data for reduction to "principles of aging." For biologists and physicians, the aim is to gather information, propose theories, test theories, and gather more data, and so on.

While biologists explore the mysteries of mortality, other gerontologists are concerned with the quality of human life in the later years. There is little point in expanding longevity if there is no meaningful place for the resulting elderly population in society. There must be work, pleasure, medical care, and a role to play for life to be worth it.

Since the focus of this text is on human aging, with background material on aging in other life forms, some material has been included that is sociological and psychological. This material is included to illustrate the point that biological aging has direct behavioral and social consequences and also that some social situations have direct biological consequences. The boundaries are hazy between the parts of gerontology. The medical sections are included to illustrate the relations between aging and disease and are not intended as introductions into geriatric medicine.

It is hoped that each instructor will be able to use the text as a point of departure in developing the biology of aging in his or her own way. Advances in areas such as Alzheimer's disease and osteoporosis are so rapid that the time required to produce a book will automatically date the text. Again, the instructor must fill the voids.

The text is aimed at courses in the biology of aging often found in the biology department. I recognize that many if not most biology majors are preprofessional students, mainly in health-related fields, hence the focus on human aging. I also expect that psychology, sociology, and chemistry majors may find their way into such a course, and the level of this text is suitable for them.

Finally, I wish to thank the following reviewers who assisted in the development of this text: Professor Ray Wilson, Baylor University; Dr. James T. Glesel, University of Florida; Professor Robert Mitchell, Penn State University; Professor Dorothy Moses, University of Akron; Dr. Richard G. Ham, University of Colorado; Dr. Allen Allenspach, Miami University; and Professor John F. McCue, St. Cloud State University.

John W. Brookbank

Chapter
1
Aging in
the United States

INTRODUCTION

Gerontology as an organized discipline is now only about 40 years old. In attaining its present state of development, the science has progressed through an important phase of descriptive studies from which have emerged a variety of concepts and definitions of aging. In 1974 the National Institute on Aging (NIA) was established within the National Institutes of Health under the directorship of Dr. Robert Butler. The NIA was established in response to increases in the numbers of elderly people and is mandated by the Research on Aging Act of 1974 to deal with biomedical, social, and behavioral research. It is concerned not only with the biological basis of aging, but with the quality of the lives of elderly Americans.

Despite the advances in biology and medicine over the past 50 years, the alternative views regarding the relationship between aging and disease in humans remain much the same. One view holds that aging is primarily a genetically programmed process, but diseases of aging are primarily chance events largely attributable to environmental factors. Another view regards aging and diseases of aging as inseparable, intrinsic phenomena, with environmental factors playing a secondary role. Disease in this sense can be an infection, a change of organ function, a malignant growth, or a result of exposure to toxic materials (for example, alcohol and tobacco). Aging modifies the response of the body to external insults and modifies the bodily functions themselves.

Whatever is found to be the cause of age changes within the body, it remains that aging and diseases associated with aging are inextricably interwoven, and how they relate to each other is, at present, largely a matter of definitions. Since aging may enhance, minimize, or alter the presentation of disease in humans, a background understanding of the biology of aging is critical for those in the biomedical fields.

There have been many attempts to identify a single causal mechanism of aging—attempts that remain unsuccessful at this writing. It is certainly recognized that a diversity of factors is associated with aging, although the possibility remains that these diverse factors may be a manifestation of a single or at most a few causes. It is well recognized that individual humans age at different rates and that different organs in the same individual age at different rates. It is therefore difficult to conceive of any single, overall master control "clock." There is such a clock, or series of clocks, that operates during embryonic development. Organs are formed in a precise order in time as the embryo progresses from an undifferentiated state to its final form as a fetus. During embryonic development there is a sequential expression of genes that elicits the unfolding of the developmental program. It is tempting to think of aging as an extension of developmental phenomena.

A different theory of aging is that there are progressively greater alterations in body proteins with advancing years due to alterations or failures of gene expression, and these genetic changes may account for observed functional changes with age. Whether these changes are due to accumulation of presumably random damage or to a programmed senescence remains an open question. Increased susceptibility to some infections, cancers, and perhaps even such diseases as arteriosclerosis, diabetes, hypertension, and senile dementia are included among those conditions perhaps related to the alterations in structural and functional proteins that may occur with age. As with all theories of aging proposed to date, this "error theory" has serious shortcomings (Chapters 4 and 5). The contention remains that, in some as yet unknown way, genetically based biological aging has a significant, direct role in the origin of many of the bodily changes and diseases associated with aging.

In this chapter we will attempt to establish a vocabulary to deal with biological aging. We will also present a statistical approach to the study of aging in human populations. We will characterize the elderly population of the United States as to numbers, geography, sex, race, and level of disability.

DEFINITIONS

Extrinsic and Intrinsic Factors in Aging

It has proved useful, in studying life expectancies, to consider aging factors as either *extrinsic* (outside the body) or *intrinsic* (inside the body). Extrinsic factors include exercise, nutrition, some diseases, accident, and physical and mental stresses imposed by the environment. Intrinsic factors include the genetically determined life span and the program of embryonic development. True aging in the biological sense is limited to intrinsic factors, since they are the only restrictions on longevity of a life form existing under ideal, protective environmental conditions. Obviously, these conditions are met fully only in the laboratory, where small mammals can be raised with optimal diet under germ-free conditions. True aging is also progressive and almost universal among living things.

Aging and Senescence

In spite of medical and technological advances, all humans still grow old and die. The changes that happen in time (growth, sexual maturation, the accumulated wisdom of advancing years) are results of aging. The general decline of body systems in later years is referred to as *senescence.* The symptoms of old age vary greatly from one person to another. Some die from diseases affecting specific organs, such as the heart or kidneys. Others die from cancerous growths that destroy normal tissues. Some die from a generalized failure of more than one body system. Some succumb to infection or suffer accidental death. *Aging* beginning in the adult years, and the accompanying gradual impairment of body functions with advancing years (senescence), can therefore be defined as a process or processes that result(s) in increasing probability of death due to organ system failure, including failure or impairment of the immune system, which protects against infections.

Most wild animal populations show aging, but do not show senescence. Predation and environmental stress result in a constant loss of the weaker members of a wild population. In contrast, humans have a high rate of survival during the years of growth and maturation, followed by a period of declining survival in old age. Lack of predators and the presence of a protective environment lead to a sizable population of senescing human beings which is without parallel in wild animal populations.

Aging and Genetics

In some areas of the world genetic background is more relevant to the duration of life than environmental conditions. Modern civilization has reduced the impact of environment on longevity. The genetic basis for aging and longevity is not disputed. Longevity and rate of aging are species traits and are heritable as are other characteristics of the particular organism. The ascendant importance of genetics to human longevity is the result of medical progress in controlling detrimental environmental factors, including disease, malnutrition, and neonatal mortality.

The role of genetics is well illustrated by classical studies of the age at death of 58 sets of identical twins (Kallman and Sander, 1949). Identical twins arise from a single egg and are identical genetically. They show an average intrapair difference in age at death of about 37 months, whereas the difference in age at death of fraternal (two-egg) twins of the same sex is close to 78 months. The difference between identical twins is clearly smaller than the difference between two-egg twins. These results have been reviewed and confirmed by Bank and Jarvik (1978). Also, humans with long-lived parents and grandparents live, on the average, 6 years longer than those with parents and grandparents who died before the age of 50 (Abbott, Murphy, Bolling, and Abbey, 1974; Murphy, 1978).The observed greater longevity of females is not completely understood, but it may have a strong genetic component. It is possibly related to factors on the X chromosome.

In all these instances environment does play a role, but genetic background is unquestionably of critical importance.

Life Expectancy and Life Span

Humans have few natural predators, save themselves. Thus, in many areas of the world humans have a life expectancy that approaches the limiting life span of *Homo sapiens*. *Life expectancy* (or survivorship) is the average survival (in years) of individuals within a group all born on the same date. It is conventionally defined by the age at which 50 percent of the initial population are found as survivors. Life expectancy can be expressed for any age. At birth it is less than at 65 years, since at 65 an individual has lived through childhood diseases and has exhibited a capacity for survival in the face of increasing age (Table 1.1). In contrast, *life span* indicates the maximum age attained by the last surviving member of a group. A comparison between the two terms is represented graphically in Figure 1.1.

Life span values are difficult to compute in wild populations, since senescence rarely occurs. As the animal grows older, it becomes increasingly subject to environmental pressures and predation and rarely lives to the point of senescence. In human populations the life expectancy has been increased by 20 years since 1900 by reduction of infant mortality and by improved control of disease; the life span has remained unaffected. In the wild the life expectancy for animals can be increased by the disappearance of a predator, again without affecting the life span. Maximum longevity data are best obtained from captive populations of wild species. Domesticated animals usually have a longer life expectancy and life span than related wild species.

Another form of life expectancy data of considerable use to insurance companies can be generated by plotting the logarithm of the probability of death as a function of chronological age; the slope of this line is called the *age-specific death rate*. The mathematical expression was first expounded by Gompertz in 1825 (Jones, 1956). In present times the Gompertz function illustrates that after age 35 the probability of death doubles every seven years (Figure 1.2). A decrease in the slope of the Gompertz line means a decrease in the age-specific death rate or, in other words, a greater age interval between doublings of the probability of death. A shift

Table 1.1 EXPECTATION OF LIFE (IN YEARS) AT SELECTED AGES BY RACE AND
SEX; DEATH-REGISTRATION STATES, 1900–1902, AND UNITED STATES,
1959–1961, 1969–1971, 1979–1981, AND 1984

| Age and period | Total | White | | All other: | | | |
| | | Male | Female | Total | | Black | |
				Male	Female	Male	Female
At birth							
1984	74.7	71.8	78.7	67.4	75.0	65.6	73.7
1979–1981	73.88	70.82	78.22	65.63	74.00	64.10	72.88
1969–1971	70.75	67.94	75.49	60.98	69.05	60.00	68.32
1959–1961	69.89	67.55	74.19	61.48	66.47	—	—
1900–1902	49.24	48.23	51.08	—	—	32.54	35.04
At age 1 year							
1984	74.6	71.6	78.4	67.5	75.2	65.9	74.0
1979–1981	73.82	70.70	77.98	66.01	74.31	64.60	73.31
1969–1971	71.19	68.33	75.66	62.13	70.01	61.24	69.37
1959–1961	70.75	68.34	74.68	63.50	68.10	—	—
1900–1902	55.20	54.61	56.39	—	—	42.46	43.54
At age 20 years							
1984	56.1	53.3	59.8	49.3	56.7	47.6	55.5
1979–1981	55.46	52.45	59.44	47.87	55.88	46.48	54.90
1969–1971	53.00	50.22	57.24	44.37	51.85	43.49	51.22
1959–1961	52.58	50.25	56.29	45.78	50.07	—	—
1900–1902	42.79	42.19	43.77	—	—	35.11	36.89
At age 65 years							
1984	16.8	14.6	18.7	14.1	17.8	13.5	17.2
1979–1981	16.51	14.26	18.55	13.83	17.60	13.29	17.13
1969–1971	15.00	13.02	16.93	12.87	15.99	12.53	15.67
1959–1961	14.39	12.97	15.88	12.84	15.12	—	—
1900–1902	11.86	11.51	12.23	—	—	10.38	11.38

Source: U.S. Bureau of the Census, 1985.

to the left changes (increases) the intercept or death rate extrapolated to
age zero. This Y axis intercept is thus sometimes called the "vulnerability"
of a population. This empirical equation forms the basis for the actuarial
tables of the life insurance industry.

Effects of Improving Survivorship

As life expectancy approaches life span, we are improving survivorship
through lowering the number of deaths by disease and accident, a process
resulting in the "rectangularization" of the survivorship curve. Though at
first glance it would seem desirable for humans to push this process to the
limit, increased survivorship does have far-reaching consequences other
than life extension for the individual. The increase in numbers of people

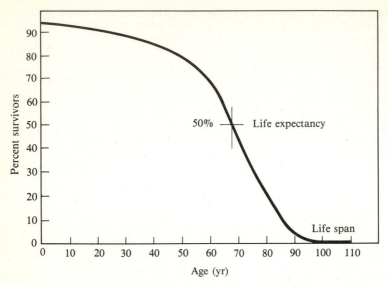

Figure 1.1 Survival curve; data from U.S. Census mortality tables of U.S. white males, 1939–1941. Life expectancy is the average age at 50 percent survival. Life span is the age maximum longevity (oldest known individual).

over age 65 resulting from increased life expectancy would be in addition to similar increases in the elderly population expected from the "baby boom" of the 1950s. One would hope that any improved survival rates would be accompanied by better health among elderly people, with concomitant higher productivity and employment and lower dependency. However, such changes would place severe stress on the economy by elderly people's remaining in the work force, and dependency would be shifted to younger workers competing for fewer open positions. The economy as a whole is extremely sensitive to changes in the distribution of the population among the various age categories.

NUMBERS OF ELDERLY PEOPLE

For simplicity we define the elderly population as those persons 65 years of age or older. At the same time it is important to realize that this population is not a homogeneous group with respect to social or biological factors. In a comparison of the population over 80 with the population in the 60 to 69 age bracket, there are many sharp differences in health, marital status, income, education, use of leisure time, and living arrangements. These differences are population differences and do not include the variation in rate of aging between individuals of the same age. Aging proceeds at different rates in different people. Functional disabilities appear earlier in life for some than for others. Such disabilities inevitably

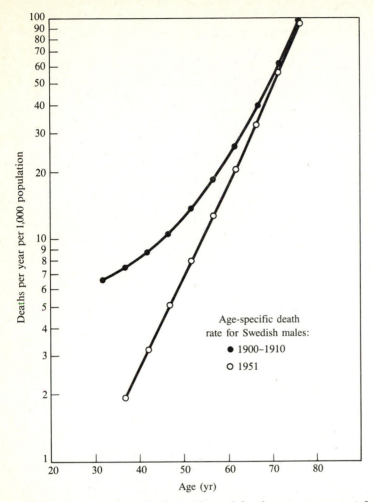

Figure 1.2 Gompertz plot (logarithm of death rate versus age) for Swedish males in 1900–1910 and in 1951. The slope is defined as the age-specific death rate. The Y intercept is defined as the vulnerability of the population (death rate at age zero). (From H. B. Jones. *Advances in Biol Med Physics,* 4:281 1956 Copyright 1956 by Academic Press, New York. Used with permission.)

appear in all with passage of time. Population studies of age groups are necessarily defined in terms of the chronological age of the population. In these populations the aggregate aging process, physiological age, and functional age follow chronological age closely. Studies of populations mask individual variability.

In 1900 there were approximately 3.1 million people over age 65 in the United States. By 1980 the number had increased to 27.1 million. Census bureau predictions indicate that by 2000 those over 65 will number 32 million. Not only has the number of elderly increased, but also the proportion of elderly in the population has changed from 4.1 percent in 1900 to 11 percent in 1980 and to a projected 11.9 percent in 2000 (assuming constant mortality rates over time). The proportion is obtained by dividing the number of persons over 65 by the total population. In addition to increasing in both proportion of population and number, the population over 65 has in itself grown older. For example, the portion of the over 65 who are 75 and older will continue to increase until the year 2000. In 1976 38 percent were over 75; by 2000 this will rise to somewhere near 45 percent.

The proportion of elderly in the population is more difficult to project than the number over 65 since to obtain the proportion one must also project fertility rates for the population as a whole (Table 1.2). Projections assuming three different fertility rates (low rate, replacement rate, and high rate) are shown in Figure 1.3. From a postwar high of 3.8 births per woman at the peak of the baby boom, the total fertility rate in the United States has fallen to 1.8, where it has remained unchanged for almost a decade (Westoff, 1986). This is below the replacement rate (the rate that, excluding in- and out-migrations of the population, would keep the population at a constant level). The decline is characteristic of most Western countries (Figures 1.4, 1.5, 1.6),some of which have fallen to below 1.5 births per woman. The U.S. population is showing the effects of aging brought about by the low fertility rate. Were it not for the continued

Table 1.2 PROJECTIONS OF THE U.S. POPULATION BY 2025 AND 2080

Assumed fertility rate	Projections (millions) with assumed net annual immigration of		
	250,000	450,000	750,000
Year 2025			
1.6	266	276	293
1.9	291	301	320
2.3	318	330	349
Year 2080			
1.6	203	224	261
1.9	286	311	355
2.3	422	453	509

Projections on the assumption of moderate improvement in longevity (life expectancy at birth is assumed to increase gradually from 77 to 81) with different assumptions about future fertility and net immigration.

Source: C. F. Westoff, Science 234:554, 1986. Copyright 1986 by AAAS. Used with permission.

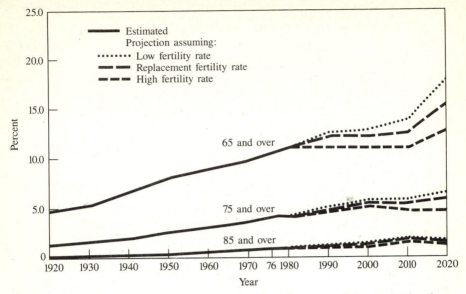

Figure 1.3 Projections of percentages of total population at older ages. The three fertility rates on which projections are based are low, or 1.6 births per woman; replacement, 2.0 births; and high, 2.3 births. (From J. S. Siegel. In Haynes and Feinleib, eds., *Epidemiology of Aging.* NIH Publication No. 80-969. 1980.)

in-migration, the U.S. population would stop growing and begin to decline before the middle of the next century. The low fertility rate is due mainly to the delay of marriage and to the widespread use of contraception, with heavy reliance on surgical sterilization as a contraceptive method. Judging from events in other Western countries and our own historical experience of two centuries of fertility decline, the prognosis is for continued low fertility in the United States. There is an absence of social trends that would counteract the forces contributing to the decline in birth rate.

The declining birth rate will have effects on the *dependency ratio,* the number of elderly people divided by the numbers of younger people remaining in the work force as supporters of the elderly population. There will be more retirees drawing social security in proportion to those paying into it than would be the case where there was a higher birth rate. What actually happens in the future will depend to some extent on the age profile of the immigrants to the United States.

POPULATION CHARACTERISTICS

This section considers vital and social statistics, or the demography, of the present U.S. population. A useful overall reference on demographic trends is Siegel (1980).

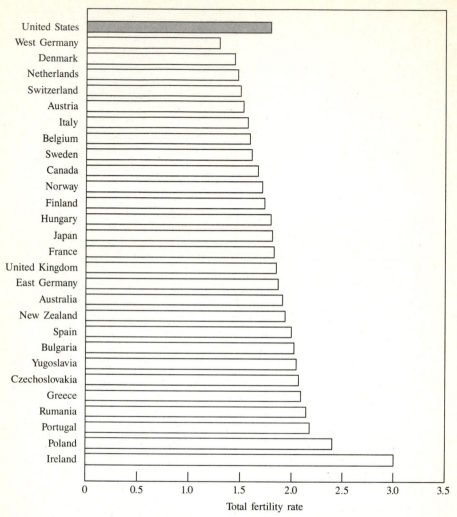

Figure 1.4 Total fertility rate in developed countries in the early 1980s. (From C. F. Westoff, *Science* 234:554, 1986. Copyright by AAAS. Used with permission.)

Composition by Sex

For each successive age group over age 65, females outnumber males by increasing margins. In the 65 to 69 age group the number of females per 100 males is 123. This increases to 250 in the population 85 and over. These data have considerable significance for the medical care system, since females are heavier users of services than males. The increased survival value of females is found, to a lesser extent, in all advanced human societies in the world. In fact, female survival is one of the most pervasive age-related phenomena in the entire animal kingdom. In humans there

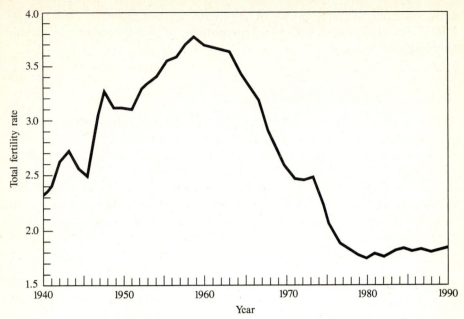

Figure 1.5 U.S. total fertility rate, 1940 to 1985. (From C. F. Westoff. *Science* 234:554, 1986. Copyright 1986 by AAAS. Used with permission.)

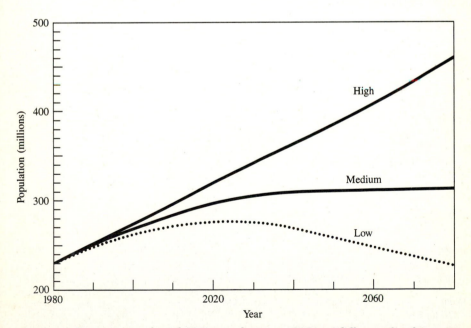

Figure 1.6 Projections of total U.S. population to 2080 at different fertility rates. (From C. F. Westoff. Science 234:554, 1986. Copyright 1986 by AAAS. Used with permission.)

is no evidence of convergence of the death rates of the two sexes (Siegel, 1980). Sex differences provide a promising area for research into the mechanisms of aging.

Geographical Distribution

There are three ways in which the percentage of elderly in a state or region can change: by out-migration of younger people, by in-migration of older people, and by a change in fertility rates. Interstate migration rates tend to be low; older people tend to remain in rural areas or large urban centers. The high proportion of elderly people in rural, nonfarm areas is mainly due to the departure of younger people from the small towns and the movement off the farm of those elderly people who have become unable with age to manage their farms. The low percent of people over 65 on farms is thus due to their leaving the farms and also to the higher birth rate among those remaining on farms. About 34 percent of the older population live in large cities (52 percent of blacks). About 27 percent live in rural areas. In many states with a high proportion of the over 65 population (for example, Florida, Arkansas), the dominant factors are the out-migration of younger people and the in-migration of the elderly (Table 1.3). A recent review of migratory patterns and their economic implications is provided in Crown (1988).

Table 1.3 MIGRATION OF U.S. POPULATION BY REGIONS, 1975–1980

Region and age (yr)	Net migrants (thousands)
Northeast	
Under 65	−1,348
Over 65	−138
Northcentral	
Under 65	−1,008
Over 65	−165
South	
Under 65	+1,557
Over 65	+207
West	
Under 65	+797
Over 65	+96

Source: U.S. Bureau of the Census, 1981.

Institutional Care

According to census data, some 5 percent of those over 65 reside in institutions, 96 percent of this 5 percent in nursing homes. Most of these residents are white (94 percent) females (65 percent). Minorities and males tend to be underrepresented in institutions compared with their percentages in the population as a whole. Within the over-65 population, 20 percent will be institutionalized in a nursing home at some time in their lives.

Mortality

In general, longevity in the United States has increased considerably in the twentieth century. In recent years the percentage surviving of those over 65 has increased (Table 1.4). The observed age-specific decline in mortality from chronic diseases is due mainly to decreases in cardiovascular disease. As a result, there has been an increase in life expectancy among those over 65. In this section we will examine mortality rates for the elderly population for some specific diseases and the distribution of these diseases within subgroups of the over-65 population.

Causes of Death   A comparison of the 10 leading causes of death in the United States in 1900 and 1977 is given in Table 1.5. The differences are striking and reflect advances in the treatment of bacterial and viral infections using antibiotics and vaccines. Heart disease and cancer were dread diseases in the 1900s as well as in 1959; it's just that fewer people lived long enough to develop these maladies. Death from some form of pulmonary infection usually intervened in advance of the development of the pattern of senescence more characteristic of old age in present times.

Table 1.6 gives the expected gain in life expectancy after a hypothetical elimination of various causes of death.

Sex Differences   Age-specific mortality rates are higher for males. At birth males outnumber females by a ratio of 105 to 100. With advancing age the sex ratio declines continuously due to higher male mortality (see Tables 1.1, 1.4).

The difference in mortality rate has been increasing until quite recently. This divergence of male and female death rates has been occurring in spite of the fact that differences in life styles between the sexes have diminished. The divergence is found in countries where males and females occupy similar occupational roles; for example, in the USSR females enjoy a 10-year advantage over males in life expectancy at age 65. Among priests and nuns in Catholic teaching orders, similar life styles still result in an excess of male mortality. Though environmental factors are

Table 1.4 PERCENT SURVIVING FROM BIRTH TO SELECTED AGES AND MEDIAN
AGE AT DEATH BY RACE AND SEX; DEATH-REGISTRATION STATES,
1900–1902, AND UNITED STATES, 1959–1961, 1969–1971,
1979–1981, AND 1984

Age and period	Total	White		All other Total		Black	
		Male	Female	Male	Female	Male	Female
Percent surviving from birth							
To age 1 year							
1984	98.9	98.9	99.2	98.3	98.5	98.0	98.3
1979–1981	98.7	98.8	99.0	97.9	98.3	97.7	98.1
1969–1971	98.0	98.0	98.5	96.6	97.2	96.4	97.1
1959–1961	97.4	97.4	98.0	95.3	96.2	—	—
1900–1902	87.6	86.7	88.9	—	—	74.7	78.5
To age 20 years							
1984	98.1	97.9	98.6	97.1	97.8	96.7	97.5
1979–1981	97.7	97.5	98.4	96.4	97.4	96.1	97.2
1969–1971	96.7	96.5	97.6	94.3	95.9	94.1	95.7
1959–1961	96.1	95.9	97.1	93.1	94.7	—	—
1900–1902	77.2	76.4	79.0	—	—	56.7	59.1
To age 65 years							
1984	78.6	74.4	85.5	62.2	77.4	58.3	74.9
1979–1981	77.1	72.4	84.8	58.5	75.4	55.1	73.3
1969–1971	71.9	66.3	81.6	49.6	66.1	47.5	64.7
1959–1961	71.1	65.8	80.7	51.4	60.8	—	—
1900–1902	40.9	39.2	43.8	—	—	19.0	22.0
Median age at death							
1984	78.2	75.1	82.1	70.7	78.8	68.9	77.3
1979–1981	77.6	74.2	81.8	69.0	77.8	67.4	76.6
1969–1971	74.9	71.5	79.5	64.8	72.8	63.8	72.2
1959–1961	74.3	71.4	78.5	65.6	70.6	—	—
1900–1902	58.4	57.2	60.6	—	—	29.8	34.3

Source: U.S. Bureau of the Census, 1985.

important, genetics seems to be of critical importance. The observation
that the sex difference in mortality has been growing until quite recently
may reflect the changes in causes of mortality over the years; the sharp
drop in the importance of infectious diseases and maternal mortality and
the increased importance of degenerative conditions as causes of death
serve to focus attention on the effects of genetic and biological factors as

Table 1.5   10 LEADING CAUSES OF DEATH IN TOTAL
                  U.S. POPULATION, 1900 AND 1977

Rank	Cause of death	Death rate per 100,000 population
	1900	
1	Pneumonia, influenza	202
2	Tuberculosis	194
3	Diarrhea, enteritis	143
4	Heart disease	137
5	Stroke	107
6	Nephritis	89
7	Accidents	72
8	Cancer	64
9	Diphtheria	40
10	Meningitis	34
	1977	
1	Heart disease	332
2	Cancer	179
3	Stroke	84
4	Accidents, motor vehicle	23
	Accidents, all other	25
5	Pneumonia, influenza	24
6	Diabetes	15
7	Cirrhosis of liver	14
8.5	Arteriosclerosis	13
8.5	Suicide	13
10	Early infancy disease	11

Source: From J. S. Siegel. In S. G. Haynes and M. Feinleib, eds., *Epidemiology of Aging.* NIH Publication No. 80-969. U.S. Government Printing Office, Washington, D.C., 1980.

causes of death. Longevity is a heritable species trait, and it appears that the difference in longevity between the sexes has a strong genetic component as well.

Racial Differences   Comparing whites with blacks and other races, one finds the death rates higher for nonwhites below age 65 and between the ages of 65 and 74. Between the ages of 75 and 79 there is a crossover in the data resulting in lower death rates for nonwhites.

Little information exists regarding the relative contributions of environment and genetics to the racial mortality gap. Much may be accounted

Table 1.6   GAIN IN LIFE EXPECTANCY IN THE UNITED STATES
AFTER ELIMINATION OF VARIOUS CAUSES OF DEATH

Cause of death	Gain (yr)	
	At birth	At age 65
Major cardiovascular disease	11.8	11.4
Malignant neoplasms	2.5	1.4
Motor vehicle accidents	0.7	0.1
Influenza, pneumonia	0.5	0.2
Diabetes mellitus	0.2	0.2
Infective and parasitic disease	0.2	0.1

Source: From J. S. Siegel. In S. G. Haynes and M. Feinleib, eds., *Epidemiology of Aging.* NIH Publication No. 80-969. U.S. Government Printing Office, Washington, D.C., 1980.

for by differences in socioeconomic status. In recent years there have been greater improvements in black mortality under age 65 than in white mortality. Over age 65 there has been little change in the differences between races with time.

Morbidity and Disability

As life expectancy increases, intrinsic or endogenous disease also increases. Unfortunately, data on morbidity and disability due to these conditions are limited, making an assessment of the functional status of the elderly population difficult. The data here derive from the National Health Interview Survey (NHIS), as compiled by Colvez and Blanchet (1981). The survey has been conducted continually since 1957 on a probability sample of 120,000 noninstitutionalized respondents.

Disabilities can be short or long term. Short-term disability is measured in numbers of restricted activity days per 100 persons. We will focus on long-term disability, which is expressed as a prevalence per 10,000 persons (Table 1.7). It is broken down into three categories: severe (unable to carry out main activity), moderate (limited in amount or kind of main activity), and slight (not limited in main activity, but otherwise limited). The data are for all ages. Main activity includes work, school, and housework.

Long-term disability has increased in the time selected in the table (1966–1974), with greatest increases in severe long-term disability. For those 65 and older the prevalence of limitation of activity was high, but there was little change in this prevalence over the period. Changes have occurred in the causes of disability over age 65. Mental and nervous conditions have decreased, while circulatory diseases (excluding heart and hypertension) have increased as causes of disability.

Table 1.7 VARIATION IN THE PREVALENCE OF LIMITATION OF ACTIVITY IN THE UNITED STATES BETWEEN 1966 AND 1974 BY SEX, AGE, AND CATEGORY OF LIMITATION OF ACTIVITY

Limitation of activity	Under 17 years		17–44 years		45–64 years		Over 65 years	
	Male	Female	Male	Female	Male	Female	Male	Female
Severe: main activity impossible								
Prevalence 1974*	25	17	143	67	937	214	2,983	816
Variation 1966–1974 (%)	+32	+21	+57	+76	+106	+78	+38	+6
Moderate: main activity restricted								
Prevalence 1974	187	150	402	511	1,046	1,595	1,506	2,718
Variation 1966–1974 (%)	+148	+118	+12	+41	−12	+46	−44	+9
Slight: not limited in main activity, but other types of restrictions								
Prevalence 1974	188	163	371	278	545	493	485	780
Variation 1966–1974 (%)	+69	+66	+51	+2	+25	−13	+6	−3

*Prevalence per 10,000 inhabitants.

Source: Adapted from A. Colvez and M. Blanchet. American Journal of Public Health 71:464, 1981.

METHODS OF STUDY

The principal methods of study of the effects of aging on populations are the cross-sectional and longitudinal designs. The *cross-sectional method* employs measurements made at the same time on a large number of subjects, presumed to be matched for other variables to exclude environmental effects. The *longitudinal method* involves serial measurements of specific variables on the same subjects as aging occurs. It thus identifies age changes in individuals as well as average differences between groups of subjects of different ages but otherwise similar backgrounds.

Cross-Sectional Method

Age changes in individuals are not evaluated by the cross-sectional method. Rather, the researcher arrives at an average value for any particular aging variable measured. Caution is necessary in interpreting results, since cross-sectional changes include changes due to particular social or environmental conditions which may be confounded with age-related changes; specific conditions occur differentially in subjects from different birth cohorts. The primary advantage of the cross-sectional approach is the speed with which age-related changes can be measured in groups of subjects of different ages.

Effects Due to Birth Cohort Differences   A birth cohort is a group of persons all of whom were born in a given year. Obviously, different cohorts differ from each other in ways that have nothing to do with aging. A cohort group born in 1900 would have a smaller percentage of members who finished high school compared with a 1940 cohort. Thus any test based on mental performance will be measuring effects of educational level as well as aging. Economic conditions early in life also affect older subjects differently from younger ones. Those who were 70 in 1980 were exposed to the depression beginning in 1929, when they were 20 years old. Those born in 1940 have no comparable event in their early life history. Interruptions of life course due to wars, epidemics, and other major events also create cohort differences that influence test results in ways that cannot be isolated from age-related results using the cross-sectional method.

Effects Due to Differential Mortality   As a population ages in cross-sectional studies, it becomes more and more selected for those who survive. Death occurs more frequently among older subjects than among the young. By 70 years the cohort population available for study has been halved. The averages based on populations of young adults are based on observations of people, some of whom will not live to their seventieth year; data from older subjects represent data from the select group that has survived. Death does not occur randomly in a population; it is more frequent among those whose traits add up to greater susceptibility to serious disease and death.

Effects Due to Disease   The aim of cross-sectional studies is the assessment of changes due to aging and senescence. Many diseases increase in frequency with advancing age and may influence results of tests designed to measure changes due solely to age. Subjects suffering from impaired respiratory function due to lung disease or smoking will not give accurate data in tests designed to measure level of physical endurance as a function of age alone. Disease-impaired subjects should be excluded from such test groups, and there is no reliable way to ensure that this has been done.

Many investigators concerned with social and behavioral problems simply ignore the disease problem, while others set health criteria for inclusion in the study that are either too exclusive or superficial. Commonly, a few specific diseases such as coronary artery disease or diabetes are identified. Unfortunately, in many studies health status is self-evaluated; if a subject says he or she is in good health, the investigator accepts this. Detailed screening by a physician is critical to future interpretation of any of these studies.

Longitudinal Method

Longitudinal studies overcome some of the limitations of the cross-sectional method, but they require much more time, since variables are measured in the same individuals as they age. A rate of aging may be obtained by the longitudinal method for any particular variable the investigator wants to follow. Instead of making several measurements over time, a researcher might obtain information about past events by taking a history at the first visit, make a current assessment, and measure the outcome or subsequent condition at a later date. Such evaluations will, of course, be limited by the accuracy of the history, which is limited by the accuracy of the subjects' recall of remote events. Ideally, a longitudinal study should involve periodic objective assessments of many variables to assess the effects of aging in individuals and groups.

Problems with Longitudinal Data   A problem faced by investigators using the longitudinal method is the difficulty in finding a large sample of people willing to commit to long-term evaluation and in maintaining the sample size throughout; subjects may move away or die or simply drop out. Studies should be designed to maintain a constant sample size within each age decade during the ongoing investigation. New subjects must resemble those they replace as closely as possible. One study, the Baltimore Longitudinal Study of Aging (BLSA), uses a self-selection strategy in recruitment of subjects that tends to maintain a uniform character of the population subgroups. Many participants are recommended by friends or relatives already in the study.

Screening of subjects is a critical aspect in the design of longitudinal studies if one is to be able to say that certain changes observed in performance over time are due to aging.

It is also difficult to find funding for such large undertakings. Support agencies cannot expect to see significant results early in the project; the data are simply not there. Many investigators have opted to restrict themselves to specific life periods for longitudinal analysis, to overcome difficulties with staffing, recruitment, attrition, and financing.

Longitudinal studies have been initiated by a number of groups of investigators with different interests and goals, and communication among investigators of different groups has often been minimal. A series of six conferences held between 1972 and 1975 brought together the investigators from the major longitudinal study groups. The meetings provided a forum for exchange and discussion of the problems associated with the operation of such studies. The idea of pooling data from these various studies was considered and found to be impractical because of systematic differences in methods of selection of subjects for study and methods of measurement of variables. Even though direct pooling of data is not feasible, comparison of aging trends discovered by the different groups can be made. To date women have been grossly underrepresented, and no studies have utilized blacks or other ethnic groups as identifiable subsets. Data on these groups derive from cross-sectional studies, such as census data.

Use of Longitudinal Data   Longitudinal studies, properly designed, may be expected to answer certain critical questions over an extended period of operation: (1) What is the rate of change in individuals for certain variables? (2) What is the diversity among individuals measured for the same variable? (3) Is there a general aging factor, or does each organ system age independently of all others? (4) How are changes in different variables related in different subjects? (5) Do critical events in the life cycle affect aging? (6) Can levels of performance at a given age be used as predictors of life expectancy? (7) Can aging be distinguished from disease? (8) Does age per se influence the progression of disease states such as arteriosclerosis?

Longitudinal studies also provide cross-sectional data about age-dependent differences in groups of normal individuals. Average differences between groups or the average regression of a variable with age can be derived from longitudinal data. To assess the outcome for a particular individual or the effects of specific events on later performance, the subjects must be reexamined at a later time.

A major use of longitudinal information is in the search for risk factors related to disease and death. Risk factors include the presence or absence of such habits as smoking, dietary intake of fat, blood pressure, and family longevity. Longitudinal studies also make possible the assessment of critical levels of performance. Kidney clearance, for example, may show a decline with age, but the clinical significance of such a decline lies in whether or not it relates directly to an increased likelihood of death or disease. One can also search longitudinally for the effects of specific events in life history, such as cessation of smoking, death of a spouse, retirement, loss of mobility, by comparing measurements of vital functions before the event with those made afterward.

The Baltimore Longitudinal Study of Aging   The Baltimore Longitudinal Study of Aging (BLSA) was begun in 1958 to trace the effects of aging in humans (Shock et al., 1984). It attempts to distinguish between true aging and other factors, such as disease, socioeconomic conditions, and educational background, that may become pronounced with time but have little to do with the underlying mechanisms of human aging. The study was begun with 1,000 male volunteers ranging in age from 17 to 96. Most are from the upper-middle class segment of the general population.

The BLSA scientists have adopted the theory that aging is distinct from disease, unlike many who maintain that there is no unique biological process of aging distinct from disease. The BLSA has therefore excluded data obtained from subjects with specific diseases when those diseases would alter the function under consideration. This does not mean that the disease effect on aging has been eliminated, only that this artifact has been maximally controlled and minimized. Mistakes can be made, and disease conditions can be inadvertently overlooked. The BLSA has contributed to knowledge of normal aging, and some of the data in Chapters 6 and 7 are derived from this study.

The Duke Studies   The Duke Studies consist of two longitudinal investigations. The first, started in 1955, addressed the basic physical, mental, and social processes involved in normal aging and the causes of variation in these processes. The study involved 267 men and women aged 60 to 90 years. The results are summarized in Busse and Maddox (1980). Remarkably, the results contradict averages found in cross-sectional studies in that there were a number of subjects in the longitudinal study who showed no decline in health status or intellectual function over a number of years.

The second study (1983 report) consisted of 261 men and 241 women aged 45 to 70 years. It measured the effects of spousal death, serious illness, and menopause on normal individuals living in the community. This study added more detail to the first study and the general conclusions were not substantially altered.

The Framingham Study   The Framingham Study was designed specifically to measure the determining factors in the development of heart disease. It was initiated in 1949 by the U.S. Public Health Service and was later transferred to the National Heart Institute. Two-thirds of the 30- to 59-year-old population of Framingham, Massachusetts, was selected from published lists of all residents, it being recognized that serial examination of a large number of subjects would be required.

Some risk factors have been identified, and it was demonstrated that these factors may be additive in their effects on the heart. The factors identified are cigarette smoking, elevated blood pressure, elevated serum cholesterol, low density lipoproteins, low vital capacity, obesity, and diabetes. These findings are relected in public health programs designed to reduce the incidence of cardiovascular disease (Framingham Study, 1978).

SUMMARY

The terms aging and senescence are sometimes incorrectly used interchangeably. Aging refers to all events happening within time following birth and includes growth, sexual maturation, and the acquisition of knowledge and experience. Senescence refers to the changes occurring toward the end of a normal life span which are associated with a decline of vigor and increased probability of death. Life span is defined as a genetic characteristic of a species, while life expectancy is strongly dependent on environmental factors. The longevity (life span) of females is greater than that of males, a fact presumably related to genetic factors.

The proportion of elderly people in the population of the United States and most Western countries is increasing. This increase is due mainly to increased life expectancy and lowered birth rate. In the United States rural, nonfarm communities and large metropolitan centers have a high proportion of elderly people.

The causes of death have changed during the twentieth century, reflecting medical advances in neonatal care and treatment of infectious diseases.

The methods of study of aging in human populations are of two basic sorts, longitudinal and cross-sectional. Longitudinal studies offer the best means of evaluating changes over time that are solely the product of aging. The difficulties lie in selecting disease-free subjects who are representative of the population as a whole, in maintaining a group of test subjects once selected, in maintaining staff continuity, and in finding adequate funding over long periods of time. Longitudinal studies also yield cross-sectional data.

REFERENCES

Abbott, M. H., E. A. Murphy, D. R. Bolling, and H. Abbey. The familial component of longevity. A study of offspring of nonagenarians. *Johns Hopkins Medical Journal* 134:1, 1974.

Bank, L., and L. F. Jarvik. A longitudinal study of aging human twins. In E. L. Schneider, ed., *Genetics of Aging.* Plenum Press, New York, 1978.

Busse, E. W., and G. L. Maddox. *Final Report, the Duke Longitudinal Studies. 1955–80.* Duke University Medical Center, Center for Study of Aging and Development, Durham, N.C., 1980.

———. *The Duke Longitudinal Studies on Aging and the Aged.* Springer Verlag, New York, 1983.

Colvez, A., and M. Blanchet. Disability trends in the United States population, 1966–76. *American Journal of Public Health* 71:464, 1981.

Crown, W. H. State economic implications of elderly interstate migration. *The Gerontologist* 28:533, 1988.

Framingham Study. USHEW Publication No. (NIH) 74–599. U.S. Government Printing Office, Washington, D.C., 1978.

Jones, H. B. A special consideration of the aging process, disease, and life expectancy. *Advances in Biological and Medical Physics* 4:281, 1956.

Kallman, F. J., and G. Sander. Twin studies on senescence. *American Journal of Psychiatry* 106:29, 1949.

Murphy, E. A. Genetics of longevity in man. In E. L. Schneider, ed., *The Genetics of Aging.* Plenum Press, New York, 1978

Shock, N. W., R. C. Greulich, R. Andres, D. Arenberg, P. T. Costa Jr., E. G. Lakatta, and J. D. Tobin. *Normal Human Aging, the Baltimore Longitudinal Study.* NIH Publication No. 84–2450. U.S. Government Printing Office, Washington, D.C., 1984.

Siegel, J. S. Recent and prospective demographic trends for the elderly population and some indications for health care. In S. G. Haynes and M. Feinleib, eds., *Epidemiology of Aging.* NIH Publication No. 80–969. U.S. Government Printing Office, Washington, D.C., 1980.

Westoff, C. F. Fertility in the United States. *Science* 234:554, 1986.

Chapter
2
Aging in
Lower Life Forms

PERSPECTIVES FOR HUMAN AGING

We are specifically concerned with aging and life span in humans. In later chapters we will discuss a number of theories of aging derived from studies of intact mammals and cells of mammals, and we will discover that there exists no definitive information that favors one particular theory of human aging and senescence to the exclusion of all others. The lack of a unified theory of biological aging is frustrating to biologists and physicians.

The use of model systems has provided the means of understanding other enigmas in biology. The most notable example of this approach was the use of the bacterium *Escherichia coli* for unraveling the mystery of the universal genetic code. Thus, while we remain in this quandry concerning the nature of human aging, it might be valuable to review all potentially relevant biological systems that might serve as models for human aging. For example, we will see that some living things do not seem to undergo senescence at all. Studies of such life forms might shed some light on the nature of their immortality and lead to better understanding of how it is that other forms of life senesce with age. It is perhaps unlikely that the diverse world of living things has a single, universal basis of mortality, but knowledge of the patterns of senescence that do exist is essential to a complete understanding of the problem.

In this chapter life forms other than mammals will be considered— plants, the major groups of invertebrate animals, and the nonmammalian vertebrates (fish, amphibians, reptiles, and birds). Mammals have Chapter 3 all to themselves. A valuable reference for material covered in this chapter is Comfort (1979). Senescence in plants is well summarized by Nooden and Thompson (1985). A short review of model systems amenable to genetic analysis of aging is provided by Martin and Turker (1988).

Table 2.1 shows the extremes of life span encountered among living creatures. For purposes of comparison, a short list of life spans for various mammals is given in Table 2.2. Variability among plants is most extreme. Animal groups are diverse in tissue organization, reproduction, temperature regulation, and metabolic rate—all of which are related to life span in one way or another. It is reasonable to assume that all animal groups (phyla) include some species with relatively long life spans that end in senescence, though it is difficult to distinguish death by accident from aging and senescence in natural populations. It is not reasonable to assume that senescence results from identical causes in all cases.

From an evolutionary point of view, it has been convincingly argued that only those species showing partitioning between germ line and somatic cells will show senescence. Species producing solely by asexual means, such as by fission, do not show senescence since a decline in vigor of the parent unit would lead, by natural selection, to the elimination of that life form. It has also been postulated that lack of selective pressure following the reproductive phase leads to accumulation of deleterious traits that result in senescence, whereas selection for positive attributes is more rigorous in those stages of life preceding and at the beginning of the reproductive phase. It has been suggested that some genes may be selected for positive effects in early life that have negative effects in later years after reproductive activity has declined. Selection for delayed fertility should in theory lead to selection for delayed senescence (Rose, 1984; Rose and Graves, 1989). We will encounter support for these evolutionary viewpoints in connection with studies involving the fruit fly, Drosophila.

To summarize, if aging and senescence are byproducts of natural selection acting on fitness characters, there is then no more reason to expect universality in aging mechanisms than there is to expect universality in underlying mechanisms of reproduction. Senescence is not physiologically necessary, and it arises only when selective pressure fades with increasing age. For this reason, it is concluded that aging is not a general cell property (Rose and Graves, 1989). Aging is as likely, or unlikely, to have a uniform mechanistic basis as flight, respiration, or vision. Among mammals, there is some uniformity in reproductive mechanisms relating to derivation from common ancestral stock. Thus, mammalian species should share some uniform aging mechanisms. But there is no reason to expect the same mechanisms to arise in other, unrelated phyla. In this light, the search for a *universal* mechanism of senescence is likely to continue to be futile.

AGING AND SENESCENCE IN PLANTS AND INVERTEBRATE ANIMALS

Plants

Senescence is an active, internally controlled process that leads to death. The process occurs at all levels of plant life, from cells through organs to whole organisms, and is intimately associated with many phases of plant

Table 2.1 LIFE SPANS OF VARIOUS PLANTS AND ANIMALS

Group	Species	Approximate maximum age (yr)
Plants		
Trees and shrubs	Italian cypress	2,000
	Bristlecone pine	5,000+
	Alder	100
	Rhododendron	50
Animals		
Protozoa	Various ciliates	1
	Amoeba	2
Sponges	Commercial	50
Coelenterates	Anemone	90
	Hydra	2
	Coral	28
Flatworms	Tapeworm	35+
	Planaria	2
Nematodes	*Filaria bancrofti*	17
	Hookworm	12
Annelids	Sabellid tube worm	10
	Earthworm	10
	Leech	27
Rotifers	Various species	60 days
Spiders	*Tarantula*	15
Insects	Termites	40
	Fruit fly	80 days
	Honey bee (queen)	6
Echinoderms	Starfish	7
Mollusks	Octopus (female), dies after mating)	3
	Octopus (male)	4
	Chiton	12
Vertebrates		
Various fish		1–60+
Various amphibians		1–52+
Reptiles	Tortoise	170
	Rattlesnake	19
	Alligator	56
Birds	Eagle owl	65+
	Canada goose	32

Source: Compiled from several sources.

Table 2.2   LIFE SPANS OF VARIOUS MAMMALS

Group	Common name	Approximate maximum age (yr)
Primates	Human	113
	Gorilla	39
	Rhesus monkey	29
Ungulates	Horse	60
	Domestic cattle	30
	Sheep	20
Proboscids	Indian elephant	70
Carnivores	Domestic cat	28
	Domestic dog	34
	Brown bear	37
	Leopard	25
Cetaceans	(Blue) whale	80
Rodents	Gray squirrel	15
	Laboratory mouse	2
	House rat	5
	Rabbit	13
	Golden hamster	4
	Shrew	2

Source: Compiled from several sources.

development. It seems to have more distinct and diverse functions in the plant life cycle than in the animal life cycle. Cell death plays a role in plant development, as when xylem cells form water-conducting vascular bundles; the protoplasts of xylem cells autolyse during their development, leaving the cells empty. Leaves, petals, stamens, branches, and shoots senesce, die, and abscise, all as an orderly process in the life cycle. Senescence of plant organs, such as leaves, plays a role in preparation for an adverse season by disposing of vulnerable parts. The abrupt senescence of entire plants may represent turnover at the community level to provide room for offspring and to allow expression of the genetic combinations of the progeny.

Physiological changes in plants, all actively controlled, include loss of ribosomes and protein synthesis, loss of chloroplasts, changes in membrane permeability, all leading to a breakdown of cellular homeostasis. These degenerative changes are brought about by hydrolytic enzymes synthesized for the purpose in advance. Small quantities of plant hormones, particularly ethylene and the cytokinins, exert dramatic effects on senescence by poorly understood mechanisms.

One extreme of life span is represented by annual plants (plants that live for one growing season). These plants have a genetically programmed rapid senescence and death caused by synthesis and release of hormones (primarily ethylene). At the other extreme are the perennials, including the practically immortal sequoia and bristlecone pine trees (Figure 2.1). Most of the tissues of these trees are dead wood and bark. The oldest differentiated cells are in the needles; these are probably no more than 30 years old. Germinal lines of cells exist in the confines of the wood, namely, the reserve cells (the stem cells or cambium) of the shoots, roots, and vascular tissues. Germinal or stem cells are undifferentiated, dividing populations of cells that contribute to all differentiated plant tissues during growth. In addition, plants have a line of stem cells in the reproductive tissues (germ cells), giving rise to pollen and seeds which will perpetuate the species for generations to come.

Single-Celled Life Forms

Populations of bacteria can be considered to be non-aging. Survivorship of the population under optimal conditions is essentially limitless and reflects the equally limitless capacity of bacteria for reproduction through cell division. One-celled animals (protozoa) and plants (unicellular algae) do undergo senescence and death. Some cells give rise to clones (groups of identical progeny) which rapidly die out. Studies of these organisms lead

Figure 2.1 A bristlecone pine. This tree may be "as old as Methusela," perhaps 5000 years old. Photo courtesy of Dr. D. K. Bailey.

to the conclusion that some species require sexual crossing to maintain the vigor of the line, while others do not.

In the ciliates (*Paramecium,* for example), more than 6,000 species have been described. Most species have been found to have a definite clonal life span of a characteristic number of cell divisions (starting with one cell) before degenerative changes and death appear. One species (*Tetrahymena thermophilis*) is immortal. The limited clonal life span of most ciliates parallels the limited clonal life of mammalian cells in culture, which we will discuss in Chapter 5.

Ciliates in general possess two kinds of nuclei, a germ line micronucleus and a somatic macronucleus. The micronucleus shows little transcription activity during the asexual (binary fission) cycle. The macronucleus is highly polyploid (800 times the haploid value in DNA content). During conjugation the cells come together side by side and exchange nuclear gametes (Figure 2.2). Micronuclei undergo meiosis producing four gamete nuclei, three of which degenerate. The one remaining divides and one of the resulting pair is exchanged with the conjugating partner. The macronuclei disintegrate. The resulting individuals part as genetically identical (but heterozygous) individuals.

The same procedure is followed during autogamy, wherein the paramecia undergo conjugation with themselves. If we start with *AA* and *aa* strains, the result after conjugation is *Aa* individuals. After autogamy in heterozygous individuals, *AA* or *aa* individuals result. New micronuclei and macronuclei are formed from the zygote nucleus.

Following conjugation or autogamy, binary fission of single zygotes produces a clone of cells, the size of which depends on the number of divisions. This number is genetically fixed. If clones of a species of *Paramecium* are allowed to cross-mate, offspring from this sexual phase are rejuvenated for a clonal life as long as the previous one. However, this "clonal rejuvenation" declines with the age of the cells selected as parent cells. Clonal aging differs from environmentally induced changes and

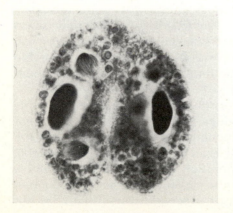

Figure 2.2 Conjugation in paramecium. Shown are the meiotic divisions (reduction divisions) of micronuclei. (From P. Wiesz. *Science of Biology.* 4th ed. Figure 25.14. Copyright 1971 by McGraw-Hill, New York. Used with permission.)

death caused by adverse culture conditions such as starvation. Clonal life span limits are expressed in a constant (optimal) environment. In some measure, the clonal senescence and the rejuvenation through sexual reproduction found in *Paramecium* parallels the situation found in higher forms. In mammals the zygote formed by egg and sperm grows to maturity and senesces, but in the meantime may have started a new clone (individual) through sexual reproduction, and so on through the generations of the species.

Species of *Tetrahymena* can exhibit an indefinite or definite life span. Those species not normally manifesting age-related somatic decline (senescence) show other time-ordered aspects of the life cycle. As examples, the onset of mating behavior (maturity), the expression of certain cell surface molecules, and the synthesis of various enzymes are all closely regulated in time. A separation of differentiation and aging is apparent in these immortal clones in that differentiation occurs in these forms in the absence of senescence. It has been theorized (see Smith-Sonneborn, 1985) that the macronucleus of these ciliates is able, by selective expression, to suppress the activity of certain deleterious "senescence" genes.

The apparent immortality among the various amoebae is observed only when these cells are grown exponentially (constant maximum rate). A growth-limiting, minimal diet induces a finite life span, consisting of two kinds of mortal cells. Type A, at division, produces one viable and one nonviable cell. Type B produces two equally viable cells. Recombination experiments between nucleus and cytoplasm of immortal cell lines and those cell lines with defined life span indicate that both nucleus and cytoplasm contribute to the limitation of life span.

Coelenterates and Flatworms

Aging superficially resembling that found in humans and other more highly evolved forms is first encountered in the coelenterates (hydras, sea anemones, corals, jellyfish). Within this group are some apparently nonaging species, such as some anemones (Figure 2.3); some animals, such as *Hydra sp.*, that do not appear to have senescence as part of the life cycle; some species of hydroid colonies that show resorption of individuals into the colony under adverse conditions; and some animals that show a period of senescence prior to death. This group as a whole possesses considerable power for regeneration of lost parts and for asexual reproduction by budding or fragmentation from the adult.

Among the flatworms, a characteristic ability to replace lost parts along with continued ability to reproduce by asexual means is again encountered. In this case asexual reproduction is by transverse fission of the adult worm into two or more identical animals (another cloning process). Senescence appears only when regeneration or asexual reproduction is prevented. Though these animals are also capable of sexual reproduction by eggs and sperm, it seems the sexual process in this instance is not necessary for rejuvenation to take place.

Figure 2.3 Long-lived anemones, *Sagartia troglodytes.* From R. L. Manuel. British Anthozoa. 1981 © Academic Press, London. Used with permission.

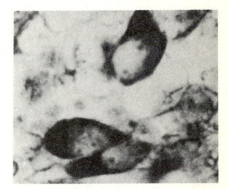

Figure 2.4 Neoblasts of *Planaria* worms. The heavily stained cytoplasm and clear nuclei reflect large amounts of cytoplasmic RNA. (From R. Goss. *Regeneration.* Copyright 1969 by Academic Press, New York. Used with permission.)

In both coelenterates and flatworms, adult animals are found to have a population of reserve, undifferentiated cells called neoblasts, somewhat like the stem cells of plants (Figure 2.4), which are used during regeneration. No such population of reserve cells has been found in any of the vertebrates. Some vertebrates are nevertheless capable of regeneration by a process of reverse differentiation of the cells next to the wound, followed by redifferentiation of the missing tissues. In any event, while there appears to be a positive correlation between the capacity for asexual replacement of all body tissues and life span, there appears to be little correlation between regenerative ability and longevity among animals.

Animals with Fixed Cell Number

The roundworms (nematodes, including vinegar eels and some parasites) and rotifers ("wheel animals") are unique in that the adults have a fixed, predetermined number of cells. Cell division in the adult is unknown. Information regarding the genetics of these organisms is rapidly expanding.

The occurrence of structurally altered enzyme molecules in aging vinegar eels (*Turbatrix aceti,* Figure 2.5) is a well-known example of an aging phenomenon first discovered in nematodes and later demonstrated in mammals. The investigations were probably prompted by the "error catastrophe" hypothesis of Orgel (1963) and by the theory of altered, inactive molecules (Gershon and Gershon, 1970). The investigations were later extended to mouse liver enzymes and to other *Turbatrix* enzymes. Since altered enzymes coexist with unaltered forms of other enzymes, it was difficult to see how some proteins and not others could be protected from primary sequence errors. Indeed, evidence gathered by Sharma and Rothstein (1980) indicated that the age-related decline in specific activity of pure enzymes arose from alterations in tertiary structure and not from errors in translation or transcription. It has therefore been postulated that posttranslational modification coupled with decreases in rate of protein turnover in older nematodes accounts for the accumulation of altered molecules. It is not clear if decreased protein turnover results from changes in amounts of proteolytic enzymes or from changes in accessibility of target proteins to degradative compartments (lysosomes). (See the discussion of error theory in Chapter 4.)

The roundworms accumulate age pigments similar to those accumulated by cells of senescing humans. In rotifers it has been shown that underfeeding promotes longevity, as does low temperature. Both rotifers and roundworms manifest the effects of aging by decreased efficiency of some enzyme systems. Such animals have provided model systems for studies of aging at the molecular level.

Recent work has revealed mutants of *Caenorhabditis elegans* that display an extended life span (Friedman and Johnson, 1988). Three long-

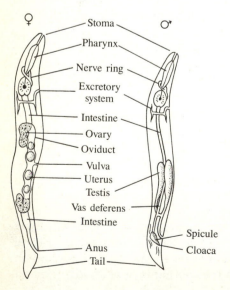

♀   ♂
Stoma
Pharynx
Nerve ring
Excretory
system
Intestine
Ovary
Oviduct
Vulva
Uterus
Testis
Vas deferens
Intestine
Spicule
Cloaca
Anus
Tail

Figure 2.5 Generalized internal anatomy of nematodes.

lived strains were isolated following chemical mutagenesis treatment. It was initially thought that these mutants had greater longevity because they ate less. Subsequent observations showed that feeding rate of the mutants is comparable to normal controls. The strains are thought to involve allelic genes of a major gene called age-1. The wild type allele of age-1 specifies a product resulting in a 15-day life span. A recessive mutation at the age-1 locus results in a 10- to 15-day extension of the life span, with accompanying decrease in self-fertility (these animals are hermaphroditic, a trait that aids in generation of in-bred strains). The gene products involved with normal and extended longevity have not as yet been identified.

Mollusks (Clams, Snails, Octopuses)

The mollusks include species living for one year, for a number of years, and for an indefinite number of years. The last group includes giant clams of the South Pacific, which show continued growth throughout life as well as an indefinite life span. In contrast, the female octopus mates only once and dies within a short time of mating and brooding the eggs. The female eats little during the brooding of the eggs even though she may forage for and find food. The modified feeding behavior has an endocrinological base in a structure called the optic gland. Surgical removal of this gland alters brooding behavior and leads to resumption of feeding and a greatly extended life expectancy.

Arthropods

Studies on aging in this group focus primarily on two forms—various water fleas (*Daphnia*) and the fruit fly (*Drosophila*). In the water fleas it was found that dietary restriction to near starvation increases life span and decreases heart rate. The water fleas also possess reserve cells and a capacity for regeneration, though the life span is limited to 2 weeks.

The most studied arthropod with respect to aging is *Drosophila* (Figure 2.6). This fly has been studied genetically for many years and provides a most suitable subject for a variety of aging studies. The life span of some species can be as long as 60 to 80 days. The effects on longevity of environmental factors such as low temperature (increases) and starvation (increases) have been extensively studied. In addition, the effect of genetic background, nutrition, maternal age, population density, alcohol, and thermal shock have been separately assessed. Tolerance for alcohol, for example, decreases exponentially with age. Pantothenic acid added to adult food increases life span by as much as 46 percent, an observation that may have led (or misled) some nutritionists to recommend royal jelly from bee hives for increasing human longevity. Royal jelly is the mixture fed to the developing queen bee by the workers and is rich in pantothenic acid. The queen lives for 6 years, the workers for only 9 months.

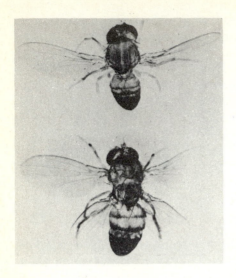

Figure 2.6 *Drosophila,* wild type and bithorax (2 sets of wings) mutant. (From L.W. Browder. Developmental Biology, © 1984 by Saunders, Philadelphia. Used with permission.)

The most significant factor for longevity in the fruit fly is the genetic background of the fly. Most recessive genes encountered in laboratory stocks (vestigial wings or white eye, for example) have reduced survival. Inbreeding in general depresses life span. Two inbred strains with similar survival curves will, when crossed, often yield offspring with increased survival (heterosis). It is generally assumed that inbreeding increases homozygosity for deleterious genes, whereas heterosis is assumed to be due to gene interaction in heterozygotes. Both these phenomena imply some sort of genetic control and deal with the entire phenotype of the organism as well as longevity. From such data it is not possible to distinguish between control of longevity by a set of genes or control by the entire genome. Similar phenomena are observed in inbred strains of laboratory mice (Chapter 3). In connection with non-adaptive theories of the evolution of senescence, in *Drosophila* there are experimental results showing successful selection over generations for a prolonged life span. Selection for increased fertility at progressively later ages over 15 generations in laboratory experiments with *D. melanogaster* leads to a 30 percent increase in mean longevity (Rose, 1984).

Several theories of aging (Chapter 4) postulate that there are age-related changes in gene expression and that these changes contribute to the decline in viability of senescent cells. This hypothesis was tested directly in *Drosophila* using high-resolution, two-dimensional gel electrophoresis of radiolabeled proteins (Fleming et al., 1986). Although resolution of small differences in electrophoretic mobility between proteins can be obtained with this technique, detection of small quantities of possibly important proteins is not guaranteed. The results failed to reveal qualitative age-related changes in *Drosophila* proteins, but it was found that profound quantitative variations occur in the expression of proteins during the life span of this insect. It is not possible to say anything about the basis for these quantitative fluctuations and whether they play a causal role in aging or are themselves the results of other aging processes.

Structural changes occur in insects with age. *Drosophila* has, as do all insects, a rigid chitinous exoskeleton, three compartments to the body (head, thorax, and abdomen), a hemocoel or cavity containing the hemolymph, a tracheal system for conduction of respiratory gases, and a ventral nerve cord with segmental ganglia. The volume of hemolymph increases at the expense of the volume occupied by various tissues as the fly ages. There is a decrease in cytoplasmic basophilia, probably reflecting a decrease in ribosomal RNA. Age pigments appear in association with lysosomes and degenerating mitochondria (Chapter 5). There is a decrease in the amount of stored fat. The brain shrinks in size, and a number of neurosecretory cells of the brain may be lost. The changes parallel in many ways the changes in higher organisms, even though the body plan is quite different. Mating behavior, which is quite elaborate, also declines with age.

The insects provide some clues as to the influence of sex on longevity. Among wasps (Habrobracon), both haploid and diploid males exist. The life spans of the haploid and diploid males are identical. These life spans are shorter by 50 percent than those of diploid females. This sort of information does not support the assumption that sex-related longevity differences are based on specific sex chromosomes or chromosome number. In addition, in experiments where both haploid and diploid males are irradiated to produce mutations, the decrease in life span observed is related to chromosomal damage and the decrease in life span of haploids is greater than that observed in diploids, as would be expected. A somatic mutation theory of aging would require, therefore, that haploids should be shorter-lived than diploids. In fact, nonirradiated haploids and diploids have identical life spans (see Lints, 1985).

Though tissue and body organization are diverse, the invertebrates show many parallels with aging in vertebrates. A difference one would do well to remember is the lack in invertebrates of an immune system as it appears in the vertebrates. Genetic background is of obvious importance, and environmental stress, such as restricted food supply, has analogous results. Additional studies of these forms may indicate which, if any, of these aging factors are shared with higher organisms and which are fortuitous parallels of evolution.

VERTEBRATES

Fish

Most species of fish undergo a real senescence. Exceptions seem to be those fish which apparently have unlimited growth (sturgeon, plaice). In the female plaice (Figure 2.7), no specific maximum size is reached, and no specific mortality is associated with increasing size (Bidder, 1932). Un-

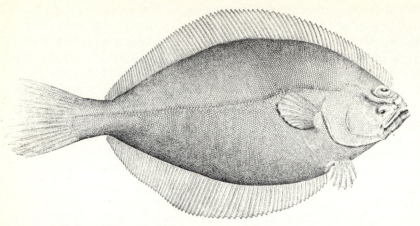

Figure 2.7 Plaice. (From an 1897 monograph.)

fortunately, predation on wild populations of any fish make it almost impossible to determine their mortality statistics; the female plaice may be killed before evidence of senescence appears. Though the female out-lives the male, she may not be potentially immortal. As the female plaice grows, all tissues and organs are increased in size. The phenomenon of indeterminate growth thus seems to resemble the ability of some lower forms to replace all body parts. The male plaice stops growing after some years and shows increased mortality upon attaining maximal size.

Amphibians

Amphibians show temperature effects in that species living in the tropics typically have shorter life spans than those living in temperate climates. In the South African clawed frog (*Xenopus*), one long-term study records a life span of about 15 years. The female shows continuous growth, whereas the male does not. In both sexes the elasticity of connective tissue diminishes with age; a similar phenomenon occurs in humans. Among the salamanders, the Mexican axolotl reaches sexual maturity as a larva, a phenomenon known as neoteny. These animals never change into adult form though they may senesce (Moment, 1982).

Tortoises and Birds

The reptiles include the longest-lived animals among the vertebrates, the tortoises and turtles. Shells of Galapagos tortoises (Figure 2.8) from the Bronx Zoo analyzed using carbon-14 dating technique were found to be 170 to 250 years of age at the time of death. These tortoises continue to grow throughout life.

Figure 2.8 Galapagos tortoise. (From J.R. Slevin, California Academy of Sciences 17: Plate 17. 1931.) Title: Theology of The Schooner *Academy*.

Among the birds, the eagle owl has been reported to live in excess of 65 years. The chicken, because of its economic importance and life span of about 10 years, has been more thoroughly studied. A biological clock appears to be reflected in egg production. The number of eggs laid by a hen is a fixed percentage (about 70 percent) of the number of eggs laid the previous year. This decrement in egg production seems to parallel aging in these birds. Aging continues at a comparable rate after removal of the ovary. Chickens raised on a diet deficient in the amino acid tryptophan exhibit increased life span along with diminished growth. Finally, it has been established that blood pressure tends to increase with age in chickens much as it does in humans.

CONCLUSIONS

There seems to be no doubt that species with sexual reproduction, from single-celled animals to vertebrates, show aging and senescence. The only instances of a seemingly indefinite life span are found among those life forms showing predominantly asexual reproduction and continued growth or replacement of all body parts throughout life. The ability to regenerate lost parts of the body does not correlate with longevity.

Genetics seems to be of critical importance wherever it has been studied as a variable. This requires some clarification. The genes of a particular species determine the species characteristics, including life span. Within a species the genes of individuals vary in a relatively minor way compared with interspecies variation. Yet it is this smaller genetic variability that accounts for variability in life span between genetically unrelated members of the same species. Certain environmental variables also show consistent positive effects on longevity, notably restriction of food supply and lowering of body temperature.

The choice of an animal for research in aging is influenced by the feasibility of genetic research, by the parallels between the proposed model and human aging, and by the life span of the experimental organism. The life span of the organism in relation to the life span of the investigator is of particular importance. The shorter the generation time of the experimental model, the more experiments that can be performed.

The prime objective of all gerontological studies is the understanding of human aging. The information available on aging in other life forms is somewhat sparse compared to that available on mammals. Since anatomy and physiology of the various life forms varies considerably, there is perhaps no reason to assume that aging in humans is based on the same principles as aging in other forms. For example, some fish apparently show indeterminate growth and consequent delayed onset of senescence to the point where predation and accidental death may obscure senescence. Also, birds and mammals, in contrast to lower forms, are warm blooded and maintain a constant body temperature along with a higher metabolic rate. Since the rate at which an animal lives metabolically is inversely correlated with life span, it is important to keep this situation in mind when comparing longevity in humans with longevity in tortoises, for example.

REFERENCES

Bidder, G. P. Senescence. *British Medical Journal* 2:583, 1932.

Comfort, A. *The Biology of Senescence.* 3rd ed. Churchill Livingstone, Edinburgh, 1979.

Fleming, J. E., E. Quattrocki, G. Latter, J. Miguel, R. Marcuson, E. Zuckerkandl, and K. G. Bensch. Age dependent changes in proteins of *Drosophila melanogaster. Science* 231:1157, 1986.

Friedman, D. B., and T. E. Johnson. Three mutants that extend both mean and maximal life span of the nematode, *Caenorhabditis elegans,* define the age-1 gene. *Journal of Gerontology* 43:B102, 1988.

Gershon, H., and D. Gershon. Detection of inactive enzyme molecules in aging organisms. *Nature* 227:1214, 1970.

Lints, F. A. Insects. In C. E. Finch and E. L. Schneider, eds., *Handbook of the Biology of Aging.* Van Nostrand Reinhold, New York, 1985.

Martin, G. W., and M. S. Turker. Model systems for the genetic analysis of mechanisms of aging. *Journal of Gerontology* 43:B33, 1988.

Moment, G. B. Theories of aging: An overview. In R. C. Adelman and G. S. Roth, eds., *Testing the Theories of Aging.* CRC Press, Boca Raton, Fla., 1982.

Nooden, L. D., and J. E. Thompson. Aging and senescence in plants. In C. E. Finch and E. L. Schneider, eds., *Handbook of the Biology of Aging.* Van Nostrand Reinhold, New York, 1985.

Orgel, L. E. The maintenance of the accuracy of protein synthesis and its relevance to ageing. *Proceedings of the National Academy of Science, USA* 47:609, 1963.

Rose, M. R. The evolution of animal senescence. *Canadian Journal of Zoology* 62:1661, 1984.

Rose, M. R., and J. L. Graves, Jr. What evolutionary biology can do for gerontology. *Journal of Gerontology* 44:B27, 1989.

Sharma, H. K., and M. Rothstein. Altered enolase in aged *Turbatrix aceti* results from conformational changes in the enzyme. *Proceedings of the National Academy of Science, USA* 77:5865, 1980.

Smith-Sonneborn, J. Aging in unicellular organisms. In C. E. Finch and E. L. Schneider, eds., *Handbook of the Biology of Aging.* Van Nostrand Reinhold, New York, 1985.

Chapter
3

Aging in Mammals

INTRODUCTION

The problem of human aging has been approached indirectly by using laboratory animals and directly by observing aging in humans. Some studies are longitudinal; an experimental group, all born at the same time (a cohort), is observed as a group throughout the life span of the members. Other studies are cross-sectional; several age cohorts within a population are observed at a particular time (Chapter 1). The cross-sectional study is more frequent and the only type that can be done practically on long-lived species, although there are longitudinal studies in progress on humans. Some studies, for ethical reasons, cannot be carried out using human subjects. For example, assaying the effect of limited caloric intake on senescence, an experiment requiring near starvation of the experimental subjects, is ethically feasible only with laboratory mammals, and some would question the ethics of such an experiment even in animals. In discussing aging in humans, it is therefore reasonable to include what is known about aging in other mammals and particularly the most frequently used model system, the laboratory mouse.

All mammals show a period of senescence prior to death. During old age nonhuman species exhibit much the same alterations in tissues and age-associated diseases as are encountered in humans. The fact that life span is a species trait indicates that life span is in large measure genetically controlled. In mammals a relationship exists between the ratio of brain weight to body weight and life span. The larger the brain in relation to body size, the longer the life span. In addition, metabolic rate varies inversely with life span, and since smaller mammals have higher metabolic rates than larger mammals, it also follows that for a given ratio of brain size to body weight, the smaller mammal will have a shorter life span. Also important to consider is the proportion of life spent in the prereproductive stage; the more delayed the onset of reproductive life, the longer the life span (and the later the onset of senescence).

LIFE SPAN IN HUMAN EVOLUTION

Changes with Time

Neither life expectancy nor life span has remained constant over the millennia of human history. Life expectancy varies with the environment within the maximum allowed by the life span. Both life expectancy and life span have changed with time. Life expectancy strongly reflects the severity of the environment. Changes in life span reflect changes in the genetics of the species.

A comparison over the years for hominid ancestors and humans is given in Figure 3.1. The maximum rate of increase of life span occurred about 100,000 years ago, when estimates indicate a surprisingly rapid rate of increase of 1.4 years in life span for each 10,000-year period (Cutler,

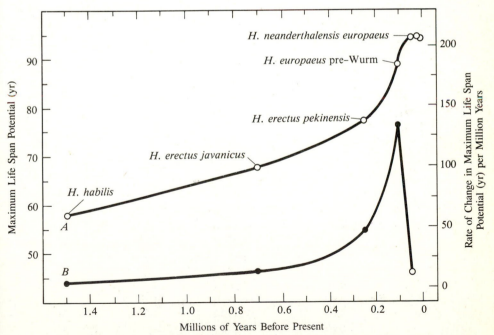

Figure 3.1 Evolution of maximal life span of ancestral humans. *A,* Increase in life span versus time. *B,* Rate of change of maximal life span with time. (From R. G. Cutler, *Journal of Human Evolution* 5:169, 1976. Copyright 1976 by Academic Press, New York. Used with permission.)

1975). The calculation of life span for extinct species can be made using estimates of brain size and body weight from fossil material; similar calculations on living species provide estimates of life span which check well with observed maximum survival (Table 3.1). The correlations in mammals between the ratio of brain weight to body weight and life span was most fully developed by Sacher (1959, 1975). From the early stone age (70,000 to 30,000 years ago) to the present, it is assumed that the life span of humans has slowly increased from about 75 years to about 114 years (this number reflects the age of the oldest surviving human and may increase slightly as newer medical records are available). The life expectancy over the same period shows a dramatic increase from about 30 years to more than 70 years (Table 3.2).

Evolution of Longevity

The term *longevity* is used as synonymous with maximal life span. Since evolution operates on the basis of the survival of the fittest, the increased life span of humans over the years of evolution might be expected to be related in some way to evolutionary survival and fitness. The precise way in which longevity is related to the survival of primitive humans is not understood. The positive relationship between brain size (in relation to body size) and longevity is seen by some (Moment, 1982) to reflect greater flexibility, or adaptability, of the proportionally larger brain, which in turn promotes a longer life in the face of a changing environment. Some argue (Strehler, 1977) that the program of delayed reproduction, slow maturation and learning, and the accompanying forced dependency, all associated with the larger brain, are key factors in the development of human longevity. Not only are the young slow to mature, but also the older members must be around to instruct them. A balance must be struck between accumulated experience and gradual senescence. Especially im-

Table 3.1   PREDICTION OF LIFE SPAN OF MODERN PRIMATES ON BASIS OF BODY AND BRAIN WEIGHT

Common name	Brain size (cm³)	Body weight (g)	Life span (yr)	
			Observed	Predicted
Tree shrew	4.3	275	7	7.7
Rhesus monkey	106	8,719	29	27
Orangutang	420	69,000	50	41
Chimpanzee	410	49,000	45	43
Gorilla	550	140,000	40	42
Human	1,446	65,000	95–100	92

Source: Data modified from R. G. Cutler. A. R. Behnke, C. Finch, and G. Moment, eds., *Biology of Aging.* Copyright 1978 by Plenum Publishing Corporation, New York. Used with permission.

Table 3.2 AVERAGE MORTALITY RATE OF *HOMO SAPIENS* IN PAST
AND RECENT ENVIRONMENTS

Time period	Life expectancy (yr)	Approximate maximum life span (yr)
70,000–30,000 B.C.	29.4	70
30,000–12,000 B.C.	32.4	100
12,000–10,000 B.C.	31.5	100
10,000–8,000 B.C.	38.2	100
Greece (1100 B.C.–A.D. 1)	35	100
Rome (753 B.C.–A.D. 476)	32	100
England (1276)	48	100
England (1376–1400)	38	100
United States (1900–1902)	61.5	100
United States (1950)	70	100
United States (1970)	72	100
United States (1980)	73	100

Source: Data modified from R. G. Cutler. *Journal of Human Evolution* 5:169, 1976.

portant for this consideration is the development of speech during the evolution of humans (more about that later).

Regardless of such speculation, it does seem likely that relatively few genes are involved—somewhere in the neighborhood of 250 at most (Cutler, 1975). Senescence is qualitatively similar in most mammals, but the rate of aging varies over a 40-fold range. This suggests that the genes controlling the rate of aging may be rather few. Position effects, or relocation (transposition) of genetic elements within the genome, may be of great importance, since position effects are known to affect gene activity without gene mutation. The exact nature of these changes is among the fundamental questions that remain to be answered. Some of the most likely candidates, as we shall see in Chapter 4, are those genes governing the efficiency of DNA repair in somatic cells.

Senescence, to view the question from the other side, can be viewed as an evolved change in the time of onset of the declining phase of life. One may then ask if there is adaptive advantage, in the evolutionary sense, to longevity, as implied above; or if there is adaptive advantage to elimination, through senescence, of the older members of a population; or if senescence is nonadaptive (without direct survival value). There are cogent arguments against the adaptive viewpoint. First, accidental mortality is high enough in most species in the wild to obviate the need for any intrinsic mechanism to terminate life. Second, given two species A and B, which differ only in that A has a fixed life span and B does not, B is selectively better fit than A (Kirkwood, 1981). It seems that senescence is best explained in nonadaptive terms. Most theories of this type hold that senescence begins after reproductive life is over and must be the result of an accumulation of genes that have deleterious effects only in later years. Thus, senescence might result from the activity of genes that act positively during growth and development (for example, promote calcification of bones) but have deleterious actions later in life, after the reproductive phase (for example, promote calcification of arteries), provided that the deleterious effect is manifest sufficiently late in life not to interfere with reproduction and care of offspring (Williams, 1957).

LONGEVITY IN SMALL AND LARGE MAMMALS

Small Mammals

Most small mammals (the size of mice) have a maximum life span of about 2 or 3 years, while elephants live nearly as long as humans. Within the genetic framework of life span, mice do not have a long period of gradual senescence following their reproductive period. In wild populations of mice the important consideration is the production of large numbers of new genetic combinations through random matings. New combinations are necessary to provide the raw material for evolutionary selection and survival of the fittest. Fitness in this case would refer to disease resistance, overall strength, and freedom from congenital abnormality. Mice become reproductively competent at 6 to 8 weeks of age. There is no period of extended parental care or "adolescence" as in longer-lived species. Overpopulation is controlled by disease, predators, availability of food, and natural disasters such as fire and flood, all of which are balanced by reproductive activity if the population as a whole is to survive (Cole, 1954). There does not appear to be a "survival factor" in mice associated with living to an age much beyond the reproductive period. Aging, senescence, life span, and maturation age all seem to be interrelated in some way.

Large Mammals

Elephants and humans have much longer life spans. Female elephants have a gestation period of 20 to 22 months, with a space of about 4 to 9 years between calves. Young elephants spend 12 to 20 years as prereproductive individuals. During this time they receive care and instruction from their mothers. Elephants are relatively intelligent animals and can be taught to avoid catastrophe and to cooperate within the herd. The only predator to be feared by a grown elephant is the human. Herd size is largely determined by predation on young stragglers, disease, natural catastrophe, and accident. The evolutionary rules still hold that genetic diversity must be maximized and that eventually the old will be replaced by the more vigorous young after the young have been "tutored." The leader of the herd is most often an old female with experience in handling situations that threaten the calves of the herd.

Teaching and leadership by older individuals are also characteristic of primates. The leader of a troop of baboons is regularly an old male or group of males. Leadership in human society is characteristically not relegated to the younger members. Among the primates, we humans have a life span some two to four times longer than our not-so-distant ancestors; the longevity of humans thus evolved from relatively short-lived predecessors. It seems that modern humans also mature more slowly than their ancestors. This period of adolescence is a period of learning from the older members of human society as well as a period of biological maturation.

Humans have, during the same evolutionary period, increased the number of neurons in the cerebral cortex by a factor of nearly 100 over lower primates (Cutler, 1975). This number of extra neurons is sometimes referred to as "biological intelligence" and refers only to the fact that cortical neurons beyond the number required for control and integration of normal body functions have appeared in increasing numbers during primate and human evolution. Some of these increases in cortical neurons most certainly had to do with the development of the human speech center in the left cerebral cortex. Instruction of the slowly maturing young would be greatly facilitated by the ability to communicate generalizations and abstractions between parents and children. Here, with the expansion of the cortex, one begins to see a possible reason for the relationship between the ratio of brain size to body weight and longevity during the evolution of modern humans. Still, there is really no clue as to which came first—the evolution of speech and relatively greater brain size or longevity. The increase in number of cortical neurons and the increase in life span during human evolution are summarized in Figure 3.2.

A recent view of the origin of the modern human mind (Lewin, 1987) favors a mechanism of group-against-group competition as the driving force behind the evolution of human intelligence (and perhaps, therefore, human longevity). Early humans perhaps had their greatest competition from other groups of humans. The hostile forces of nature may not, in this view, have provided nearly the evolutionary pressure as that provided by competition with other human minds. The competitors would be closely matched, leading to evolution through a positive drive of human against human. The idea is consistent with the fact that humans alone competitively play group against group on a large and complex scale. This theory may provide a basis for the rapid evolution of the human mind and the parallel rapid evolution of longevity.

It was mentioned that there may be no more than 250 genes associated with the evolution of human longevity. These numbers are based on estimated mutation rates over the past 100,000 years of human evolutionary history. Since the evolutionary changes are dramatic and the time allotted for evolution relatively short, it follows from such projections of

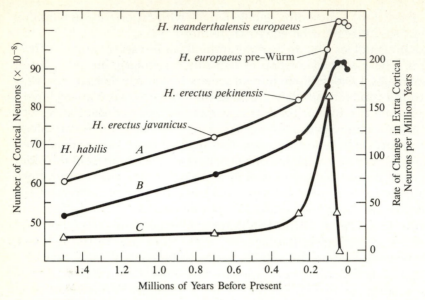

Figure 3.2 Evolution of life span and extra cortical neurons during human evolution. *A,* Maximal life span. *B,* Number of cortical neurons. *C,* Rate of change of number of cortical neurons. (From R. G. Cutler, *Journal of Human Evolution* 5:169, 1976. Copyright 1976 by Academic Press, New York. Used with permission.)

mutation rates into the past that relatively few genetic loci could be involved. Recall that during human evolution within the group of primates, the maximum rate of increase in life span was 1.4 years per 10,000 years, occurring about 100,000 years ago. Estimates indicate that 0.6 percent of the total functional genes became altered to code for altered peptide sequences during this 100,000-year period (Cutler, 1975). These calculations suggest that two of the most complex features of humans, longevity and intelligence, evolved extremely rapidly with relatively few changes in the genome. Other interpretations suggest that gene rearrangements, with few mutations, could account for the evolutionary changes. Thus, evolutionary changes could, at least in part, be the result of changes in regulation of existing genes which have been repositioned adjacent to segments of regulatory DNA located in other parts of the genome.

Effect of Diet on Mammalian Senescence

The dramatic effect of diet was first noticed in rats in 1915 by Osborne and Mendel. McKay, Crowell, and Maynard (1935) greatly extended the work. The effect of dietary restriction in laboratory mice is to increase both the mean age at death and life span by as much as 50 percent. Restriction of food intake slows the rate of aging, delays a spectrum of age-related diseases, and delays age-related physiological deterioration. Such restriction does not change the age-related increase in systolic blood pressure in the mice. Though some questions remain unanswered, current evidence suggests that food restriction may act by lowering plasma glucose levels of food-restricted mice, presumably also lowering levels of glycation of proteins and nucleic acids (Masoro et al., 1989). The role of glycation in aging is discussed with other theories of aging in Chapter 4. Earlier work (Masoro, 1988; Masoro et al., 1982) has shown that food-restricted mice live longer than ad libitum fed controls without reducing the caloric intake per gram of body weight. Moreover, the food-restricted mice consumed a greater number of calories per gram of body weight over their lifetime than ad lib fed mice, yet lived longer (Figure 3.3).

The profound effects of food intake on longevity have strong human implications. It may well turn out that the well-fed populations of the world are in fact overfed. Some instances of extreme longevity in humans may be related to diets low in cholesterol, high in vegetable protein, and marginal in terms of caloric intake. Studies of the effects of caloric restriction on human life expectancy might be done through examination of the eating patterns of various human cultures.

THE MOUSE AS A MODEL SYSTEM

Genetics and Inbred Strains

Regardless of the evolutionary conjectures about why mice don't live longer lives, it remains that they do senesce and die within two to three years of birth, dependent on the strain, and that many of the features of this senescence resemble the process of aging in humans (Sacher and Staffeldt, 1974). Much is known about mouse and rat genetics, and genetically defined inbred strains are easily available. These considerations make both mice and rats attractive as a model system in which to study the biology of aging. The hope for every model system is that it will provide information about the human situation without the necessity of experimentation on human subjects while probing for basic data. The proper study of mankind may indeed be man, but practicality and ethical considerations dictate otherwise. It is impossible for the investigator of human aging to survive for more than one generation of a longitudinal study of human aging; the same investigator could observe aging in mice for 20 or more generations!

Inbred strains of mice are maintained by brother-sister matings and provide a large number of individuals that are genetically identical in all respects within a strain, save that they are, of course, either male or female. Mice can be raised under controlled environmental and dietary conditions, including the germ-free state.

It is somewhat paradoxical to use inbred mice as objects of research

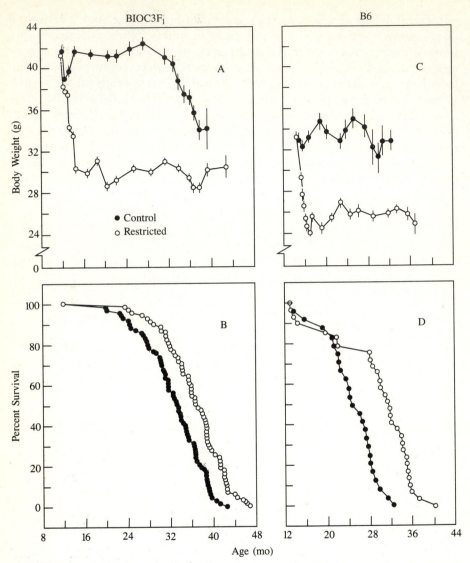

Figure 3.3 Body weights (A and C) and survival (B and D) of two strains of mice (B10C3F1 and B6) on restricted and control diets. Weights are plotted as means $\pm$ standard error. Each point in the survival curves represents one mouse. (From Weinduch and Walford, 1982. Copyright 1982 by AAAS, used with permission.)

on aging in humans. Humans are genetically diverse; the inbred strains of mice are genetically uniform. Humans are exposed from birth to various infection-causing viruses and bacteria; the mice are maintained germ-free (or at least free of known specific pathogenic microorganisms). Humans resemble wild populations of mammals much more than the experimental mice do.

There are some compelling reasons for using mice, however, in spite of the vast difference between them and human populations. Humans die of a variety of causes. Death may have an accidental cause, such as an automobile collision, lightning, and snake bite, or it may occur from a quiet, simple stopping of the heart during sleep. In between these extremes lie countless ways of dying from what are termed "natural causes." A little thought should convince most of us that natural death is essentially genetic death (Burnet, 1978). In the absence of accident and infectious disease, the timing of death is dependent on an individual's genes. Since our aim is to study natural or genetic death, it is useful and appropriate to utilize several inbred strains of mice which have been shielded from infections and grown in the protective environment of the laboratory. As we shall see, there is diversity in the cause of death within single inbred strains of mice as well as in human populations.

Survivorship of Laboratory Mice

The typical survivorship curve for an inbred strain of mice begins with 100 males and 100 females maintained separately (Figure 3.4). The curve begins with adolescent mice; infant mortality is virtually nonexistent due to germ-free conditions. Food is sterilized and is carefully prepared to insure an adequate diet. Deaths are recorded each day until the last survivor succumbs. Few deaths are observed until approximately 60 percent of the life span has been lived. The curve then bends downward until 50 percent survive and then gradually approaches the limiting life span for the strain. The placement of the curve may differ between two different strains, depending on genetic factors within the strains. In other

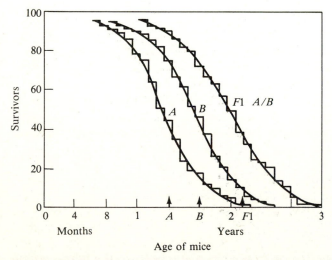

Figure 3.4 Survival curve for inbred mouse strains *A* and *B* and F1 generation hybrid *A/B*. (From F. M. Burnet. *Endurance of Life*. 1978. Copyright 1978 by Cambridge University Press, New York. Used with permission.)

words, the life expectancy may vary, though the life span may remain the same.

The offspring of the first generation (F1) of a cross between two inbred strains frequently live longer than either parent strain. The life expectancy and the life span of the F1 in these cases is greater than either parent strain. This is called hybrid vigor (heterosis) and is due in part to gene interactions and to the covering of some "bad" allelic genes (genes occupying the same location in maternal and paternal chromosomes) of one strain by different alleles of the other strain.

Some mouse strains have unusually short life spans. These stocks are genetically abnormal, and it is possible to identify discreet pathological changes associated with one or another body system. One strain dies routinely from a form of leukemia and carries a cancer virus integrated into the DNA, which is transmitted through the reproductive cells to subsequent generations. The virus manifests itself in white blood cells of adults through an uncontrolled proliferation of these cells to a point where the host animals are killed. Another strain is highly susceptible to kidney disease, resulting in a life span under a year due to kidney failure.

Diversity of Cause of Death in Inbred Mice

Other pure lines (inbred strains of mice) are less uniform in the cause of death and also show a more normal life span. In all survivorship curves one finds some mice dying at half the maximum life span. In spite of all efforts to make conditions ideal and identical, these mice of the same inbred strain die from a variety of causes. A small proportion will always show cancers. Some show degenerative diseases of the blood in the form of an anemia caused by a mistaken attack on the red blood cells by the immune system (autoimmunity). Some show kidney or lung disease or failures of the circulatory system and heart. In other words, the uniformity of inbred strains breaks down when one analyzes the cause of natural death, and the mice resemble humans in that there is a general breakdown in the structure and function of the various organ systems, any one of which can account for the death of a particular mouse. A central problem of the biology of aging is this diversity of cause of natural death in genetically uniform animals.

Thus, much of senescence in mice resembles that observed in humans in spite of our more diverse genetic background. In humans a relatively long period of maturity (in the absence of accident) is followed by a period in which difficulties arise, seemingly at random, and become more and more evident until, in one way or another, the life is ended.

Inbred Strains Versus Wild Species

Sacher and Hart (1978) describe a system that compares the house mouse (*Mus*) with wild populations of the white-footed mouse (*Peromyscus*) (Figure 3.5). The two are similar in size. In brain weight the advantage goes to

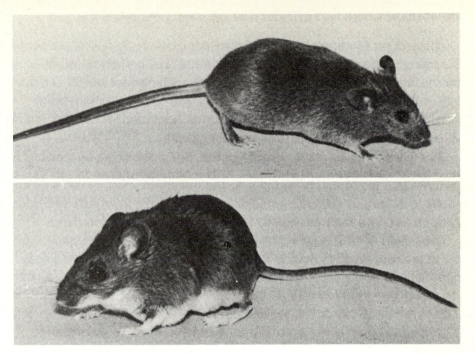

Figure 3.5 Laboratory mouse, *Mus musculus* (top); wild mouse, *Peromyscus leucopus* (bottom). (From G. Sacher, *The Gerontologist* 14:268, 1974. Copyright 1974 by the Gerontological Society of America. Used with permission.)

Peromyscus by a factor of 1.6. The metabolic rate is one-third higher in *Mus.* The life span of *Mus* is about 3.4 years, whereas *Peromyscus* lives nearly 2.5 times longer. There is a 2.5-fold difference in repair of ultraviolet-induced DNA damage (Hart, D'Ambrosio, Ng, and Modaak, 1979). These data would tend to support the theory that life span relates in some way to efficiency of DNA repair mechanisms (see Chapter 4). The number of divisions (doublings) of cells maintained in culture outside the body has shown to be correlated with life span in animals. This phenomenon is described more fully in Chapter 4. The cells of these two species of mouse maintained in culture show the differences expected in numbers of doublings; *Peromyscus* cells survive for twice as many doublings as cells of *Mus*.

HUMAN LONGEVITY IN MODERN TIMES

Survival Among Primitive People in Modern Times

Having discussed the evolution of longevity of humans as large, long-lived mammals and also having dealt with the life span of early humans and their more remote ancestors, we now turn to considerations of aging in

Homo sapiens in the present century. A hunter-gatherer culture persisted among the Australian aboriginals until less than a hundred years ago. This is presumed to be the state of human culture prior to the development of agriculture some 10,000 years ago. In the New Guinea highlands, also within the past hundred years, there existed an example of tropical garden cultivation. These two groups could be considered as being as close to "natural man" as one can get in recent times. The life span potential in these two groups is the same as is found in other human populations in modern times. In other words, given the same environmental advantages as those enjoyed by modern people in terms of medical and health care, these culturally primitive but biologically modern humans show the same life span as their culturally different counterparts in the modern world. The genetics controlling longevity is universal among modern members of *Homo sapiens.*

In both types of primitive culture the highest incidence of mortality occurred in the early years. Infancy was a period of high mortality, and it was followed by a second period of danger after weaning. Weaning was the time when children lost protection from poisonous or spoiled food and also lost protection against disease by maternal antibodies (antibodies are transferred to human offspring through the placenta during intrauterine life and to some extent through the mammary gland during early neonatal life). Disease and accidents continued to cause childhood death, but once adulthood was reached, immunity against common diseases such as malaria was firmly established among survivors. Throughout adult life infections of a less common sort, famines, homicides, and accidents contributed to the mortality rate. Survival beyond 50 was rare, though possible. Survival testified to strength and wisdom, and the elders tended to be honored by their community or tribe.

Life Expectancy of Modern Humans

In present times the life expectancy of humans in developed countries has far surpassed the 40 to 50 years of members of a hunter-gatherer culture. Public health policies, modern medicine, and improved "health consciousness," to name the major factors, allow thousands to reach an age that only one or two individuals would have reached in a more primitive society (Figure 3.6). Toughness and resistance to disease are no longer requisites for survival. There still exist, however, individuals with the genetic qualities that kept primitive inidividuals alive long enough to become tribal leaders.

There are striking differences in longevity between the sexes. In the total United States population the life expectancy of females at birth is about 77 years, while that of males is about 70 years. No satisfactory biological explanation has been found for this difference in survival, though the reasons seem to be both behavioral and biological. In general, though women are more likely to be sick than men, their illnesses are less likely to be fatal. Women have more acute illnesses and nonfatal chronic conditions, such as arthritis, sinusitis, colitis, chronic constipation, and bunions. Men lead in emphysema, ischemic heart disease, atherosclerosis, asthma, cerebrovascular disease, and injuries. In the first half of life masculine tendencies to violence, as measured in homicides, suicides, and accidents, take an excess toll. In the latter half of life cardiovascular disease accounts for most of the difference in viability. In situations where other variables have been held constant, the difference in longevity between men and women persists.

Possible explanations for this might involve hormonal differences, differences in life roles, the absence of a Y chromosome in females, or the presence of two X chromosomes in females, one of which is inactive, as the Barr body. Females are thus a mosaic with respect to the X chromosome, and deleterious information carried on one X might lead to selection of cell lines bearing the more advantageous X-linked genes. With respect to possible influence of the Y chromosome, studies of death rates in one Amish family reveal some interesting data. The males of this family are missing the long arm of their Y chromosomes (Smith, 1988). The longevities of four generations of this family were compared with longevities of neighboring families with males having normal Y chromosomes. In the families with the normal chromosome, the women lived to their mid 70s and the men died five or six years earlier. In the family with the deleted arm of the Y chromosome, the women lived to an average age of 77.4 and the men substantially outlived them to an age of 82.3. The sample size is small, and even though the results are intriguing, Smith himself states that these data of themselves provide no basis for assuming any role of the Y chromosome in aging other than the determination of sex. The investigation continues utilizing other kindred families in which males show a similar Y chromosome morphology.

It is also worth noting that DNA polymerase alpha, an enzyme associated with replication and repair of DNA in animal cells, is X-linked. Whatever the causal factor or combination of factors, the result of this differential mortality between the sexes is an increasing imbalance in the sex ratio as life progresses.

Exceptional Longevity in Modern Populations

Though some of the data may be suspect, there are a few places on earth where exceptional longevity seems to occur with greater frequency than elsewhere. These locations are Abkhasia of the Georgian Socialist Republic (USSR), the Hunza valley of the Himalayas, and the Ecuadorian Valley of Vilcabamba (Leaf, 1973). The claims of long life from these areas are striking. Benet (1974) states that 2.6 percent of Abkhasians were over 90, compared with only 0.1 percent in the USSR as whole. Nine persons out of 819 residents of a Vilcabamba village claimed to be over 100 years old. Some of the Vilcabamba residents claimed to be 120 to 130 years old. A recent attempt to verify ages in Vilcabamba found systematic age exaggeration after age 70 (Mazess and Forman, 1979). Nonetheless, there are twice the number of people over 60 in Vilcabamba than are found in the nation as a whole.

Two of these groups (not Abkhasia) are high-altitude communities. All are peasant communities. The elderly characteristically not only take an active part in the everyday life of the village, but also retain considerable authority in the family. Diet tends to be low in fat and high in vegetable protein. The people tend to be relatively low in body fat and engage in constant physical labor. Among the Abkhasians, being fat is viewed as an illness. The Abkhasian culture is also characterized by minimal stress, a lack of competition, and a stoic life style.

Environment and Diet

It is obviously a mistake to place sole responsibility for living to an advanced age on genetic constitution and to ignore environmental factors. Popular attitudes hold that environment and diet have much to do with longevity, if not everything. It is sufficient to point out that eating properly, exercising, and avoiding environmental hazards will go a long way toward maximizing whatever genetic potential an individual possesses. From the work on diet restriction in rats, it is clear that diet has a strong effect on longevity in mammals. As we shall see later (Chapter 9), there is definitely something to be gained by giving up bad habits such as smoking and maintaining physical and mental fitness. It should be remembered that only a tiny fraction of people live to realize the life span to which their genes may have entitled them. Death comes in a wide variety of ways, and the only meaningful way to look at the effects of aging is as an ever-increasing vulnerability.

GENETIC CONDITIONS ASSOCIATED WITH PREMATURE AGING IN HUMANS

In much the same way as was observed for various inbred strains of mice having shorter than normal life spans, it is possible to catalog a number of human genetic conditions that lead to an abnormally short life. These conditions are referred to as "diseases" in the sense that they represent pathological departures from the normal course of aging and are not the direct consequence of infection or injury. These diseases have been called "segmental progeroid syndromes" in that each represents a segment of the spectrum of changes associated with senescence (Martin, 1978).

It has been estimated that there are possibly 7 to 70 genetic factors at separate locations in the DNA of the cell that control the major aspects of senescence. These genetic loci may be distinct from or the same as those concerned with longevity. Evolutionary data suggest the existence of relatively few genes concerned with life span. These same data do *not* suggest what causes senescence or how the aging rate might be controlled.

The several diseases catalogued below represent changes or mutations in normal human genes producing abnormal aging in one or several body systems. (So far, no mutation resulting in longer life has been described, though these have obviously occurred in the past.) The existence of these conditions emphasizes that there may exist relatively few genes responsible for longevity in normal individuals. These genetic conditions are described more completely in Chapter 6 where cellular details are included. At present, we will confine ourselves to a listing of the conditions and their presumed mode of inheritance. Hereditary syndromes (a syndrome is a collection of symptoms or manifestations that characterize a particular disease) are controlled in most instances by an autosomal dominant gene.

The *Hutchinson-Gilford progeria syndrome* is a rare human genetic disease with many features mimicking accelerated aging (Figure 3.7). These individuals appear normal at birth, but age prematurely in their teens. The condition is presumably inherited as an autosomal dominant (DeBusk, 1972; Schneider and Bynum, 1983).

Werner's syndrome (WS) is another collection of symptoms indicative of premature aging. In contrast to progeria, Werner's syndrome does not

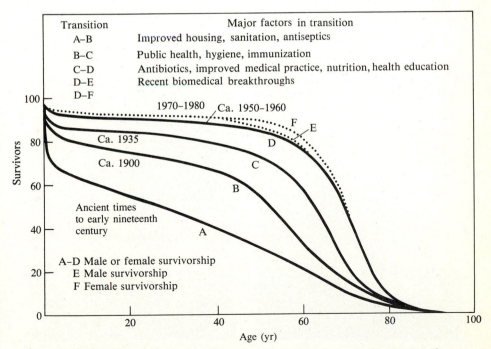

Figure 3.6 Human survival curves from ancient times through the twentieth century, with major transition factors. (From B. L. Strehler, *Federation Proceedings* 34, 1975. Copyright 1975 by Federation Proceedings. Used with permission.)

become manifest until later in life, at about 20 years, although some signs may appear in the late teens. It is inherited as an autosomal recessive (Epstein, Martin, Schultz, and Motulsky, 1966).

Alzheimer's disease (presenile dementia) and *senile dementia* fill a third or more of the nursing-home beds in this country. Alzheimer's disease comprises about half of all dementias of older people (Sinex and Merril, 1982). The diseases are sometimes collectively referred to as senile dementia of the Alzheimer type (SDAT) regardless of the age of onset. Some forms of SDAT are inherited as a dominant gene on chromosome 21.

Pick's disease is rarer than Alzheimer's disease and difficult to distinguish from Alzheimer's except at autopsy. Women are affected more often than men. It is also thought to be inherited as a rare autosomal dominant factor (Burnet, 1983).

Trisomy 21 (Down's syndrome, also once known as mongolism) results from having an extra autosome, specifically an extra chromosome 21. If individuals with this condition live to age 40, they frequently develop senile dementia of the Alzheimer type (Whalley, 1982).

Huntington's chorea is a relatively rare nervous disorder controlled by an autosomal dominant gene, located on chromosome number 4 (Burnet, 1983). Symptoms usually begin during the 40s or 50s.

Ataxia telanqiectasia is a degenerative disease. Afflicted individuals

 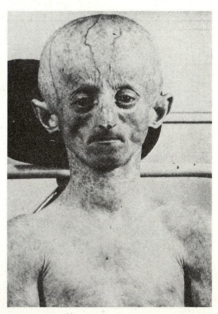

Figure 3.7 Progeria patient. *(a)* At 10 months of age, apparently normal. *(b)* At 14.5 years. From F. L. DeBusk, *Journal of Pediatrics* 80:697, 1972. Copyright 1972 by C. V. Mosby Co., St. Louis. Used with permission.)

appear normal at birth, but show ataxic (failure of coordination) symptoms in late infancy. The condition is apparently inherited as an autosomal recessive.

Amyotrophic lateral sclerosis, Friedreich's ataxia, and *Parkinsonism-dementia complex* are all characterized by early loss of neurons from some segment of the brain or spinal cord (Burnet, 1983). Amyotrophic disease and Friedreich's ataxia are both inherited as autosomal recessives. The Parkinsonism-dementia complex is a prevalent condition of the Chamorro people of Guam; it kills an estimated 15 percent of the population. It is thought to be carried as a dominant gene with a variable expression in females (some females may have the gene, but show no symptoms), but 100 percent expression in males.

Xeroderma pigmentosum is another rare disease, affecting approximately 1 in 250,000. Infants are born without visible abnormality, but later are predisposed to multiple skin cancers. The basic lesion, carried as a recessive gene, is related directly to a defect in the mechanisms of DNA repair.

Autoimmune disease is a general term encompassing many conditions. Many inexplicable diseases of the past have now been shown to be basically the result of a genetic predisposition in which the immune system mistakenly attacks the tissues of the body which houses it, leading to a wide spectrum of disease states (Burnet, 1983).

Familial amyloidosis is described as the accumulation in various tissues of an amorphous, acellular material composed of multiple proteins related to immunoglobulins.

DISEASES OF NORMAL SENESCENCE

The genetic abnormalities discussed above are all indicative of the genetic control of normal aging. They also all bring about premature aging and death and represent "mutant" genetic conditions having normal genetic counterparts in normally senescing individuals. This leaves open the question of the genetic or nongenetic nature of the diseases associated with "normal" mortality, specifically cardiovascular disease and the various types of malignant neoplasms (cancers). These two disease categories rank highest as causes of death in all age categories in the United States (see Table 1.5). Table 1.6 illustrates the importance of various diseases and accidents in terms of the effect of their elimination on life expectancy.

Cardiovascular Disease

More people die of disease affecting the heart and blood vessels than from any other group of diseases. The causes of death include coronary artery disease of the heart, strokes (hemorrhage of or blocking of arteries in the brain), aneurysms (weakening and dilation of large arteries, followed by rupture), and high blood pressure. High blood pressure (hypertension) contributes to all the other conditions in addition to doing damage on its own to the kidneys and eyes. Atherosclerosis is the leading cause of death in the United States and is the most common disorder included under the general term arteriosclerosis. It is a disease of larger arteries involving hardening and narrowing of the arteries due to accumulation of plaques of fatty material in the lining of the vessel; it is also indicted, along with hypertension, as being the cause of most cardiovascular disease.

There are a number of dietary and environmental factors involved in the development of hypertension and atherosclerosis. High dietary cholesterol tends to lead to arterial plaque; high salt predisposes to hypertension. In the United States, England, and Australia, smoking is definitely linked to cardiovascular disease, especially coronary artery disease; this is not indicated in data from Greece, Yugoslavia, Italy, Finland, or the Netherlands. The situation is complex, and it is difficult to sort out the environmental factors from the genetic.

There does appear to be a tendency, apart from diet, for cardiovascular diseases to run in families. There exists a revolutionary notion that atherosclerosis may arise in a manner similar to cancers. This notion is based on the single observation that a large fraction of atherosclerotic lesions appears to arise initially from changes in a single cell, which goes on to form a clone of altered cells by cell division (Benditt and Benditt, 1973).

Vascular Brain Syndromes

Arteriosclerosis (with attendant decrease in blood supply to the brain), poor nutrition, some cancers, and chronic alcoholism may cause dementias. The brain changes associated with vascular brain syndromes are perplexing. Usually, there is a correlation between the degree of dementia and the amount of degenerative change in the brain. However, at autopsy the brains of some extremely demented people show little pathology, and the brains of some people lucid during life are found to be riddled with degenerative changes.

Cancers

Cancers represent a complex of diseases, primarily of old age. Some cancers are clearly inherited, such as retinoblastoma, an eye tumor found in children. There also appear to be genetic factors leading to resistance to formation of cancers. It seems that cancers develop from changes or mutations in segments of DNA that regulate the activation and repression of the developmental program. Some of these changes are mediated by cancer viruses. Some cancers are characterized by production of proteins found in earlier developmental periods. All are characterized by uncontrolled cell division.

One of the functions of the immune system is the recognition and elimination of cancerous cells. Development of cancer can thus be thought of as failure of repair of damage to regulatory DNA and secondarily as failure or inability of immune system cells to detect and eliminate the altered cell(s). A further discussion of the cell biology of cancer will be found in Chapter 6.

CONCLUSIONS

In the long run, all body cells are susceptible to degeneration and death. Within genetically uniform strains of mice, the cause of natural death frequently appears to be a random failure in one or another organ system. Longevity may have evolved through the survival advantage imparted by the experience of old age in training the youth in long-lived species. Biological intelligence, as measured by the number of extra cortical neurons, and longevity seem to go hand in hand. Genetically uniform, germ-free mice provide a reasonable model for the study of human aging. Death in genetically uniform strains may follow a random pattern similar to that found in genetically diverse strains.

There appear to be a number of genes controlling the life span of the various cell types of the body, and many genetic diseases reflect the presence of abnormal and presumably mutant counterparts to normal genes. Mutations leading to segmental progeroid syndromes and early mortality in mice and in humans provide support for the idea that a specific number of genes are involved in aging.

From the evolutionary point of view, animal senescence is viewed as the result of diminished selection during the post-reproductive period and accumulation of genes acting detrimentally in the post-reproductive period, as discussed in Chapter 2.

Increased life expectancy of modern humans is due to improved health and medical practices, not to genetically altered life span. In modern times survival is not solely a function of strength and disease resistance. In the absence of infectious disease and accident, natural death is genetic death. Most claims for exceptionally long life in human populations are unsubstantiated, though living habits in some geographical areas are conducive to realization of maximal life span. In some diseases of senescence it is possible that one of the basic lesions is a breakdown of DNA repair systems.

REFERENCES

Benditt, E. P., and J. M. Benditt. Evidence for a monoclonal origin of human atherosclerotic plaques. *Proceedings of the National Academy of Science, USA* 70:1753–1756, 1973.

Benet, S. *Abkhasians: The Long-Living People of the Caucasus.* Holt, Reinhart and Winston, New York, 1974.

Burnet, F. M. Age-associated heredo-degenerative conditions of the central nervous system. In H. T. Blumenthal, ed., *Handbook of Diseases of Aging.* Van Nostrand, New York, 1983.

Burnet, F. M. *Endurance of Life.* Cambridge University Press, London, 1978.

Cole, L. C. D. The population consequences of life history phenomena. *Quarterly Review of Biology* 29:103–137, 1954.

Cutler, R. G. Evolution of human longevity and the genetic complexity governing aging rate. *Proceedings of the National Academy of Science, USA* 72:4664, 1975.

DeBusk, F. L. The Hutchinson-Gilford progeria syndrome. *Journal of Pediatrics* 80:697–724, 1972.

Epstein, C. J., G. M. Martin, A. L. Schultz, and A. G. Motulsky. Werner's syndrome. A review of its symptomology, natural history, pathologic features, genetics, and relationship to the natural aging process. *Medicine* 45:177–221, 1966.

Hart, R. W., S. M. D'Ambrosio, K. J. Ng, S. P. Modaak. Longevity, stability and DNA repair. *Mechanisms of Ageing and Development* 9:203, 1979.

Kirkwood, T. B. L. Repair and its evolution: Survival versus reproduction. In C. R. Townsend and P. Calow, eds., *Physiological Ecology: An Evolutionary Approach to Resource Use.* Blackwell, Oxford.

Leaf, A. Every day is a gift when you are over 100. *National Geographic* 143:93–118, 1973.

Lewin, R. The origin of the modern human mind. *Science* 236:668, 1987.

McKay, C. M., M. F. Crowell, and L. A. Maynard. The effect of retarded growth upon the length of life span and upon the ultimate body size. *Journal of Nutrition* 10:63–79, 1935.

Martin, G. M. Genetic syndromes in man with potential relevance to the pathobiology of aging. In D. Bergsma and D. E. Harrison, eds., *Genetic Effects of Aging.* The National Foundation—March of Dimes. *Birth Defects: Original Article Series,* 14(1), 1978. Alan R. Liss, New York, 1978.

Marttila, R. J., P. Arstila, J. Nikoskelainen, P. E. Halonen, and U. K. Rinne. Viral antibodies in the sera of patients with Parkinson's disease. *European Neurology* 15:25, 1977.

Masoro, E. J. Food restriction in rodents: An evaluation of its role in the study of aging. *Journal of Gerontology* 43:B59, 1988.

Masoro, E. J., B. P. Yu, and H. A. Bertrand. Action of food restriction in delaying the aging process. *Proceedings of the National Academy of Science, USA* 79:4239, 1982.

Masoro, E. J., M. S. Katz, and C. A. McMahan. Evidence for the glycation hypothesis of aging from the food-restricted rodent model. *Journal of Gerontology* 44:B20, 1989.

Mazess, R., and S. Forman. Longevity and age by exaggeration in Vilcabamba, Ecuador. *Journal of Gerontology* 34:94–98, 1979.

Moment, G. B. Theories of Aging: An Overview. In Adelman and Roth, eds., *Testing the Theories of Aging.* CRC Press, Boca Raton, Fla., 1982.

Osborne, T. B., and L. B. Mendel. The resumption of growth after continued failure to grow. *Journal of Biological Chemistry* 23:439–447, 1915.

Sacher, G. A. Maturation and longevity in relation to cranial capacity in hominid evolution. In R. H. Tuttle, ed., *Antecedents of Man and After.* Vol. 1. Mouton, The Hague, 1975.

Sacher, G. A. Relation of lifespan to brain weight and body weight in mammals. *Ciba Foundation Colloquy on Ageing* 5:115, 1959.

Sacher, G. A., and R. W. Hart. Longevity, aging and comparative cellular and molecular biology of the house mouse, *Mus musculus,* and the white-footed mouse, *Peromyscus leucopus.* In D. Bergsma and D. E. Harrison, eds., *Genetic Effects of Aging.* The National Foundation—March of Dimes. *Birth Defects: Original Article Series.,* 14(1). Alan R. Liss, New York, 1978.

Sacher, G. A., and E. F. Staffeldt. Relation of gestation time to brain weight for placental mammals. Implications for the theory of vertebrate growth. *American Naturalist* 108:593–615, 1974.

Schneider, E. L., and G. D. Bynum. Diseases that feature alterations resembling premature aging. In H. T. Blumenthal, ed., *Handbook of Diseases of Aging.* Van Nostrand, New York, 1983.

Sinex, F. M., and C. R. Merril. Preface. In F. M. Sinex and C. R. Merril, eds. Alzheimer's disease, Down's syndrome, and aging. *Annals of the New York Academy of Science* 396, 1982.

Smith, K. Personal communication. 1988.

Strehler, B. L. *Time Cells and Aging.* 2nd ed. Academic Press, New York, 1977.

Tanzi, R. E., et al. Amyloid beta protein gene: cDNA, mRNA distribution, and genetic linkage near the Alzheimer locus. *Science* 235:880, 1987.

Weindruch, R., and R. L. Walford. Dietary restriction in mice beginning at 1 year of age: Effect on life-span and spontaneous cancer incidence. *Science* 215:-1415, 1982.

Whalley, L. J. The dementia of Down's syndrome and its relevance to aetiological studies of Alzheimer's disease. In F. M. Sinex and C. R. Merril, eds., Alzheimer's disease, Down's syndrome, and aging. *Annals of the New York Academy of Science* 396, 1982.

Williams, G. C. Pleiotropy, natural selection, and the evolution of senescence. *Evolution* 11:398, 1957.

Chapter
4

Genetics and Theories of Aging

DNA AND MOLECULAR GENETICS

Conservation of DNA

From the discussion to this point, it is increasingly obvious that genetics and aging are inextricably interwoven and that an understanding of the rudiments of genetics is critical to an understanding of the central role of genetics in aging.

The metabolic stability of the genetic material, deoxyribonucleic acid (DNA), is unique. While most molecules of cells turn over (are degraded and replaced) with regularity, DNA is not replaced (neglecting for the moment the process of DNA repair). Most cells do not synthesize new DNA. The cells of the epithelia and mesothelia (skin, gut, connective tissue) do divide and DNA replication is therefore found. The DNA of the nerve cells, heart and other muscle cells, and other cells (termed *postmitotic* cells, since they do not divide after birth) of a 65-year-old person is essentially the same macromolecule that was present at his or her birth. The lifetime stability of DNA is of prime importance in combating the aging process.

The DNA of the nucleus is the repository of all genetic information which eventually, when decoded into proteins, finds its way into the cell machinery in the cytoplasm (Figure 4.1). At the level of the cell, these genetic products function as units of cell structure and as components of the energy-generating systems that maintain life. The conservation of DNA is critical for the proper structure and function of the units of life, the cells. To this end, there are complex cellular mechanisms for the repair of damage or errors that befall DNA molecules during the course of life.

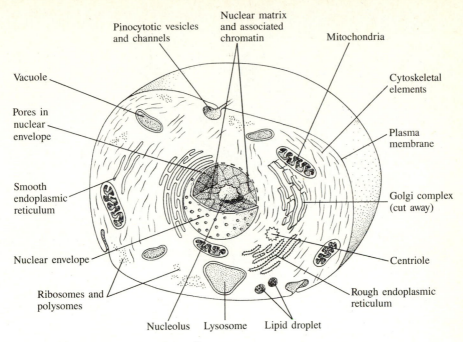

Figure 4.1 Normal eukaryotic cell.

However, even as DNA is being conserved (repaired) for the performance of vital life functions, it may also be falling victim to errors in DNA repair as the individual ages.

Chromosomes and DNA

Modern genetics is based on the studies of Avery and his associates (Avery, McLeod, and McCarty, 1944), who first successfully correlated the physical and chemical properties of DNA with the genetic role of DNA in living organisms, and on the studies of Watson and Crick (1953), who unraveled the mysteries of DNA structure and replication.

Everything a plant or animal is, both structurally and functionally, depends on the kind of DNA (genes) with which it is endowed. Each gene is a linear, specifically ordered sequence of the DNA subunits. DNA is a component of the chromosomes found in the nucleus of the cell (Figure 4.2). Chromosomes are paired structures (one member of each pair from the father, one from the mother) which contain the genes along their length. Humans have 23 pairs of chromosomes (Figure 4.3), each pair differing from the others in shape and size as well as in genetic content. Each gene is represented twice, reflecting contributions from both parents. Each gene may also take on several different forms; for example, eye color comes in blue, brown, hazel, etc. Such alternate forms of genes occupying a particular position in a chromosome are called alleles, or

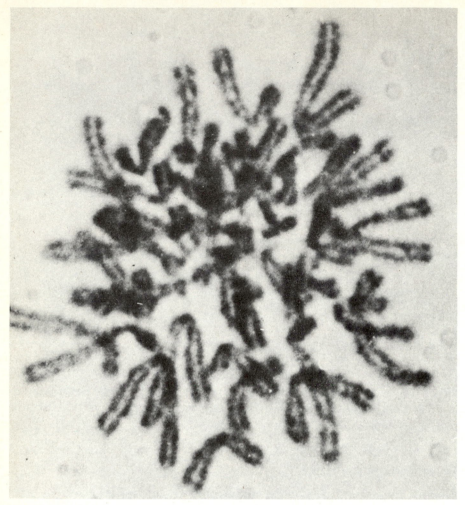

Figure 4.2 Human metaphase chromosomes. (From D. L. Hartl. *Human Genetics.* Copyright 1983 by Harper & Row, New York. Used with permission.)

allelic genes. Some alleles dominate over others, as brown eyes "cover" blue. Other alleles act in concert to produce a blend. The information for expressing specialized proteins, such as hemoglobin of the red blood cells, or for controling the developmental pathway of an organism is encoded in the DNA in the chromosomes.

The Cell Cycle

Cell division, or mitosis, is divided into several subphases (Figure 4.4). During prophase the chromosomes prepare for division by condensing into shorter, fatter structures. During metaphase the nuclear envelope

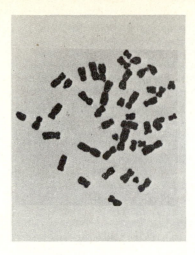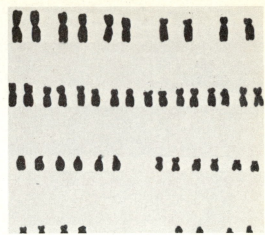

Figure 4.3 Human female karyotype. *(a)* Spread of 23 pairs of chromosomes during metaphase. *(b)* Arrangements into 22 pairs of autosomes and 1 pair (XX) of sex chromosomes. (From D. L. Hartl. *Human Genetics.* Copyright 1983 by Harper & Row, New York. Used with permission.)

disappears, and the chromosomes assume a position in the center of the cell and attach to microtubules by their centromeres. By virtue of the microtubules, the centromeres are in turn attached to cell division centers, the centrioles, located at the poles of the cell. At anaphase the chromosomes move to the poles, and the cell cytoplasm constricts under the influence of microfilaments (cell fibrils that form a contractile ring around the girth of the cell). At telophase the nuclei reconstitute themselves as interphase nuclei, and the separation of daughter cells is completed.

Most of the life of a cell is spent in interphase. During interphase and prior to the next ensuing cell division, DNA is replicated. Prior to replication of DNA, cells are said to be in G1 of interphase. After replication, interphase cells as are spoken of as G2 cells. The synthesis of DNA occurs between G1 and G2, during the S phase (synthesis phase). Most body cells are functional in the G1 phase of interphase; they are termed postmitotic cells since they have completed their divisions. Some tissues (for example, skin) maintain some cells in G2 for rapid division during wound healing. Liver tissue contains some interphase cells which are tetraploid and octaploid. These cells do not divide and remain as functional liver cells throughout life.

DNA Structure, Replication, Transcription, and Repair

In order to better understand current theories of aging, it is necessary to have some idea of how genes are expressed at the molecular level. A human cell contains a DNA library with instructions on how to produce

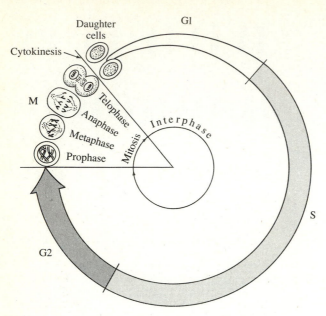

Figure 4.4 The cell cycle, mitosis (M) and interphase. Interphase is divided into G1, before replication of DNA; G2, after replication of DNA; and S, synthesis (replication) of DNA.

and maintain humans. This library is normally almost errorless, though, as we will see, there are places in the genetic system for errors to creep in. The central dogma of molecular genetics holds that the information contained in the genes is expressed through the directed synthesis of specific types of protein molecules.

The genetic information of a species is encoded into the structure of the DNA of the cells of that species. DNA in cells is organized as a double-stranded helix with the coding elements arranged tandemly along the length of the DNA molecule (Figure 4.5). Many double helices are organized into a chromosome, which also contains structural elements that serve to bind the DNA strands into the larger chromosomal packages.

To get the information out of DNA for use by the cell, the DNA strands, or tapes, are transcribed, or rewritten, into a closely related molecule, RNA (ribonucleic acid). Only a selected few genes are transcribed at a time in any given cell type. These transcripts are originally very large molecules termed heterogeneous nuclear RNA (HnRNA). Prior to transport, these molecules are processed and reduced in size and then exported from the nucleus of the cell, where the chromosomes are located, to the cytoplasm of the cell, where the protein-manufacturing machinery is found (see Figure 4.5). The RNA transcripts of the gene are called messenger RNA (mRNA) because these molecules carry a message of genetic information from the gene in the chromosome to the cytoplasm of the cell.

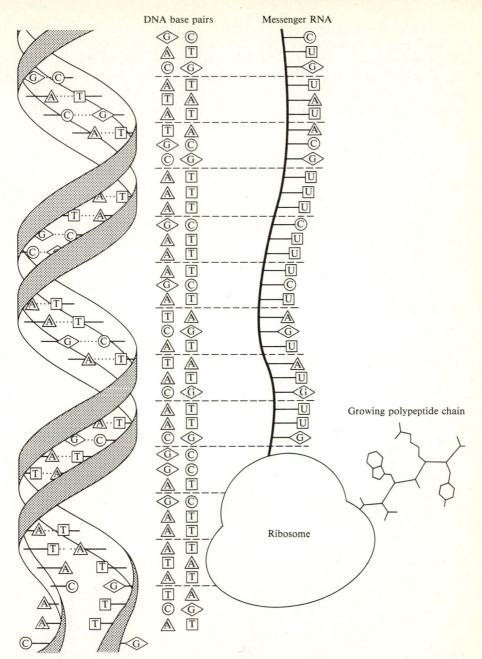

Figure 4.5 DNA structure. Left to right: DNA double helix; DNA helix straight-ened out and divided into triplet code "words"; mRNA transcript (from the left DNA strand) attached to one ribosome of the polysome. (From R. Dickerson and L. Geis, *The Structure and Action of Proteins.* Harper & Row, New York, 1969.)

Most mRNA is polyadenylated by addition of 50 to 200 adenosine residues at the 3′ end of the molecule. The purpose of polyadenylation is speculative, but the polyA content is useful for identifying mRNA. In the cytoplasm mRNA associates with bodies called ribosomes to form polyribosomes or polysomes, which are the active macromolecules for protein synthesis. Ribosomes are particles composed of RNA subunits combined with proteins. Ribosomal RNAs (rRNA) are transcribed from tandemly repeated genes collectively termed ribosomal DNA (rDNA), which in turn is associated with the nucleolus.

Structure of Chromatin

Chromatin is a complex of DNA and proteins located in the chromosomes. Among the proteins associated with DNA in chromatin, histones have a major role in the structural and functional organization of the genetic material (Figure 4.6). There are five classes of histones defined by their electrophoretic mobility and by their content of the amino acids lysine and arginine. The H1 class is richest in lysine, and H3 and H4 are richest

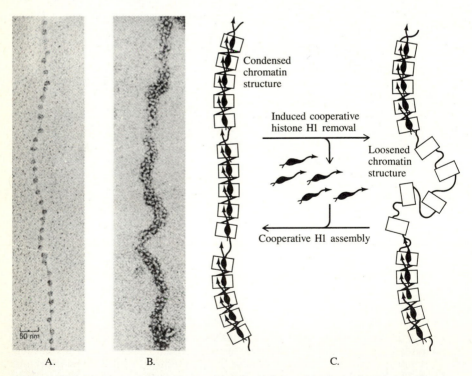

A.   B.   C.

Figure 4.6 Structure of chromatin. *(a)* Decondensed active chromatin showing nucleosomes (beads on a string). *(b)* Native structure (inactive) of chromatin. *(c)* Nucleosome structure involving histone molecules. (Photographs courtesy of Dr. V. Foe (a) and Dr. B. Hamkalo (b)).

in arginine. Slightly rich in lysine are the H2A and H2B classes. Histones H2 through H4 are the "core" histones in Figure 4.6c. The H1 class contains up to six distinct subtypes differing in their primary structure. The other histone classes are highly conserved and contain fewer subtypes; the subtypes are attributed primarily to modifications made after synthesis of these molecules and not to their primary structure.

Histones may have a role in gene expression. Gene expression may be controlled at the level of transcription, of processing and transporting the transcript, of translation of the transcript into protein, or of posttranslational modification of the protein product. In their search for the means by which the expression of genes is controlled, molecular biologists theorize that histones, especially H1, are an integral part of the total process involved in promoting or repressing gene transcription.

It is apparent that histone molecules do not contain sufficient information within themselves for the initiation of the schedule of chromatin changes during the program of gene activation. It is equally apparent that drastic alterations in chromatin structure accompany gene activation. During development of the sea urchin (and other forms) the subtype of H1 produced is drastically changed from the morula (late cleavage) stage to the gastrula. The existence of heterogeneity among H1 molecules provides a mechanism for control of the physical state of chromatin at different times in the life history of a cell. Cole (1984) has recently likened the role of H1 histone in gene activity to that of the disulfide bridge in stabilizing the folding of a protein. Assuming the various subtypes of H1 differ in their ability to condense DNA, and perhaps chromatin as well, they could act to stabilize patterns of cell activity and cell differentiation dependent on specific gene readout by opening and closing segments of the genome to transcription. The system that sets in motion the changes in H1 and core histones requisite for transcription of DNA remains unknown.

Histones are conserved during aging, though they certainly may play a role in any changing patterns of transcription with age. Histone acetylation undergoes an age-related decrease, a modification that leads to a structure of chromatin not conducive to transcription. At the same time the quantity and kind of histones associated with DNA in chromatin do not seem to change with age.

Protein Synthesis (Translation)

In the cytoplasm proteins are assembled, or translated, into polymers or chains of amino acids under the guidance of the messenger RNA transcript (Figure 4.7). There are 20 distinct varieties of amino acids. Messenger RNA combines with cytoplasmic ribosomes to form polyribosomes, with the ribosomal particles linearly arranged along the message. Transfer RNAs (tRNAs), one for each amino acid, bind to amino acids forming aminoacyl-tRNAs. These compounds then locate at the specific sites along the codon (mRNA) in the specified sequence by virtue of a nucleotide

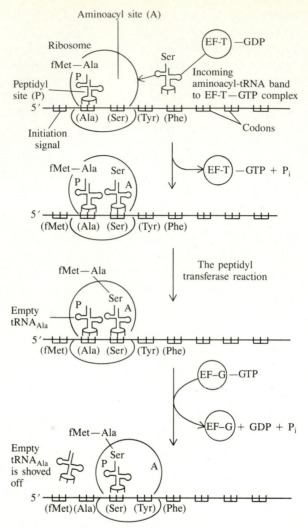

Figure 4.7 The elongation steps in protein synthesis. The ribosome contains proteins EF-T and EF-G (elongation factors T and G) which couple the reaction to the GTP high energy phosphate bond. From A. Lehninger. Biochemistry (2nd Ed.) © 1975 by Worth Pub. Co. New York. Used with permission.

triplet (the anticodon) in the tRNA. The sequence and kinds of amino acids impart the special properties characteristic of a specific protein and are determined by the type and sequence of the coding elements of the original DNA genes. The genetic code was cracked by the elegant experiments of Nirenberg, Watson, Crick, and others (see The Genetic Code, 1966).

Proteins may be structural, as in the case of collagen, or enzymatic, as in the case of the digestive enzymes pepsin and trypsin. Some other specific proteins contribute to chromosome structure, while others may act to regulate transcription.

Repair of DNA

DNA replicates itself during the S phase of mitosis by using the two helical strands as templates for the synthesis of new complementary strands. Errors of replication occur during a lifetime and are induced by a variety of environmental agents such as ionizing radiation and harmful chemicals encountered in a world of advanced technology. These errors are repaired by excision of the erroneous DNA segments and resynthesis of new complementary strands, using the second strand as a template. The process is complex and is governed by a series of enzymes for chaining or polymerizing the molecular components of DNA into large molecules, for excising segments, and for tying strands together end to end (Figure 4.8). Bear in mind that all these replication and repair enzymes for DNA are proteins and are themselves encoded and governed by specific genes in DNA—a marvelous system that seems to lift itself up by its own bootstraps.

Reiterated and Single-Copy DNA

Some DNA sequences are unique, represented only once in the genome. Other sequences are reiterated many times, at least 10^4 copies. In between are sequences that are moderately reiterated. The moderately repeated sequences are involved with production of tRNAs, rRNAs, and mRNAs for basic proteins (histones). Included in the unique sequences are genes coding for proteins other than histones. A large fraction of the genome is organized with reiterated sequences interspersed with single-copy sequences. The highly repeated sequences may in fact serve a regulatory function over the neighboring single-copy regions.

DNA Methylation

Methylation of cytosine residues of DNA relates to gene expression and thus might be important for aging phenomena. Gene activity during embryogenesis is associated with demethylation of the transcriptionally active DNA. Wilson and Jones (1983) compared mortal and immortal cells and methylation patterns. The level of methylation in senescing mouse cells was found to decrease (perhaps due to demethylation during previous cell divisions), while the level in viral-transformed immortal lines of mouse cells is stable. The changes may be indicative of aberrant gene expression in senescent cells or may simply reflect culture conditions.

Transposable DNA and Tumor Viruses

Some elements of the repeated DNA are capable of moving from one chromosome to another. The insertion of such a transposable element may be accompanied by disturbances in the expression of genes in that region of the chromosome, leading to changes in phenotype. These transposition effects were first described by McClintock, who received the 1983 Nobel

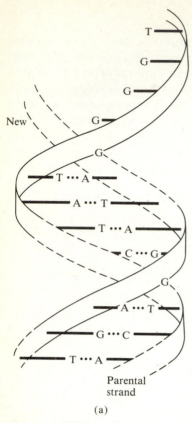

T

G

G

New   G

G

T ··· A

A ··· T

T ··· A

C ··· G

G

A ··· T

G ··· C

T ··· A

Parental
strand

(a)

Figure 4.8 DNA replication and repair. *(a)* DNA replication via semiconservative copying of parent strand into complementary daughter strand. Based on Figure 4.5. *(b)* Excision repair of DNA. (From F. M. Burnet. *Endurance of Life.* Copyright 1978 by Cambridge University Press, New York. Used with permission.)

Prize for her work on transposable elements in the genome of maize. It is important in this connection that the DNA of tumor viruses is also able to insert itself into the human genome virtually at random. We will deal more with this in our discussion of cancer cells in Chapter 6.

RELEVANCE OF EMBRYONIC DEVELOPMENT

Some students of biological aging hold that the aging process (but not necessarily senescence) begins at conception or even prior to fertilization of the egg. In the first case, fertilization begins a series of events that transform the fertilized egg into a newborn human, a series that includes both cell multiplication and cell death. In the second case, aging of the oocyte (potential mature egg) within the mother's ovary may have conse-

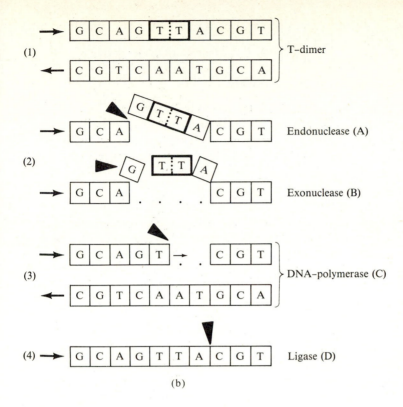

(b)

quences for age-related effects observed later in the life of the individual developing from that egg.

Program of Embryonic Development

The program of embryonic development is that series of events by which a fertilized egg, or zygote, is transformed into a newborn infant. This program is under genetic control and includes provision for the death of certain cells, as will be seen below. The fertilized human egg undergoes a number of cell divisions (mitoses) to generate a ball of cells. By a process of cell migrations and foldings of sheets of cells, an embryo composed of concentric layers of three basic cell types is formed. These three cell lines give rise to all the tissues and organs of the body.

From a single fertilized egg cell, an adult human composed of about 10^{14} (100 trillion) specialized cells arises. The embryonic cells destined to form different adult organs gradually assume the shape and function of those organs. Primitive heart cells become heart muscle and heart lining; liver cells assume characteristic functions and shapes; intestinal cells specialize for the secretion of enzymes for the digestion and absorption of nutrients. This process of cell change is called differentiation, and it occurs simultaneously with the assumption of characteristic form (anatomy) during embryonic development.

Cell Death During Early Development

Development includes differential cell death in its program. For example, the digits of the hand are molded by death and resorption of cells between the fingers (Saunders, 1966). Certain nerve cells (neurons) of the spinal cord are lost (Hamburger, 1958). Organs reminiscent of earlier evolutionary stages (the early primitive kidneys, the arteries concerned with gill respiration) are formed and then discarded.

Since the developmental pattern is a species-specific trait and therefore under genetic control, it follows that the programmed death of cells during embryonic development is also genetically controlled. The genetic program resulting in the differentiation of a cell ironically includes provision for the death of some cells in order to arrive at some aspects of body form characteristic of the species. One area programmed for death in the chick embryo is a zone of cells located where the future wing joins the body, an area called the posterior necrotic zone (Figure 4.9). These cells are programmed for death at a specific time in development and will also die in organ culture outside the body at the same time as their programmed death in the intact embryo. Other cells are selected for death by their inherent susceptibility to hormonal action, the same hormones that cause growth in other body cells.

It is abundantly clear that regressive phenomena during embryonic

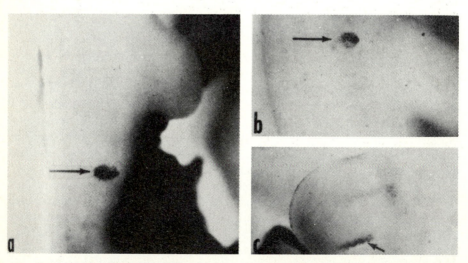

Figure 4.9 Cell necrosis (posterior necrotic zone) during development of the wing of the chick. (From J. W. Saunders, Jr. *Science* 154:604, 1966.)

development are programmed to occur in a highly predictable manner and under genetic control. As might be expected, there exist mutant genes that achieve expression by extending or contracting the normal pattern of cellular death or even by causing death of tissues or organs in which such changes do not normally occur. For example, a mutation in fowl called rumpless results from the extension of a restricted but normal zone of cell death leading ultimately to the destruction of tail vertebrae and associated tail structures. In contrast, some mutations lead to abnormalities through failure of normal degenerations to occur, as in the rare persistence of the embryonic tail or webbing between fingers and toes in humans. These mutations, involving either abnormal cell death or abnormal cell survival, are heritable in the classical Mendelian mode as single or sometimes multiple gene differences.

In general among the vertebrates, the mechanism of cell death seems to be suicide rather than assassination by "killer" cells. Cells possess internal membrane-bound vesicles (lysosomes) containing enzymes capable of digesting critical portions of the cell. Maintenance of the membrane boundary of these vesicles is thus crucial to cell life; breakdown of the lysosomal membrane results in rapid cell death. Though the suicide "trigger" remains unknown, the mechanism may well ultimately operate at the level of genetic copying resulting in failure of genetic information to reach the synthetic machinery of the cell (Saunders, 1966). This of course still leaves open the question of the cause of failure of genetic readout.

From the developmental or embryological point of view, genetically programmed cell death is one of many mechanisms utilized to arrive at normal body form. The relevance of this kind of developmental change for aging is clear. Perhaps all cells of the body are genetically programmed for death at some definite time in the life course. We will encounter evidence for this in Chapter 5, when we will examine aging at the cellular level. All human cells so far tested have been shown to have a finite life span when grown outside the body in tissue culture. After some 50 cell generations, all cells lose the ability to divide and enter into a period of senescence followed by cell death. The cells of other mammals have similar restrictions on life span in culture. The significant fact is that the life span of cells in culture is directly related to the life span of the donor species. The relationship of senescence in cell culture to senescence in the whole animal is unclear, since most body cells are postmitotic, especially during adult life.

Recessive Nature of Immortality

Cell fusion studies (Pereira-Smith and Smith, 1983) between normal human diploid cells and transformed, immortal fibroblasts yield cell hybrids with finite life spans. It was also found, in complementation studies, that at least two separate events can result in immortality. These experiments involved fusions between two distinct lines of immortal parent cells, where it was discovered that these lines complement each other yielding a hybrid line with finite division capacity (see also Chapter 6).

Gene Activity During Development

The modern theory of development holds that different genes are active in different cells as a result of the differentiation process in those cells. Control of gene activation is likely a function of the histones of chromatin as a coarse control, with fine control supplied by other elements of the genome, perhaps associated with reiterated sequences. The nuclei during early development are interchangeable. During development, with the exception of the vertebrate immune system, the DNA remains unchanged. Genes that are destined to remain silent in differentiated cells of different tissues are retained intact and may be reactivated. These concepts derive from nuclear transplantation studies, cell fusion studies, and studies of circumstances where the function of a cell is altered, as happens during regeneration. Nuclear transplants involve removal of nuclei from advanced tissue cells and their subsequent introduction into enucleated eggs. In this experimental situation the genes that are active in the differentiated state are repressed, and the genes that are active early in development, but silent later, are reactivated. The egg with its transplanted nucleus may then undergo normal development.

Another line of evidence regarding the unchanging DNA content of differentiated cells comes from studies of teratocarcinomas derived from mouse testis. These malignant tumors derive from abnormal primordial germ cells and can be cultured outside the body where they take on two forms. One, the embryoid body, resembles an early mouse embryo with early embryonic tissues defined. The other is a rapidly dividing cell population that may be transplanted into the testis of another mouse where it will give rise to additional tumors. It has also proved possible to transplant the malignant cell type into a developing mouse embryo, one cell at a time. Host and tumor cell can come from different strains, and this property can be used to genetically mark host and donor tissues in the resulting chimera (a tissue mosaic derived from two fused, genetically diverse, individuals). The tumor cell in this case is normal as to chromosome complement. The amazing result is that the tumor cell is "tamed" in the embryonic environment and directed to participate in the formation of many different tissues in the chimera, the most remarkable of which is the formation of sperm in male hosts. This can be verified using coat color as a genetic marker. Zygotes formed by a sperm ultimately derived from a black mouse via the tumor transplant display the proper genetics of their strain of origin. It is quite properly said that such a zygote, which develops in completely normal fashion, had a tumor for a father!

In summary, the genome during development is altered in activity, meaning altered as to which genes are expressed and which are suppressed in reversible fashion. The exception is the vertebrate immune system.

The Immune System and Genetic Rearrangements

The immune system, as one of its first steps in differentiation, learns to distinguish "self" from "not self." The aim of this process is to exclude the production of antibodies against the cells and proteins of one's own body. The embryonic thymus in some fashion scans its surroundings and records as self the surfaces and molecules in evidence, including any tissue or substance that was experimentally introduced. This explains why the teratocarcinoma cell above is not attacked by the mouse immune system. Since it is already part of the embryo during scanning, it is treated as self, leading to a condition known as immune tolerance; any challenge of the adult chimeric mouse by tissues derived from the donor mouse strain is treated as a graft from the host mouse (an autograft). The future T cells and B cells are derived from stem cells that do not produce antibody. The T cells take up residence in the thymus and the B cells ultimately in the bone marrow in mammals. Each has its specialized function, T cells controlling cellular immunity (response to tissue grafts and tumors arising in the body) and B cells secreting serum globulins that combine with foreign molecules and bacteria to eliminate invaders. Tolerance ideally eliminates the possibility of autologous attacks, since the self scanning eliminates those cells that would have been able to become involved in an autoimmune response.

The repertoire of possible responses is a function of individual cells. Considering B cells, every antigen (substance capable of eliciting an immune response) has a corresponding B cell which, on contact with its antigen, does two things: (1) divides to found a clone of cells and (2) produces gamma globulin to neutralize the antigen. In this way each antigen induces the formation of a clone of B lymphocytes directed specifically against the cell or substance acting as antigen. This process is called clonal selection.

The genetic rearrangement alluded to above involves B cells and possibly T cells as well. Since each antibody-forming cell responds to a different antigen by production of a single type of antibody molecule, how is this encoded in the genome? Each antibody molecule is composed of a constant and variable portion. The variable portion is coded for by a family of genes responsible for one potential antigen and located away from that portion of the genome coding for the constant portion of the globulin molecule. Since specificity depends on molecular three-dimensional shape, the amino acid sequence of the variable portions is varied, leading to different three-dimensional configurations. The variable and constant genes are physically separated in germ cell DNA, but in development of T and B cells the constant and variable coding segments are moved closer together and are transcribed as a single, large unit which is processed into a messenger RNA for both portions of the molecule. Once the rearrangement has been made in a particular lymphocyte, T or B, no further rearrangements are possible, thus restricting the cell to respond to one type of antigen only.

In the mouse the germ cells are estimated to have 100 to 300 separate and distinct variable genes. Since some variety is introduced in binding the variable and constant genes together, the number of specifically different types of antibody is estimated to be in the 4,000 to 12,000 range. The basis for this mechanism is the so-called hypermutability of the globulin genes during the rearrangement. Thus a limited number of variable sequences in the germ line can give rise to a wide diversity of gene products. This mechanism has not been found in other tissue types, but has not been excluded as a working model where specialized production of one of a class of related proteins is a part of the differentiation of a specific tissue. These rearrangements could be looked upon as one form of program restriction.

THEORIES OF AGING

The following discussion considers the currently popular theories of aging. Each has its advocates and a body of supporting data. Each has limitations that detract from its universal applicability. The theories are not necessarily mutually exclusive. There exists the definite possibility that a theory yet to be formulated may be closer to the truth than any of those described here. And, the search for a single cause of senescence may be elusive; much evidence in biological gerontology favors a multiplicity of causes for age-related changes rather than a single, universal cause (Hayflick, 1985). Theories involving the finite life span of cells in culture will be considered in the next chapter.

Immune Theory

The immune theory rests on two major findings. First, the ability of the immune system to deal with foreign organisms or molecules diminishes with age, with the greatest decline in thymus-derived immunity (T cell or cellular immunity). Second, with the decline of immune system function there is a concomitant increase in "mistakes" by the immune system in treating autologous tissues as foreign (autoimmunity). Both of these conditions lead to increased vulnerability to disease and to abnormalities resulting from the autoimmune responses. It has also been demonstrated (Walford, Jawaid, and Naeim, 1983) that the number of population doublings of human T cells declines as a function of donor age. This extends the observations of Hayflick (1965) on cultured normal fibroblasts to yet another cell type.

Advocates of the immune theory of aging point out that many diseases of later life are characterized by some degree of immune system dysfunction. These diseases include cancer (failure of immune surveillance), mature-onset diabetes (autoantibody activity against insulin receptors, insulin, and islet cells of the pancreas), senile dementia (autoantibody activity against neuronal surfaces and neurofilaments), and perhaps some vascular disease.

Problems with the immune theory of aging arise when one considers the lack of immune systems (as found in vertebrates) among animals that show aging and senescence. Also, the immune system is in some measure under the control of the neuroendocrine system (Chapter 7), and age changes in the immune system may be reflections of changes in endocrine regulation. Finally, there may be changes with age in the cellular antigens of the body that would render them nonself to an unaltered immune system. Examples of this autoimmune effect are seen in changes with age in proteins such as collagen and in errors in transcription, translation, or posttranslational alterations.

Neuroendocrine Theory

No part of the body acts independently of the neurological and endocrine systems. Loss of neurons and endocrine cells with age has been documented. A 10 percent decrease in brain weight occurs over the life span in humans. This loss is not necessarily all cell loss, but may reflect losses of fluids and ground substance as well. Cell losses that are known to occur are usually restricted to discrete areas of cerebral and cerebellar cortex.

Many age changes in responses to hormones are also known. Some of these are due to changes in receptors for hormones rather than to changes in endocrine activity.

Like the immune theory, the neuroendocrine theory lacks universality and may also simply reflect changes in all body cells with age, perhaps through changes in the regulation of gene expression.

Somatic Mutation Theory

Mutations are defined as inheritable changes in the DNA of a cell. If damage to DNA is extensive, and not properly repaired, a genetic sequence may be altered. The product of such a gene will also be changed, usually in a deleterious way; few mutations prove to be advantageous.

Most cells of mammals are nondividing and produce no progeny. Mutations in these single cells can only be indirectly inferred from the demonstration of inheritable changes produced in populations of cells which divide to form a larger observable clone. Since most cells of the body are nondividing, the result of somatic mutation and a nonmutational change may be the same, cell death or gene product loss (Hirsch, 1978). The frequency of somatic mutation is low, and many feel that such genetic changes are unlikely candidates for a central role in the aging process. It is true that exposure to x-rays causes increased rate of mutation and shortens life expectancy in humans; the degree of shortening of life is directly related to dose level (Prasad, 1974). However, it has been shown that the primary lesions of aging and of radiation damage are not identical. Radiation primarily affects populations of dividing cells—the skin, the lining of the intestine, and bone marrow. In contrast, apart from the limit on number of cell divisions, age affects primarily those cell lines which do not normally divide in the adult, such as the nerve and muscle cells.

Calculations of the rate of somatic mutation in the absence of radiation above environmental background levels indicate a rate much too low to account for the overall age-related changes observed in animal proteins. The continued, accurate synthesis of hemoglobin in older humans by a population of dividing stem (precursor) cells indicates an absence of accumulated somatic mutations within the hemoglobin gene sequence. This dissimilarity between radiation effects and normal aging is especially apparent when one compares the elevated amino acid substitutions in persons exposed to radiation 20 years before studies of their hemoglobin were made. These observations show that while increased levels of radiation do lead to changes in hemoglobin, normal aging does not. It remains true that exposure to any level of radiation contributes to an accumulative effect which shortens life and increases the incidence of cancers at all ages.

In Chapter 2 we discussed the wasp Habrobracon, an animal having both haploid and diploid males. If somatic mutation were the basis of aging, haploids would be expected to exhibit more rapid accumulation of mutations and a shorter life span. In fact, the haploids and diploids have identical life spans. Haploid males are more sensitive to radiation than the diploids, yet irradiation shortens the life of diploids far more than the life of haploids. Also, tetraploid human cells have the same doubling capacity as controls, indicating that genomic redundancy does not protect, as would be expected if somatic mutations were an important factor in aging.

It has also been pointed out that no somatic mutation theory has explained the following two points: (1) The germ cell line is immortal and shows no accumulation within a generation of deleterious mutations. (2) Immortal but cancerous clones can emerge from senescent somatic cells by virus transformations. One must postulate special "cleansing" functions for the gonadal or neoplastic tissues to account for the absence of accumulated (lethal) mutations (Ohno and Nagai, 1978). However, the existence of special systems in these tissues for purging the DNA of mutations has not been demonstrated as yet.

Error and Fidelity Theory

The error and fidelity theory is an outgrowth of the somatic mutation theory. It has been pointed out that it is not necessary to postulate somatic mutations to account for the observed accumulation of altered proteins in cells. Medvedev (1980) suggested that the errors could be in functioning

DNA sequences. Orgel (1963, 1970) suggested that errors in protein synthesis without alterations of DNA could lead to an accumulation of altered protein molecules.

The error theory of aging is one of the most extensively studied molecular theories of aging. The idea behind it is simple: All aging (and perhaps cancer as well) results from a decline in the fidelity of all biological components. It is difficult in practice to discover exactly where a given error originally took place—at the DNA level or at the level of transcription, translation, or posttranslation. The cell is a highly complex structure, governed ultimately by its genetic code. Fidelity as used here means the faithful reproduction of proper proteins from transcription of genes and translation of the messenger RNA into the proteins that act as catalysts or as components of cell structure. The decrease in fidelity of transcription or translation is termed error and is distinct from DNA-based mutations. Errors in transcription or translation result in the insertion of improper amino acids into the sequence comprising a particular protein.

This hypothesis led to a series of experiments designed to measure whether or not aging could be accelerated by addition of analogues for amino acids during protein synthesis and by studies designed to reveal whether or not altered proteins accumulated in aging cells. The theory is in general disfavor despite the demonstrated existence of altered proteins in aging cells, including human cells. Recall in Chapter 2 we learned of an alternative explanation for the persistence of such altered molecules: diminished turnover rates resulting in the accumulation of posttranslational modifications in some proteins (see the section on nematodes, p. 31). We will see in Chapter 5 that there is little evidence in support of increased rates of missynthesis with age.

A study of virus replication has been done in human fibroblast cultures. Holland, Kohne, and Doyle (1973) argued that the accumulation of large amounts of abnormal proteins should interfere with virus replication due to altered replicases and structural proteins involved in the self-assembly of virus particles. Utilizing early and late passage cells (the late passage cells were nondividing), these authors were able to demonstrate that viral yields from early and late passage cells were equal. The infectivity of the resulting virus particles was also the same regardless of the state of aging of the host cells.

Utilizing two-dimensional electrophoresis for resolution of normal and altered proteins, Harley and coworkers (1980) have demonstrated that the number of errors in protein synthesis does not increase with aging in normal human fibroblasts in culture. Cells derived from patients suffering from progeria or Werner's syndrome were also analyzed and found not to have increased errors when compared with early passage cells from young donors. In contrast, an immortal line of cells derived by SV40 virus transformation show increased error frequency when compared with mortal lines of fibroblasts in culture.

On the other hand, Murray and Holliday (1981) have demonstrated increased error frequency of DNA polymerases derived from senescent human fibroblasts, utilizing a method that assays the frequency of DNA polymerase–directed errors that are present as single base substitutions.

DNA repair is positively correlated with longevity. Hart and Setlow (1982) found that the efficiency with which cultured cells repaired ultraviolet damage was directly related to species life span. Chromosomal aberrations (deletions, translocations, inversions) are manifestations of DNA damage and repair. These have been studied over time (Curtis, Leith, and Tilley, 1966; Curtis and Miller, 1971); in liver they are found to increase steadily throughout life (not suddenly at the end) at a rate inversely proportional to the animal's life span. The increase in strand breakage in liver cells may occur more significantly during the early portion of an animal's life span than near the end of life (Ono, Okada, and Sugahara, 1976). This observation would indicate that a decline in DNA repair capability is not a requisite for senescence, but rather that a portion of or type of DNA lesion escapes repair, perhaps leading to irreparable damage within the cell. The increase in lesions may, however, be liver-specific and not reflective of general conditions during aging in the whole animal (see also the section on DNA repair in Chapter 5).

Medvedev (1972) proposed that loss of unique DNA sequences could produce age decrements and that the presence of selected reiterated sequences may have evolved as a means of providing redundancy necessary for preservation of vital information. Evidence in support of this view has been provided by Cutler (1974), who reported the loss of ribosomal DNA from mouse tissues during the last year of life (see the program restriction theory below).

It seems that errors may accumulate with age in cells. It is equally apparent that accumulation of errors is no guarantee of cell death. There may be a point in error accumulation where it becomes overwhelming, or catastrophic. Below this point errors may be present at noncritical levels and balanced by turnover and repair mechanisms. There is some evidence that abnormal proteins are degraded selectively by proteases. In aging cells attention might well focus on the proteases as a source of senescence should they be abnormal and thereby allow error accumulation.

It also seems apparent that these errors accumulate as random (stochastic) events and are not programmed into the genetics of the cell. The programming aspect seems inescapable, however, due to the inherently genetic nature of life spans. It must enter the picture in the form of repair or restoration systems that differ in their efficiency among the species.

As Medvedev states (1980), "The molecular biology of aging is still very much a descriptional, not an explanational, branch of gerontology."

Glycation Theory of Aging   The hypothesis that glucose acts as a mediator of aging was recently proposed by Cerami (1985). The process involves non-enzymatic reactions that occur between reducing sugars and tissue proteins and nucleic acids. The term *glycation* is preferred over the frequently encountered *glycosylation* (Roth, 1983). The end products of such reactions, in the case of proteins, leads to dehydrated and rearranged irreversible structures referred to as advanced glycation end products. Similar end products are formed between DNA and reducing sugars. Glycated proteins exhibit loss of enzyme activity, inappropriate cross-linking, and decreased degradation of abnormal proteins. The diminished capacity of diabetic cells for doublings in culture (Chapter 5), the lessened life span of diabetics, who generally exhibit higher than normal plasma glucose levels, have been used as a basis for proposing the role of glycation products in senescence (Cerami, 1985). Glycation of DNA, most usually uracil residues derived by deamination of thymine (estimated to be about 100 bases per human genome per day), if not repaired by excision-repair and uracil-DNA glycosylase, can induce mutations (Duncan and Weiss, 1978).

Hemoglobin, collagen, and lens protein are among the proteins that undergo glycation with age. Glycation of collagen may lead to elasticity changes in blood vessels, tendons, and much of the connective tissue stroma of body tissues (Kohn et al., 1984). Glycation of nucleic acids is associated with diminished activity of uracil-DNA glycosylase in late passage cells in culture, and in cells of Werner syndrome patients, which normally have a shorter *in vitro* life span than cells derived from normal patients of the same age (Bucala et al., 1984; Yamamoto and Fujiwara, 1987).

Thus, glycation would seem to have profound cumulative effects throughout the life span. The DNA effects might reasonably be explained by diminished DNA repair mechanisms in old age, and thus would fall under another theory category. The protein effects may prove to be substantial contributors to age changes, and seem, superficially, to parallel the elevated glucose levels and shorter life span of diabetics (Masoro et al., 1989), though the relationship between diabetes and aging has yet to be defined. It remains to be seen whether these glycation effects are the cause of aging or a result of changes occuring in other fundamental processes.

Program Restriction Theory

As we have discussed at some length in this chapter, it is now recognized that all genetic information depends on the base sequence of various portions of DNA. It is also known that only a small proportion of the information in DNA is utilized by cells of the various tissues. Only the sequences appropriate for a particular tissue are transcribed and translated; the remaining 95 percent or so of the DNA is "turned off." During embryonic development different segments of the genome are activated at different times. Other segments are suppressed. As a consequence, different messenger RNA molecules are synthesized at different times and appear in a temporal sequence, yielding a sequence of different proteins.

The concept of program restriction states that aging may be due to increased turn-off of DNA, leading to impaired ability of the cell to transcribe necessary RNAs, including messenger RNAs. It is also possible that some essential messages may be transcribed at all ages but that the ability to translate these messages into functional proteins is restricted in cells of older individuals. Support for the program restriction theory comes from observations that some segments of DNA, notably rDNA, which are ordinarily represented many times in the genome and which code for some of the translation machinery of the cytoplasm, are depleted with advancing age. In addition, though DNA segments may not be physically lost, chromatin structure seems to change with age in a way that favors restriction of DNA transcription. This might lead to a functional loss of portions of the gene library, though there is no evidence for selective restriction as opposed to an overall reduction in transcription.

In connection with program restriction, earlier we found that certain cells of the embryo are programmed for death during development and that this death may result from blockage of gene readout (Saunders, 1966). The cells so designated for death by the genetic program of development are located at specific places, such as between the fingers of the hand. The question was raised whether all cells of the body are similarly programmed for ultimate senescence and death. If so, then the specific program must be vastly different in different individuals of the same species because the causes of death are so diverse. Recall Chapter 3 where the central riddle of aging was posed as the variable causes of death in highly inbred strains of mice. Also, short reflection will bring to mind the fact that senescing humans suffer a broad spectrum of organ system failures. If senescence were an extension of the developmental program, one might expect a more regular and predictable sequence of organ system failures than is commonly observed.

Nongenetic Theories

These theories deal with changes in cell molecules after they have been formed, changes that are assumed to impair their function.

Effects of Temperature Chemical reactions in living systems are slowed at low temperature and accelerated with higher temperature. It has been assumed that an increased rate of living shortens life span. Some have used the observation that life span of cold-blooded animals is extended with lower temperature to explain aging in terms of the "wearing out" of components of cells.

It is known that among warm-blooded species life span is inversely proportional to metabolic rate; those mammals with high metabolic rates tend to be the smaller, shorter-lived species. This observation does not explain differences in life span within a species, the members of which have similar metabolic rates. However, if humans could manage to live with a body temperature 5° lower than the usual 98.6°F, we might expect to live about 20 percent longer (Strehler, 1975). Life would be at a very slow pace if, indeed, life could be sustained at all.

Deprivation Some theories postulate deprivation of some essential nutrient or oxygen as a cause of aging. The deprivation leads to senescence of the deprived cells. The pattern caused by such deprivation does not approximate that of normal aging. All deprived cells in a given area will die from impaired circulation. In normal aging cell death and disappearance of cells from tissues occur in a random fashion. It is more profitable to think of deprivation as being the result of aging in some individuals rather than the cause of aging.

Lipofuscin Aging humans accumulate age pigments called lipofuscin. This is another manifestation of advancing years, and it appears to be a result of senescence rather than a cause. No impairment of cell function by accumulated lipofuscin has as yet been demonstrated.

Free Radicals and Antioxidants Much has been said recently about damage to cells from free radicals. Free radicals are charged molecules produced transiently during normal metabolism or in greater numbers by radiation. Radicals from radiation may be comparatively long-lived. These free radicals are powerful oxidants and can destroy cell components. A review of the free radical theory (Balin, 1982) states that much evidence supporting this theory is circumstantial and does not allow one to distinguish whether damage by free radicals is a cause or a result of aging.

Mammalian tissues normally contain an enzyme, superoxidedismutase (SOD), which acts to remove free radicals. As expected, long-lived species are characterized by high levels of SOD. One might postulate that since the SOD of a given species is coded for in the DNA of that species, it would be better to consider damage from free radicals under the heading of genetic theories of cell aging.

There are chemicals that are free radical scavengers, among them vitamin E. These antioxidants have been tested on mice by addition to the diet. Some antioxidants increased the life expectancy or average life span of the mice; vitamin E did not. In no case was the maximal life span of the mice extended. In view of the contradictory evidence, there is no general acceptance of the free radical theory of aging, though it is reasonably certain that under extreme conditions of total body irradiation, free radicals account for a considerable amount of damage, which may go unrepaired.

Alteration (Cross-Linking) of Stable Molecules With time, certain molecules that are relatively stable, either within the cell or as part of extracellular material, become chemically altered. Proteins may become glycated or cross-linked, altering their structure of function. Cross-linking also occurs in DNA between the two strands of the helix. DNA cross-linking has been observed in cells in culture but not *in vivo.* In the living cell there are mechanisms for excising cross-linked sections of DNA as part of the usual DNA repair repertoire of the cell. No such repair mechanism exists for collagen, which is only very slowly replaced after it has been synthesized.

CONCLUSIONS

Theories of cellular aging include genetic and nongenetic theories. In view of the genetic determination for life span of the whole animal, genetic theories seem the most promising. Genetic theories include those involving DNA repair, somatic mutation, errors in protein synthesis, and genetic program restriction. It is considered unlikely that senescence is part of a continuing genetic program of cell death first encountered during embryonic development.

Random errors in information transfer do occur and seem to be handled in quantitatively different ways in different species. Specific single genes coding for immortality have eluded detection. The immortality of transformed cells does have a genetic basis and is recessive to mortality in complementation studies.

Nongenetic theories include those involving "wear and tear," essential nutrient deprivation, aging pigment accumulation, damage from oxidations by free radicals, and cross-linking, including glycation, of proteins and/or DNA. Some aspects of cross-linking and/or glycation have genetic components, such as DNA repair capacities.

No single current theory can account for all the observations of aging at the cellular level.

REFERENCES

Avery, O. T. , C. M. McLeod, and J. M. McCarty. Induction of transformation by a deoxyribonucleic acid fraction of *Pneumococcus* type III. *Journal of Experimental Medicine* 79:137, 1944.

Balin, A. K. Testing the free radical theory of aging. In R. C. Adelman and G. S. Roth, eds. *Testing the Theories of Aging.* CRC Press, Boca Raton, Fla., 1982.

Bucala, R., P. Model, and A. Cerami. Modification of DNA by reducing sugars: A possible mechanism for nucleic acid aging and age-related dysfunction in gene expression. *Proceedings of the National Academy of Sciences, USA* 81, 1984.

Cerami, A. Hypothesis: Glucose as a mediator of aging. *Journal of the American Geriatric Society* 33:626, 1985.

Cole, R. D. A minireview of microheterogeneity in H1 histone and its possible significance. *Annals of Biochemistry* 136:24–30, 1984.

Curtis, H. J., J. Leith, and J. Tilley. Chromosome aberrations in liver cells of dogs of different ages. *Journal of Gerontology* 21:268, 1966.

Curtis, H. J., and K. Miller. Chromosome aberrations in liver cells of guinea pigs. *Journal of Gerontology* 26:292, 1971.

Cutler, R. G. Redundancy of information content in the genome of mammalian species as a protective mechanism determining aging rate. *Mechanisms of Ageing and Development* 2:381, 1974.

Duncan, B. K., and B. Weiss. Uracil-DNA glycosylase mutants are mutators. In P. C. Hanawalt et al., eds., *Repair Mechanisms.* Academic Press, New York 1978.

The Genetic Code. *Cold Spring Harbor Symposium* 5:31, 1966.

Hamburger, V. Regression vs. peripheral control of differentiation in motor hypoplasia. *American Journal of Anatomy* 102:365, 1958.

Harley, C. B., J. W. Pollard, J. W. Chamberlain, C. P. Stanners, and S. Goldstein. Protein synthetic errors do not increase during aging of cultured human fibroblasts. *Proceedings of the National Academy of Science, USA* 77:1885, 1980.

Hart, R. W., and R. B. Setlow. DNA repair and life span of mammals. In P. C. Hanawalt and R. B. Setlow, eds., *Molecular Mechanisms for Repair of DNA,* Part B. Plenum, New York, 1982.

Hayflick, L. The limited *in vitro* lifetime of human diploid cell strains. *Experimental Cell Research* 37:614–636, 1965.

Hayflick, L. Theories of biological aging. *Experimental Gerontology* 20:145, 1985.

Hirsch, G. P. Somatic mutations and aging. In E. L. Schneider, ed., *The Genetics of Aging.* Plenum, New York, 1978.

Holland, J. J., D. Kohne, and M. Doyle. Analysis of virus replication in aging human fibroblast cultures. *Nature* 245:316, 1973.

Kohn, R. R., A. Cerami, and V. Monnier. Collagen aging *in vitro* by non-enzymatic glycosylation and browning. *Diabetes* 33:57, 1984.

Masoro, E. J., M. S. Katz, and C. A. McMahan. Evidence for the glycation hypothesis of aging from the food-restricted rodent model. *Journal of Gerontology* 44:B20. 1989.

McClintock, B. Controlling elements and the gene. *Cold Spring Harbor Symposium on Quantitative Biology* 21:197, 1956.

Medvedev, Z. hA. Repetition of molecular-genetic information as a possible factor in evolutionary changes in life span. *Experimental Gerontology* 7:517, 1972.

Medvedev, Z. hA. The role of infidelity of transfer of information for the accumulation of age changes in differentiated cells. *Mechanisms in Ageing and Development,* 14:1, 1980.

Murray, V., and R. Holliday. Increased error frequency of DNA polymerases from senescent human fibroblasts. *Journal of Molecular Biology* 146:55, 1981.

Ohno, S., and Y. Nagai. Genes in multiple copies as the primary cause of aging. In D. Bergsma and D. E. Harrison, eds., *Genetic Effects of Aging.* Liss, New York, 1978.

Ono, T., S. Okada, and T. Sugahara. Comparative studies of DNA in various tissues of mice during the aging process. *Experimental Gerontology* 11:127, 1976.

Orgel, L. E. The maintenance of accuracy of protein synthesis and its relevance to aging. *Proceedings of the National Academy of Science, USA* 49:5117–5521, 1963.

Orgel, L. E. The maintenance of accuracy of protein synthesis and its relevance to aging; A correction. *Proceedings of the National Academy of Science, USA* 67:1476, 1970.

Pereira-Smith, O. M., and J. R. Smith. Evidence for the recessive nature of cellular immortality. *Science* 221:964, 1983.

Prasad, K. N. *Human Radiation Biology.* Harper & Row, New York, 1974.

Roth, M. "Glycated" hemoglobin, not "glycosylated" or glucosated." Clinical Chemistry 29:1991, 1983.

Saunders, J. W., Jr. Cell death in embryonic systems. *Science* 154:604, 1966.

Strehler, B. L. Implications of aging research for society. *Federation Proceedings* 34:5–8, 1975.

Walford, R. L., S. Jawaid, and F. Naeim. Evidence for *in vitro* senescence of T-lymphocytes cultured from normal human peripheral blood. *Age* 4:67, 1983.

Watson, J. D., and F. H. C. Crick. Molecular structure of nucleic acids. A structure of deoxypentose nucleic acids. *Nature* 171:737, 1953.

Wilson, V. L., and P. A. Jones. DNA methylation decreases in aging but not in immortal cells. *Science* 220:1055, 1983.

Yamamoto, Y., and Y. Fujiwara. Culture–age effect of Uracil-DNA glycosylase activity in normal human skin fibroblasts. *Journal of Gerontology* 42:470, 1987.

Chapter
5

Aging at the Cellular Level

OVERVIEW OF CELLULAR AGING

When we consider aging at the cellular level, we are considering processes at the most basic level of molecules, cells, and tissues. Implicit in the discussion is the objective of discovering principles capable of explaining aging and senescence in the absence of disease as they are recognized in human beings. Cellular theories of aging hold that intrinsic processes occurring in cells are the fundamental cause of aging. Age-dependent changes at the cellular level are as dramatic as the changes associated with aging in the human face. Figure 5.1 illustrates the overall change in appearance that occurs with senescence in individual liver cells.

Since we are primarily interested in human aging, there is merit in limiting consideration to mammalian cells. In particular, other organisms have different kinds of cell populations and tissue organization, and many have a variable body temperature and metabolic rate. Though other life forms may help us to understand some of the general principles of senescence, the most useful approach to aging in humans lies in the study of the cells of humans and other mammals.

Those processes that are implicated in the control of aging in humans and other mammals would be expected, as basic requirements, to be irreversible, progressive, deleterious, and intrinsic cell properties and to be most conspicuous in cells derived from mammals after the reproductive age. They must also be capable of explaining such characteristic manifestations of human aging as arteriosclerosis, degenerative joint disease, increased incidence of cancers, and general physiological decline. At present, there is no single theory that can adequately explain all of the phenomena of aging.

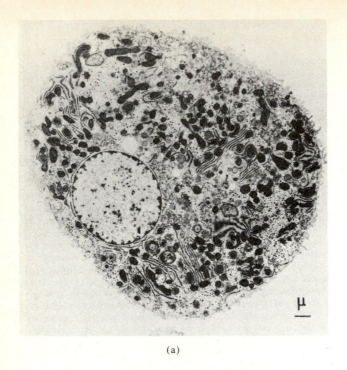

(a)

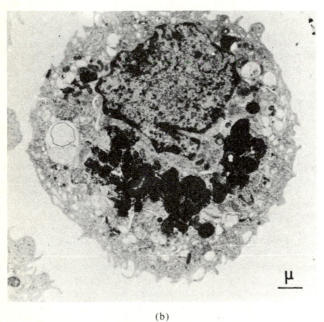

(b)

Figure 5.1 Normal rat liver cells. Bar indicates 1 micron. *(a)* 3 month old paren-chyma cell. (b) 34.5 month old kupffercell. Note heterogeneous lysosomes. (From D. L. Knook. Use of isolated parenchymal and nonparenchymal liver cells for studies of the mechanisms of cellular aging. In D. Bergsma and D. E. Harrison, eds., *Genetic Effects on Aging.* Liss for the National Foundation–March of Dimes BD:OAS XIV(1):171–180, 1978.)

Cellular theories of aging may be genetic or nongenetic; theories of aging dealing with levels of organization above the cell level are termed physiological theories. Genetic theories deal with the determination of life span by a genetic program and therefore ultimately with DNA and the synthesis of proteins coded for by DNA. Aging might thus result from changes or restrictions in the genetic program, from damage to or loss of DNA, from errors or failures in transcription of DNA to messenger RNA, from errors in translation into proteins, or from errors derived from modifications of translated proteins. Nongenetic theories focus on changes that occur in time in cellular proteins after they have been formed, changes that may be induced by environmental factors (extrinsic factors).

In this chapter we will categorize some of the major age-related happenings to cells within the body and in cell cultures. Having done this, we will try to pinpoint those cellular events that might contribute to aging in the whole animal.

AGING OF CELLS IN CULTURE

Early Tissue Culture Experiments

The invention of tissue culture is properly ascribed to the embryologist Ross Harrison, who in 1907 observed the outgrowth of nerve fibers from neurons of frog embryo spinal cord *in vitro* (literally, in glass), that is, cultured outside the body. Later, Alexis Carrel (1912) devised a means of culturing the cells of embryonic chicken heart in a similar fashion in a medium of inorganic salts, blood plasma, and "embryo extract." (Embryo extract is known to contain essential growth factors and is prepared by homogenizing chicken embryos, centrifuging the homogenate free of cells and particles, and incorporating the clear extract in the culture medium.)

Cells cultured in this manner were induced to divide, continued to divide, and were thought to be essentially immortal. The concept of immortality of cultured cells was held for some time, until it was shown by Hayflick (1965, 1980; Hayflick and Moorehead, 1961) that though cells derived from human tissues could be grown with relative ease, these cells could not be cultivated indefinitely. The original immortality of the Carrel cultures remains a mystery; it is most likely that the "embryo extract" accidentally contained embryonic cells that acted to reseed the population every time the culture was fed new medium.

The Hayflick Number

The usual method of culturing animal cells is begun by enzymatic dissociation of the donor tissue into component single cells utilizing the protease trypsin. The free cells are inoculated into plastic growth chambers containing nutrient medium and incubated. In a few hours cells attach to the plastic, and in a day or so they begin to divide. When the cell population covers the surface in a uniform monolayer, cell division ceases due to a phenomenon called contact inhibition, a property of normal cells in culture that is missing from transformed or tumor cells. The cells simply cease division when they contact each other's surfaces. At this point the culture is divided into two equal parts. One part is seeded into fresh medium; the other is retained for cell counts, microscopy, or simply discarded. This is referred to as a 1:2 subculture and is equivalent to one cell population doubling (or passage). Other subculture ratios can be used (1:4 or 1:8) provided the split ratio is properly accounted for when calculating the number of cell population doublings (CPDs).

It is now well established that populations of normal diploid human cells can proliferate in culture for only finite periods of time (Figure 5.2). Cells (fibroblasts) derived from fetal skin or lung initially divide frequently and can be subcultivated often. This growth phase is followed by a slowing of proliferative growth; the cells become granular, cellular debris accumulates, and ultimately the culture is lost. The results always show unequivocally that all tissues tested, regardless of the donor age, are incapable of unlimited proliferation. Continuous cell culture has been divided into

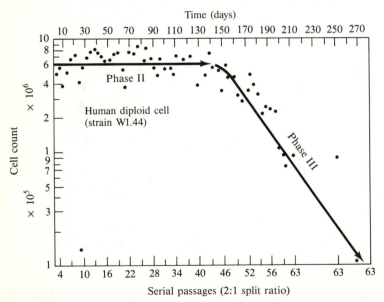

Figure 5.2 Limit on doublings of diploid human cells in culture. At each passage the cells are diluted 2:1 with fresh medium. The cell count remains constant for 46 to 50 passages, indicating 46 to 50 doublings in 150 to 160 days. (From L. Hayflick, *Experimental Cell Research* 37:614, 1965. Copyright 1965 by Academic Press, New York, and by Leonard Hayflick, University of California, San Francisco. Used with permission.)

three phases by Hayflick and Moorehead: Phase I is the initial outgrowth from the original tissue; phase II is the phase of proliferation and subculturing; phase III is the period of senescence and loss of division potential.

This degeneration is not related to nutrition, changes in acidity of the medium, accumulation of toxic wastes, or contaminants. Young cell strains are capable of vigorous proliferation in the same medium in which older strains progressively deteriorate. The lack of effect of the medium was judged by mixing cultures of viable but nondividing male cells from passage 49 with vigorously dividing female cells from passage 13. At the end of the experiment, 17 passages after mixing, the culture was found to consist entirely of female cells. These female cells entered phase III at the same time as an unmixed control culture of female cells (Hayflick and Moorehead, 1961).

In addition, if a clone of cells is frozen in liquid nitrogen at any given cell generation and then thawed at a later time for continued growth, it is found that the cells begin their life where they left off before the freeze. The "clock" counting off the cell generations has not been reset, but merely frozen in time, awaiting conditions favorable for continued cell division. It has been established that culture life span is measured by the number of completed divisions, the so-called Hayflick number, and not by the passage of time (Hayflick and Moorehead, 1961). Hydrocortisone extends the number of doublings, but does not prevent ultimate senescence.

In rodent cell culture the dying out of the cells in phase III may be superseded by renewed proliferative activity leading to a permanent, immortal cell line (Loo, Fuguay, Rawson, and Barnes, 1987). This is apparently due to transformation of one or more clones of cells to an abnormal form. This spontaneous transformation has not been observed with human cells, though human fibroblasts can be transformed into immortal lines using oncogenic viruses or carcinogenic agents (see Chapter 6).

Life Span, Donor Age, and Cell Population Doublings

It is of considerable interest that the number of doublings of various vertebrate cells in culture is correlated with life span (Figure 5.3). Human fetal cells are capable of 50 to 60 divisions (doublings, or cell population generations) prior to senescence (see Figure 5.2). The Galapagos tortoise has a long life span and fibroblasts from these animals can be cultured for 120 CPDs. As a matter of perspective, 2^{50} doublings is equivalent to about a thousand trillion cells—more than enough for 10 complete adult human beings.

Progressively older donors provide cells with proportionally fewer doublings in culture. Originally examined by Hayflick (1965), the results have been confirmed by others (Figure 5.4). Embryonic cells have greatest doubling potential. Taking the data in Figure 5.4, the relationship between donor age and number of doublings predicts that over a 90-year life span the human fibroblast division potential will fall by approximately 18

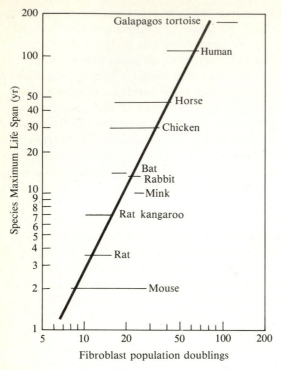

Figure 5.3 Cell doublings *in vitro* as a function of life span. (Courtesy of Leonard Hayflick. Copyright 1980 by Leonard Hayflick. Used with permission.)

population doublings. It may seem surprising that after 90 years the human body contains cells that are still capable of 20 or more divisions *in vitro*. It does, however, seem reasonable that a decline in division potential should be reached long before the replicative ability of the cells is lost completely.

The segmental progeroid syndromes (listed in Chapter 3 and discussed later in this chapter) tend to mimic one or another phase of senescence. Cells from individuals with progeria, Werner's syndrome and Down's syndrome show sharply limited *in vitro* doublings compared to age-matched controls.

Morphological and Biochemical Changes in Phase III

Young cells are uniform in size and adhere to the plastic culture dish tightly. Older cells are variable in size, are generally larger, and have a tendency to be multinucleate. They display increased nuclear size and larger numbers of lysosomes. Older cells are less tightly bound to the plastic substrate than are younger cells (Figure 5.5) and are frequently found floating in the medium. Chromosomal analysis shows that cells in

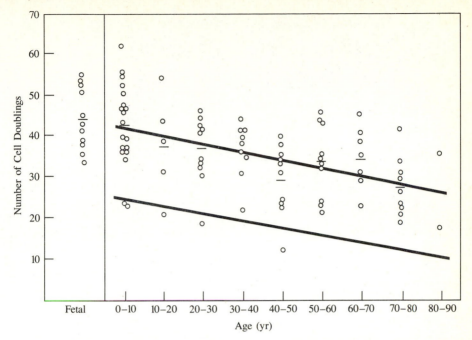

Figure 5.4 Maximum number of cell doublings as a function of donor age. (From G. M. Martin Laboratory Investigations 28:89 1970. Martin, G.M., C.A. Sprague and C. J. Epstein. CR Wm. Wilkins, Baltimore. Used with permission.)

phase III are more frequently aneuploid or polyploid than phase II cells. Decreases in rates of RNA synthesis, DNA synthesis, and DNA repair are observed in phase III. Increases in protein and RNA content are reported, perhaps the result of diminished turnover rates.

RELEVANCE OF CELL CULTURE SENESCENCE TO AGING OF THE ORGANISM

For aging, the existence of some form of aging clock would be significant. The limit on the number of cell doublings *in vitro* implies that there may be a predetermined life span of cells outside the body which is independent of changes that occur with time in the body as a whole. To put it another way, there may be no bodily change originating in one particular organ or system that induces senescence in all other parts of the body; individual cells may have a predetermined span of life as one of their intrinsic properties. It seems there is a biological clock located somewhere in the cell ticking off the cell generations before a "self-destruct" mechanism is put in operation. This would amount to a program theory of cell and organism senescence.

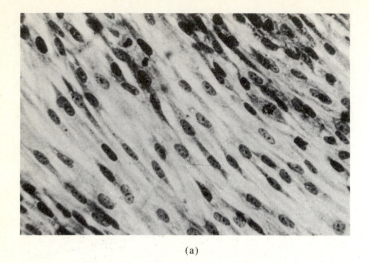

(a)

(b)

Figure 5.5 Human fibroblasts in culture. *(a)* Early passage cells. *(b)* Late (phase III) passage cells. (Courtesy of Leonard Hayflick. Copyright 1980 by Leonard Hayflick. Used with permission.)

Alternatively, it has been postulated that errors that accumulate without repair in older cells ultimately result in the death of the cell (see Chapter 4). There are many levels at which errors could creep in, including somatic mutations of DNA. As mentioned in Chapter 4, an improbably high rate of somatic mutation must be assumed to account for the errors encountered in aging cells. Mutations may be secondary to breakdowns in the fidelity of other cell synthesis and repair systems. It has been reported that DNA polymerase, for example, loses fidelity with increasing passage number in cultured human fibroblasts. Contrary claims have been made as well (Kirkwood, Holliday, and Rosenberger, 1984), and the status of the error theory remains controversial, just as we left it in Chapter 4.

On the other hand, clonal cell senescence may not be directly related to aging in the intact animal. Many body cells undergo more than 50 doublings during a human lifetime. Such cells are found in the epidermis, intestinal epithelium, connective tissues, and blood cells of the circulatory system. These cells are always under physical stress and are continually replaced throughout the life of the individual. The replacement of individual skin cells occurs about every 4 days, intestinal cells every 12 to 13 hours, and red blood cells every 4 months. If one differentiated cell and one stem cell are produced at each division, the total number of divisions in a lifetime (numbers from Strehler, 1977) would be 12,000 for intestinal cells, 5,000 for epidermal cells, and 300 for red blood cells, all clearly in excess of the 50-odd doublings permitted in culture. Clearly, the conditions *in vivo* are quite different from those obtaining *in vitro*. That number of doublings in culture relates in some way to life span is probable. The relationship is likely an indirect one. At the level of cellular aging, it seems unlikely that cells are programmed genetically to cause aging in the organism as a whole.

To relate the cell cycle in culture to the cell cycle in the living animal, it has been found *in vitro* that the proportion of cells synthesizing DNA in a given time declines with increased passage level. The interphase of the cell cycle, from G1 through DNA synthesis to G2, is prolonged in cells of later passages. The prolongation is mainly due to a protraction of the G1 phase. When division stops completely, the cells enter a permanent G1 phase, normally referred to as G0 whether in or out of the body. The S phases and division itself (mitosis) remain constant throughout the *in vitro* passages. In trisomy 21 patients the cell cycle in culture is slowed due to prolonged G2 and S phases. *In vivo*, in aging skin, there are fewer cells in division (in the mitotic, or M, phase) as compared to sections of younger skin. Frequency of an observed condition in fixed tissue is related directly to the relative amount of time spent in that particular stage in life. Thus, older, living skin shows fewer mitotic figures than younger skin because more time is spent in G1, S, and G2 in older skin (generative, or Malpighian layer). Since G1 is normally longer than G2, it would be reasonable to suppose that most nondividing skin cells would be cells in G1 of mitosis regardless of age. In the generative layer of the skin, about 10 percent of the cells are in G2 throughout life.

It appears certain that cells in culture, having completed their assigned number of doublings, do not immediately die. Cell viability can be maintained for up to two years following the cessation of cell division (Bell et al., 1980). It is of considerable interest that nondividing tissue culture cells undergo changes (for example, accumulations of altered proteins) that could be described as senescence during their postdivision existence.

Since it seems that there is a counter of some kind at the cell level, investigations of the location of the aging clock within the cell have been carried out. Technology has provided a means of exchanging nuclei between cultured cells that are approaching the limit of their doubling capacity and younger cells. This remarkable feat is accomplished in large populations of cells by subjecting them to a drug that alters the structure of cellular fibrils responsible for cell architecture (microfilaments) while simultaneously subjecting the cells to centrifugal force. The result is large numbers of enucleated cells (cytoplasts) plus their isolated nuclei (nucleoplasts), which are located further from the center of rotation of the centrifuge than the cytoplasts. These cell fractions can be reconstituted into complete cells by bringing together the isolated cytoplasts and nucleoplasts from the same or different cell cultures (Muggleton-Harris and Hayflick, 1976). Thus, a young nucleus can be placed in old cytoplasm and vice versa. The age of these recombined cells is determined by the age of both the nucleus and the cytoplasm.

A diminished growth potential was observed in combinations containing either nucleus or cytoplasm from senescent cells, indicating that *in vitro* life span is at least partly under cytoplasmic control. The conclusion is supported by later experiments in which normal embryonic lung fibroblast cytoplasts were combined with nucleoplasts from immortal SV40 virus–transformed cells. The resulting combination had a finite growth potential (Muggleton-Harris and DeSimone, 1980). Therefore, even though the number of doublings is a genetic trait fixed by nuclear gene(s), cytoplasmic factors seem to modify the expression of these genes, at least for a time, in ways that are not understood.

The relevance of cell culture senescence to aging of the organism remains controversial. It is unlikely that death of an organism is caused by failure of proliferation; 50 doublings represents a potential unlikely to be utilized in the whole animal except by continuously proliferating cell types. The changes that accompany senescence in cell cultures are undoubtedly significant clues about aging at the cellular level and proliferation per se, since this capacity does relate to life span and is a reliable though perhaps indirect index of life span potential.

TRANSPLANTATION STUDIES

Transplantation studies, theoretically, should be able to provide answers to basic questions which are inaccessible by other experimental means. Is loss of function with time controlled by a single clock or multiple clocks? Do different tissues of the same individual age at the same or different rates? Can any tissues of an individual animal continue normal function beyond the normal life span of the donor animal? It would seem that transplants of tissue from an older to a younger animal should answer some of these questions. To use a specific example, consider the somatic mutation theory of aging. If aging results from accumulated deleterious mutations, then tissue transplants of aged tissue to younger hosts would not correct functional defects in the older tissue since the defect is intrinsic to that tissue.

In such experiments the older donor tissues or cells are deemed not to have aged irreversibly if they continue to perform their functions over the younger recipient's life span. When this result is confirmed for any cell or tissue type, it shows that, even though the transplants have a finite life span, normal function is indeed possible beyond the life span of the donor. It may also imply that different cell and tissue types age at different rates with independent aging clocks, depending on how transplants of different organs fare in younger hosts.

So far so good, but there are several pitfalls to be overcome. The first of these is immune rejection of tissue grafts, which can be obviated by using highly inbred, isogenic strains of mice as experimental animals. The level of inbreeding required is estimated to be about 50 generations of brother-sister matings. Next, the assessment of function may be difficult, since one must assess the degree of normal function by the transplant. Third, one must be able to identify the transplant among donor cells in order to rule out replacement of the graft by young cells from the recipient. Finally, controls must be included to distinguish between functional loss as a result of aging and functional loss as a result of the transplant operation itself. Controls utilizing young donors and young recipients and the same tissues must be performed.

Results of some intact organ, tissue, and cell transplant studies are summarized below.

Skin Skin transplants show some intrinsic changes with age that make the skin more susceptible to tumorogenesis by coal tar derivatives than the surrounding, younger, recipient skin. On the other hand, the regrowth of hair after plucking follows a time course similar to the younger host. The participation of younger recipient cells in hair regrowth has been ruled out (Harrison, Archer, and Astle, 1982).

Ovary Ovaries of mice contain sufficient oocytes to produce several litters. In young recipients old ovaries are able to resume cycling again, though they had ceased in the donor animal. A more impressive result would be the production of offspring from the transplanted aged ovary. The converse situation is different. Old mice supplied with young ovaries fail to resume cycling and ovulation. If the older recipients had been ovarectomized early in life, the cycling pattern will resume on transplant of young donor ovaries. This suggests a clock involving the endocrine interactions between the ovarian and pituitary hormones (Nelson, Felicio, Randall, Sims, and Finch, 1982).

Thymus The mammalian thymus is the earliest organ to show age changes. In mice and humans maximum size and function of the thymus is reached soon after sexual maturity. Afterward, the organ reduces to 10 percent of it maximum size. Transplants of old thymus glands into young thymectomized, irradiated, adult recipient mice eventually restore thymic function nearly as well as transplants of young thymus. The old thymus takes longer than younger glands to accomplish the recovery (Hirokawa and Makinodan, 1975).

Spleen   In general, transplanted spleen is less able to function in the young recipient animal than in the older donor. The seemingly intrinsic changes in the transplants could be due to intrinsic age changes or to intrinsic changes induced by the transplantation process itself and an increase with age in vulnerability to transplant. The surgery is difficult, there being many vascular connections to make. It seems that most spleen transplants are limited by surgical technique, as evidenced by control studies where organs are exchanged between young subjects.

Kidney   Kidney transplants have been done in animals large enough (rats) to make the physical connections of all vascular and renal elements in their normal anatomy. Both kidneys of young rats were replaced by a pair from an older animal. The maximum function of these grafted kidneys was 46 months, measured against a normal life span of 39 months. The older kidneys functioned less well, on the average, though a few functioned as well as young, control transplants.

Single Cells   Cells or tissue can be transplanted from older donors to younger recipients and can be subcultured from the recipient through several transfers to new, young hosts. When measuring growth rate as the functional trait, it was shown that mammary epithelium can survive at least twice as long by serial transplants as the life span of the donor from which they came. This kind of experiment comes close to duplicating *in vitro* cell culture techniques described earlier.

Erythroid Hematopoetic Cells   It is generally agreed that these stem cells in older adults can function well beyond the normal life span in young hosts. In irradiated recipients transplants provided erythrocytes in life-saving numbers. Donor cells were identified by a series of criteria as distinct from recipient cells.

Lymphoid Cell Lines   The literature is long and conflicting. Most agree that lymphoid stem cells develop intrinsic defects with age using transplantation techniques (Makinodan and Kay, 1980).

Taken as a whole, a number of transplanted tissue types have been shown to have greater longevity in younger hosts than they would have had in the donor's body. Some benefit would be expected in transplants from old individuals to younger, presumably healthier hosts, but survival of donor tissue beyond the normal life span of the species remains significant. In contrast, some older tissues may be more susceptible to damage during transplantation, leading to the erroneous conclusion of intrinsic aging in such tissues because of failure to function in the young host.

DNA AND CELLULAR AGING

Loss of DNA in Aging Cells

There appears to be a loss of ribosomal DNA (rDNA) in postmitotic tissues. The rDNA represents tandemly repeated, multicopy genes that may be highly amplified beyond the level of the tandem repeats in certain cases (especially oocytes of amphibians) to allow a high rate of protein synthesis. Losses of rDNA might result in lowered amounts of protein synthesis due to the presence of fewer ribosomes in the cytoplasm. Losses with age are in fact observed in rat brain, along with a decline in protein synthesis. However, no loss of rDNA is observed in liver (rat), a tissue that does show a decline in protein synthesis. Clearly, the decline in rDNA is not the only factor that may be involved in lowered protein synthesis rates. Also, since not all tandem repeats may be active in young and middle-aged animals, loss of rDNA in older animals may not necessarily result in decreased rRNA synthesis.

Losses of rDNA have been reported from human myocardium and human cerebral cortex (Strehler and Chang, 1979). The reported loss in humans was sevenfold lower than in beagles, a ratio consistent with their relative longevities. Since a loss of rDNA could be compensated for by increased transcription of remaining tandem repeats, such loss per se does not necessarily relate to number of cytoplasmic ribosomes or to rate of protein synthesis (see the section on RNA synthesis and cellular aging below).

DNA Repair in Cells from Young and Old Donors

It might seem logical that since the nucleus contains at least a part of the aging clock, aging and senescence of cells in culture may be reflected in loss of ability to repair damage to nuclear DNA. Canine connective tissue cells from young and old donors were compared for their ability to repair damage to DNA experimentally induced by ultraviolet light (UV) *in vitro*. The results show that DNA repair mechanisms that act to correct a variety of lesions do not decline with age (Goldstein, 1971). Similar results have also been obtained with human cells in culture (Hall, Alarv, and Scherer, 1982). It has also been found that human white cells from young and old donors in culture show no detectable difference in frequency of chromosome breakage following x-ray treatment (Leiniecki, Bajerska, and Andryszek, 1971).

DNA Repair and Donor Life Span

Paradoxically, it has been shown that ability to repair damage to DNA caused by ultraviolet light correlates well with life span (Figure 5.6). Connective tissue cells from seven mammalian species of widely differing life

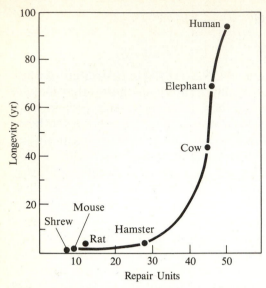

Figure 5.6 DNA repair capability and life span. (Adapted from data of Hart and Setlow. In Hanawalt and Setlow, eds., *Molecular Mechanisms of Repair of DNA, Part B*. Copyright 1974 by Plenum Publishing Corporation, New York. Used with permission.)

spans were tested for their ability to repair UV damage to DNA in culture. The elephant and human were best able to repair such damage; the mouse, shrew, rat, and hamster were least able. The cow was intermediate (Hart and Setlow, 1982). A similar correlation between repair capability and life span has been reported among mammals (Francis, Lee, and Regan, 1981) and primates specifically (Bergmann, Walford, Esra, and Hall, 1981).

The apparent paradox can be resolved. The two results are not mutually exclusive. DNA repair efficiency is high in long-lived species and lower in short-lived ones. Whatever the repair capability, it has been shown that this ability, when measured on tissue culture cells, does not decline with the age of the cell culture, at least not for human cells. In other words, it does not appear that aging among members of a species is solely a direct consequence of a decline in DNA repair capability. However, the possibility remains that the well-known differences among species in life span reflect different levels of DNA repair capability.

RNA SYNTHESIS AND CELLULAR AGING

RNA metabolism is a comparatively unexplored area in aging research. There may be a general decline in RNA synthesis with age, and there is some evidence of quantitative age changes in the metabolism of individual

RNA species. Some of the decline in transcription may result from alterations in chromosome organization, specifically at the level of chromosomal proteins that complex with DNA to form chromatin.

Chromatin changes include an increase in cross-linking between DNA and chromosomal proteins, a condition that limits transcription of DNA *in vitro*. Histone acetylation undergoes an age-related decrease, which also leads to a structure of chromatin not conducive to transcription. At the same time, the quantity and kind of histones associated with DNA in chromatin seem not to change with age.

Measurements of the complexity (the number of unique sequences of RNA or DNA in a population of molecules) of the total amount of polyadenylated RNA (both messenger and heterogeneous nuclear RNA) indicate no change with age in rats. HnRNA represents gene transcripts prior to processing and transport to the cytoplasm. A large proportion of HnRNA is turned over in the nucleus. Some amounts reach the cytoplasm as smaller molecules of mRNA. Changes in mRNA and tRNA are considered below with protein synthesis.

PROTEIN SYNTHESIS AND CELLULAR AGING

In eukaryotic organisms protein synthesis universally declines with age. It is likely that this reduction has multiple causes; all cellular components involved in protein synthesis have been implicated at one time or another.

Ribosomes

A decline in ribosomal RNA (rRNA) would be expected as a consequence of the decline in tandem repeats of rDNA (program restriction theory). This decline is supported by reports of age-related decline in total cytoplasmic RNA, of which ribosomal RNA is the largest fraction. When single ribosomes (monosomes) are isolated from whole *Drosophila*, there is a numerical decrease with age in monosomes amounting to some 23 percent over the life span. Webster, Webster, and Landis (1981) report a large decrease in polyribosomes in *Drosophila* with age. Coupled with the loss of polyribosomes is an observed loss of rough endoplasmic reticulum (a membrane system in the cytoplasm closely associated with ribosomes) in both mammals and *Drosophila*. The amount of mRNA associated with polyribosomes, as measured by polyA-RNA, seems to remain constant in the rat.

Transfer RNA

Changes in tRNA, including changes in acetylation of tRNAs (required for amino acid binding), have been reported with age. A series of experiments (Foote and Stulberg, 1981) utilized tRNAs isolated from young and old rat tissues in conjunction with an *in vitro* assay system for synthesis of viral polypeptides in which tRNA is limiting. No significant differences between the added old and young tRNAs was found in either rate or fidelity of translation, which is taken as good evidence that tRNAs are not the rate-limiting factor in the age-related decline in protein synthesis. This along with a large body of other evidence also can be interpreted as ruling against changes in the accuracy of protein synthesis with aging.

Elongation Factors

The decline in protein synthesis does not seem to be due to the availability of tRNA or mRNA or to the losses of ribosomes. Initiation of protein synthesis seems unaffected by age. The area that may be most affected by age seems to be the rate of elongation of initiated polypeptides. Elongation factors (specifically, EF1) are necessary for stabilization and continued elongation of the polypeptide chain growing from the polyribosome. EF1 decreases with age in cell-free systems derived from rat liver and brain, in parallel with decrements in protein synthesis.

Posttranslational Modifications

The three-dimensional conformation of proteins may be altered with age. In the case of enzymes the change may involve the active site of substrate binding and thus is detected as a loss of specific activity without enzyme degradation. (Enzyme conformation changes were described in the section on nematodes in Chapter 2.) Similar observations have been made on mouse tissues. It is well to emphasize that not all proteins of these animals were found to be altered in this way. Another enzyme found to have reduced activity with age while remaining essentially intact is superoxide dismutase in the mouse and rat. These enzymes do not change in electrophoretic mobility in gels that do not denature them (change their shape). Independent estimates of molecular weight also indicate no change.

   Other posttranslational changes include deamination of eye lens protein. There is no known relation between this chemical change and changes in vision with age, though it is possible that increased opacity and shape changes that occur in the lens with age may be related to these alterations. In the lens there is no protein synthesis or turnover to replace molecules of lens protein. In addition to deamination, recemization or conversion of protein amino acids from the L isomer to the D isomer has been shown to occur in tooth enamel protein. Both of these processes are extremely slow and require no turnover or low turnover for detection. Hence, they have only been described for lens and tooth protein. Recemization may be a reliable measure of chronological age, since it occurs at a rate of about 0.1 percent per year in enamel and dentine of humans (Masters, 1981).

   To summarize, the decrease in protein synthesis and the decrease in protein degradation combine to increase the half-life of proteins in older cells, rendering them more susceptible to posttranslational modification. The most likely limiting factor in protein synthesis in older cells seems to be associated with factors involved in the elongation of the polypeptide chain on the polyribosome. Finally, the errors accumulating in cells do not seem to be solely the result of errors in transcription or translation, but to alterations of molecules after translation. Though altered proteins do accumulate with advancing age, there is no good evidence that an increase in rate of missynthesis of proteins occurs with age. A considerable amount of data testifies to the accuracy of protein synthesis in old organisms.

CELL MEMBRANES AND AGING

Membranes are bimolecular layers of lipids containing embedded proteins. Cholesterol is found in higher amounts in plasma membranes than in mitochondrial membranes. The lipid moiety is composed of phospholipids and neutral fatty acids of varying chain length and varying numbers of saturated bonds (Figure 5.7).

Age Changes

There is a broad spectrum of age-associated changes in both structure and function of plasma membranes and the membranes of intracellular structures. Age-associated changes may vary among tissues of the same species and in the same tissue from different species. Total lipid decreases with age in rat and mouse liver and in rat kidney and pancreas, but remains constant in mouse and human brains.

The cholesterol-phospholipid ratio in plasma and other membranes increases with age. The change in this ratio diminishes the fluidity of the

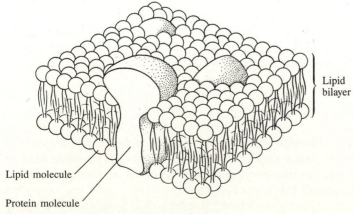

Lipid bilayer

Lipid molecule

Protein molecule

Figure 5.7 Structure of unit membrane.

membrane. This is evident in plasma membranes, endoplasmic reticulum (microsomal) membranes, and mitochondrial membranes. In addition, membranes from older animals tend to have more saturated fatty acids than young membranes, another factor diminishing fluidity. The fluidity of membranes influences the distribution of membrane proteins and thus the membrane-bound combining sites for molecules such as serotonin. Serotonin binding sites actually increase with age in human brain. Changes in fluidity may also expose antigenic groups previously hidden in the membrane and may thus influence autoimmune phenomena by exposing antigens not previously available for scanning and identification as self.

Mechanisms Behind Membrane Changes

Free radicals, such as superoxides, result in lipid peroxidation. Unsaturated fatty acids of phospholipids are especially vulnerable to oxidation. Since the fatty acids of the endoplasmic reticulum, lysosomal, and mitochondrial membranes tend to be highly unsaturated, these membranes are the primary targets for change. The nuclear envelope is closely related to the endoplasmic reticulum membrane. Membrane changes cause changes in membrane permeability of the structures. Lysosomes may leak degradative enzymes into the cytoplasm. Lipofuscins are precipitated in lysosomes and are produced by oxidation of the polyunsaturated lipids of cellular membranes.

Changes in fluidity change the relationships between membrane proteins and subcellular structures such as microtubules and microfilaments. The movement of proteins through the lipid layers is restricted in older cells, as evidenced by diminished clustering of antigens at one pole of the cells (capping) in response to the presence of specific antibody.

A chain of intracellular events based on decreased membrane fluidity has been postulated (Zs-Nagy, 1979). It is said that decreased fluidity leads to decreased potassium conductance and therefore increased intracellular potassium. The increased intracellular ionic strength should slow enzymatic reactions, as well as transcription of DNA in chromatin. All of this would lead to a decrease in protein synthesis and also to a decrease in synthesis of repair elements for membranes themselves. As we have seen, other changes may account for the decrease in protein synthesis.

CONCLUSIONS

It must be said that although there are a number of cellular changes that contribute to cellular aging, none has been established as predominant or causal. All the alterations discussed may contribute to senescence; none is capable of explaining all the observed facts.

A basic property of cells in culture is a finite life span that is directly related to both the species life span and donor age. On the face of this basic attribute there are a number of fundamental processes that do not seem to change greatly with age in mammals. Included in this list are amounts and kinds of histones, amounts of mRNA associated with polysomes, and the amount of unaltered tRNA.

Among those properties showing greatest change are membrane fluidity, posttranslational modifications of proteins including cross-linking and glycation, cross-linking and glycation of DNA, and the elongation phase of protein synthesis.

Some organs transplanted from old to young animals show extended survival beyond the normal life span, indicating perhaps some overall effect of youthful physiology on the survival of older grafts.

We are still left without a single basic cause of senescence, save for the conclusion of the evolutionists, who relate senescence to the lack of selection pressure in post-reproductive years and who see no compelling reason for a univeral mechanism underlying the phenomenon.

REFERENCES

Bell, E., L. F. Marek, C. Merrill, D. S. Livingstone, T. Young, M. Eden, and S. Sher. Loss of division potential in culture: Ageing or differentiation. *Science* 208:- 1483, 1980.

Bergmann, K., R. L. Walford, G. N. Esra, and K. Y. Hall. A correlation of repair and UV-induced DNA damage and maximum life span in primate lymphocytes. In *Thematic Sessions,* Twelfth International Congress of Gerontology 2:125, 1981.

Bohn, M. C., L. Cupit, F. Marciano, and D. M. Gash. Adrenal medulla grafts enhance recovery of striatal dopaminergic fibers. *Science* 237:913, 1987.

Carrel, A. On the permanent life of tissues outside of the organism. *Journal of Experimental Medicine* 15:516, 1912.

Foote, R. S., and M. P. Stulberg. Efficiency and fidelity of cell-free protein synthesis by transfer RNA from aged mice. *Mechanisms of Aging and Development* 13:93, 1981.

Francis, A. A., W. H. Lee, and J. D. Regan. The relationships of DNA excision-repair of UV-induced lesions to the maximum life span of mammals. *Mechanisms of Ageing and Development* 16:181, 1981.

Goldstein, S. The role of DNA repair imaging of cultured fibroblasts from xeroderma pigmentosum and normals. *Proceedings of the Society for Experimental Biology and Medicine* 137:730, 1971.

Hall, J. D., R. E. Alarv, and K. L. Scherer. DNA repair in cultured human fibroblasts does not decline with donor age. *Experimental Cell Research* 139:351, 1982.

Harrison, D. E., J. Archer, and C. M. Astle. The effect of hypophysectomy on thymic aging in mice. *Journal of Immunology* 129:2673, 1982.

Harrison, R. G. Observations on the living, developing nerve fiber. *Proceedings of the Society for Experimental Biology and Medicine* 4:140, 1907.

Hart, R. W., and R. B. Setlow. DNA repair and life span of mammals. In P. C. Hanawalt and R. B. Setlow, eds., *Molecular Mechanisms for Repair of DNA.* Part B. Plenum, New York, 1982.

Hayflick, L. The limited *in vitro* life span of human lipid cell strains. *Experimental Cell Research* 37:614, 1965.

Hayflick, L. The cell biology of human aging. *Scientific American* 242:58, 1980.

Hayflick, L., and P. S. Moorehead. The serial cultivation of human diploid cell strains. *Experimental Cell Research* 25:585, 1961.

Hirokawa, K., and T. Makinodan. Involution: Effect on T cell differentiation. *Journal of Immunology* 6:1659, 1975.

Kirkwood, T. B. L., R. Holliday, and R. F. Rosenberger. Stability of the cellular translation process. *International Review of Cytology* 1984.

Leiniecki, J., A. Bajerska, and C. Andryszek. Chromosomal aberration in human lymphocytes irradiated *in vitro* from donors (males-females) of varying age. *International Journal of Radiation Biology* 19:349, 1971.

Loo, D. T., J. I. Fuguay, C. L. Rawson, and D. W. Barnes. Extended culture of mouse embryo cells without senescence: Inhibition by serum. *Science* 236:200, 1987.

Makinodan, T., and M. M. Kay. Age influence on the immune system. *Advances in Immunology* 29:287, 1980.

Martin, G. M. Genetic syndromes in man with potential relevance to the pathobiology of aging. In Bergsma and Harrison, eds., *Genetic Effects of Aging.* Liss, New York, 1978.

Martin, G. M., C. A. Sprague, and C. J. Epstein. Replicative life-span of cultivated human cells: Effect of donor's age, tissue and genotype. *Laboratory Investigations* 23:86, 1970.

Masters, P. M. Amino acid recemization in structural proteins. In M. E. Reff and E. L. Schneider, eds., *Biological Markers of Aging Conference.* National Institute on Aging, Bethesda, Md., 1981.

Muggleton-Harris, A., and L. Hayflick. Cellular aging studied by the reconstruction of replicating cells from nuclei and cytoplasms isolated from normal human diploid cells. *Experimental Cell Research* 103:321, 1976.

Muggleton-Harris, A., and D. W. DeSimone. Replicative potentials of various fusion products between WI-38 and SV40 transformed WI-38 cells and their components. *Somatic Cell Genetics* 6:689, 1980.

Nelson, J. F., L. Felicio, P. K. Randall, C. Sims, and C. E. Finch. Longitudinal study of the estrous cycle in aging C57BL/6J mice. I. Cycle frequency, length, and vaginal cytology. *Biology of Reproduction* 27:327, 1982.

Strehler, B. L. *Time, Cells, and Aging.* 2nd ed. Academic Press, New York, 1977.

Strehler, B. L., and M.-P. Chang. Loss of hybridizable ribosomal DNA from human post-mitotic tissues during aging. Age dependent loss in human cerebral cortex-hippocampal and somatosensory cortex comparison. *Mechanisms of Ageing and Development* 11:379, 1979.

Webster, G. C., S. L. Webster, and W. A. Landis. The effect of age on the initiation of protein synthesis in *Drosophila melanogaster. Mechanisms of Ageing and Development* 16:71, 1981.

Zs-Nagy, I. The role of membrane structure and function in cellular aging. *Mechanisms of Ageing and Development* 9:237, 1979.

Chapter
6

Cancer,
Genetic Disease,
and Cellular Aging

CANCER CELLS AND CELL IMMORTALITY

Nature and Causes of Cancer

Youthful cancers aside, cancer is a collection of diseases primarily of old age (Figure 6.1). There are many different types that attack all tissues of the human body. Naturally occurring cancers of various sorts are found in many of the lower vertebrates as well as in mammals. Cancers may also be caused by external agents such as carcinogenic chemicals, sunlight, and tumor-inducing viruses. Cells that have been altered from their normal functions by carcinogenic agents are termed *transformed cells.* In most instances the tumors are monoclonal, arising from a single cell.

Under controlled culture conditions, the most striking consequence of transformation by a cancer-causing virus or other carcinogenic agent is the attendant immortality of the cancer cell. There is apparently no limit on the number of doublings in transformed cells. Normal cells in culture stop dividing through contact inhibition when the culture becomes confluent (Figure 6.2). Senescent human cells that are transformed in culture by a virus (SV40) show a resumption of DNA synthesis and continued division (Ide, Yoshiaki, Ishibashi, and Mitsui, 1983). Transformed cells in culture show no contact inhibition and continue to grow into large masses with necrotic (dying) centers. In the body this unlimited growth occurs at the expense of normal cells; most cancers are highly invasive of normal tissue.

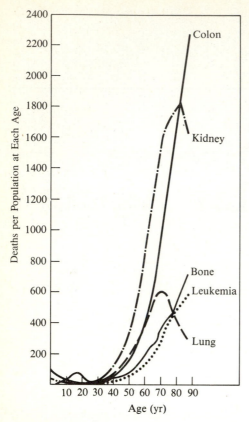

Figure 6.1 Incidence of cancer as a function of age. (From R. R. Kohn. *Principles of Mammalian Aging,* 2nd ed. Copyright 1978 by Prentice-Hall, New York. Used with permission.)

Carcinogenic Agents

Many chemicals are carcinogens, as are various forms of ionizing radiation. The common denominator uniting all these agents is mutagenesis. In order to cause cancers, an agent must be directly or indirectly capable of inducing mutations in cells. An *in vitro* test for mutagenic and carcinogenic activity looks for the induction of back mutations in bacteria by suspected compounds. Many compounds have been screened, including complex mixtures such as tobacco smoke.

In nature there is typically a latent period (sometimes measured in years) after exposure to a carcinogen before a malignancy appears. It is assumed that the initial event is a mutagenic alteration of DNA which goes unrepaired. This is followed by the latent period during which other (noncarcinogenic) events may promote the growth of a tumor. For example, coal tars induce skin cancers after multiple applications. However, a noncarcinogen (croton oil), applied after only a single coal tar application, will cause cancers, leading to the concept of an initiation phase and a

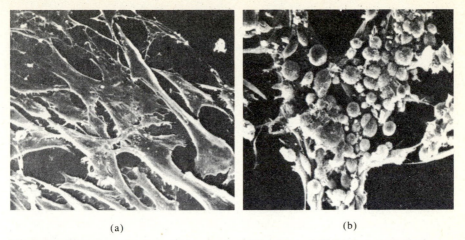

(a)   (b)

Figure 6.2 Scanning electron micrographs of *(a)* normal fibroblasts and *(b)* transformed fibroblasts growing on culture dish surface. Normal cells adhere to substrate and appear flat. Transformed cells are rounded, crowded, and nonadhesive. (Courtesy of Dr. G. S. Martin.)

promotion phase in carcinogenesis. Tumor viruses are unique as carcinogens in that they apparently induce a fully malignant state with a single event.

Tumor Viruses

Many viruses cause tumors in vertebrates, from frogs to monkeys. They are best studied using cell culture techniques. These tumor viruses contain either RNA or DNA as genetic material. The RNA viruses, as part of their life cycle, are transcribed in the host cell into the corresponding DNA by the viral enzyme reverse transcriptase. For this reason, the RNA viruses are referred to as retroviruses. The DNA-containing viruses are called adenoviruses. The DNA of adenoviruses or retroviruses may become integrated into the host cell genome, where it may be transcribed. The integration event of retroviral DNA is by itself potentially mutagenic (in which case the mutagenesis is called insertional mutagenesis) and may cause human genes to take on the properties of tumor-causing genes (called oncogenes). The transcription and translation of viral DNA results in the production of proteins including reverse transcriptase (in retroviruses), viral capsid proteins, and proteins involved in malignant transformations. The last are the products of viral oncogenes. Oncogenes may derive from the viral genome or from existing human genes by insertional mutagenesis or by action of a carcinogenic agent (see review by Bishop, 1987). A large number of oncogenes are known and they are active in a wide variety of species. The oncogenes of the DNA viruses are complex in that they are part of a set of overlapping genes, some of which are involved in virus replication.

The simplest oncogenes are those of the retroviruses, though not all retroviruses are oncogenic (Varmus, 1988). These viral genes are single genes that do not overlap with other portions of the viral genome. In the Rous sarcoma virus of chickens, the *src* gene is responsible for transforming chicken cells into malignant cells. The *src* gene is also found in normal chicken cells and indeed originated there where the normal function of its product is to act as an enzyme in the cell membrane. When carried as part of the viral genome, this related genetic sequence becomes oncogenic, presumably because of the altered environment surrounding it when it is contained in the viral genome. In other words, the expression of the gene is modified in the viral carrier situation. Retroviral genes may be integrated into the genome of the germ cell line and be transmitted vertically. Expression of the viral oncogene may follow exposure to carcinogenic agents such as ultraviolet light.

The most commonly found retroviral oncogenes isolated from human tumors or transformed human cell lines belong to the *ras* gene family and are structurally related to rat sarcoma viruses. The normal *ras* genes are involved in regulation of growth and development through the activity of their protein product. More specifically, the protein product of the normal gene is concerned with hormone and growth factor signal transmission from the surface to the interior of the cell. The mutated genes lead to cell transformation *in vitro* and to cancers of the colon and other tissues *in vivo*. The three-dimensional structure of the normal protein product (p21 protein) has been elucidated (De Vos et al., 1988). The p21 protein has a molecular weight of 21,000 and contains 188 or 189 amino acid residues. The difference between the normal gene protein and the mutated *ras* oncogene protein involves one base substitution in the mutated oncogene at one of a few critical positions. In turn, this results in a single amino acid substitution. The mutation produces p21 proteins that remain locked in the "on" position for transmission of stimulatory signals to the cell interior. The precise nature of the differences in the catalytic site of the p21 proteins from normal and cancerous cells awaits study of the three-dimensional structure of the *ras* oncogene protein.

Temperature mutants have been found among the tumor viruses. In one case the virus is sensitive to higher temperatures tolerated by the host cells (Figure 6.3). The transformed cell can be made normal by raising the temperature to 39°C and retransformed back to the malignant state by lowering the temperature to 34°C. The cytoarchitecture changes markedly. The microfilaments and microtubules of transformed cells are disorganized in contrast with the more orderly array seen in normal interphase cells.

Characteristics of Transformed Cells

Perhaps the most striking phenomenon in viral cell transformation is the immortality conferred on host cells. In the case of the large adenoviruses a portion of the viral genome distinct from the oncogene has been shown

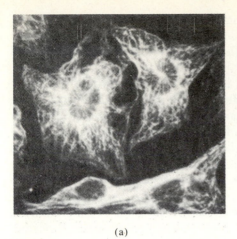
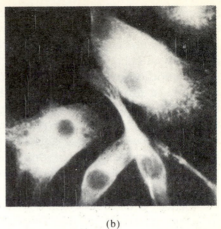

(a)   (b)

Figure 6.3 Cytoskeleton of fibroblasts infected with temperature-sensitive mutant transforming virus. *(a)* Normal cell at restrictive temperature for the virus. *(b)* Transformed cell with disorganized tubules grown at permissive temperature for the virus. (From R.L. Brown et al. Proceedings of the National Academy of Science, USA. 78:5595 1981.

to confer immortality without imparting any other aspect of the neoplastic phenotype. Viral genes are therefore important tools for the study of cell senescence as well as cell transformation. Little is known about the mechanisms that limit cell division potential and those that permit tumor-derived or virus- or carcinogen-treated cells to become immortal.

As mentioned in Chapter 4, cell fusion studies (Pereira-Smith and Smith, 1988) have been utilized to study cell immortality. Cell fusion between various immortal cell lines can be mediated *in vitro* by inactivated Sendai virus particles. Hybrid cells are selected from the mixed culture of parent and hybrid cells on a selective nutrient medium that excludes growth of mutually deficient parent cell lines. When two immortal lines were hybridized, the product sometimes was immortal and sometimes demonstrated limited growth. In cases where two immortal lines became mortal, different (recessive) genes were operating in each cell line to provide immortality. The normal, senescent hybrid, with limited potential for population doublings, is viewed as the product of complementation of two different mutant genes by their normal alleles in the two cell lines.

Through this process, Pereira-Smith and Smith were able to assign the various immortal cell lines to at least four distinct complementation groups. This indicates that immortality does not result from random events, but rather from changes in specific genes. Pereira-Smith and Smith further state that cell immortality may result from either a suppression of protein inhibitors of DNA synthesis or from an inability to respond to such inhibitors. If such protein inhibitors are involved in normal cell senescence, genes controlling these inhibitors would be prime candidates for the tumor expression inhibitor genes postulated by others (O'Brien,

Stenman, and Sager, 1986). The assignment of immortal human cells to distinct groups thus provides the basis for a focused approach to determine the genes important in normal growth regulation that have been modified in immortal cells.

In addition to unlimited growth, it seems that transformed cells have reverted in other ways to an undifferentiated or embryonic state. The transformed cell may produce inappropriate proteins, as though the control mechanisms for gene expression had been altered. As examples, cancer of the bowel is accompanied by the production by the malignant cells of a protein typical of embryonic life. Other cancers are characterized by the production of protein hormones uncharacteristic of the tissue from which the cancer originated.

Cancer cells usually begin with the normal number of chromosomes in each nucleus. Through the progressive phase of the disease, abnormal chromosome numbers and shapes are evident, presumed consequences of misreplication of DNA. Oncogenes may be amplified (selectively over-replicated) in cancer cells. Translocations between chromosomes may affect oncogene expression by position effects—bringing a segment of DNA into contact with different regulatory regions of the genome. Cancer cells become very different from normal cells, so different that, in many cases, they are attacked as foreign by the immune system of the host (immune surveillance). "Successful" cancers seem to be able to avoid this attack either because they disguise themselves as normal tissue or because the immune system is functioning at a diminished level, which occurs especially in elderly individuals.

The enhancement of immune surveillance may be an area of promising therapy. Recently, the FDA has released a naturally derived substance from human cells called interleukin 2. It is produced by gene splicing techniques. The interleukins are substances that stimulate the growth of certain T cells, especially the cytotoxic or killer T cells that are active in graft rejection and immune surveillance. The interleukin 2 binds to the surface of T cells activated by antigen and causes proliferation of the active cells indefinitely in the presence of antigen (tumor). In practice, a patient's leucocytes are separated from the plasma, treated with interleukin 2, and returned to the circulation. Regressions of tumors through activity of the increased population of killer cells has been noted.

Cancer Cells and Aging

We have a twofold problem with cancer as it relates to aging: (1) How does the apparent immortality of the cancer cell relate to overall problems of aging and senescence? (2) Why is cancer a disease of old age?

The first question is of obvious fundamental importance; the answer would contain the secret of both cancer and longevity. However, it would be well to consider some basic observations before jumping to the conclusion that cancer contains the secret of long life. First, longer-lived species do not have cells more similar to cancerous cells than shorter-lived species do. Second, it is likely that cancer cells contain viral information that modifies the expression of senescence; cancer cells may somehow suppress or lose a segment of DNA responsible for the aging clock in the nucleus. The intriguing aspect of cell transformation is that immortality so conferred seems to be independent of the malignant, invasive properties of these cells.

With respect to cancer as primarily a disease of old age, one could postulate the following: If segments of DNA that regulate gene expression are in some way altered over time by viral transformation or mutation, changes such as those outlined for malignant transformation might be expected ultimately to appear, but only after a variable latent period that may push the appearance of the tumor into the later years. In addition, if the immune system is normally responsible for eliminating cancer cells as they arise, an older immune system would be expected to be less efficient at dealing with neoplasms than a younger immune system (see Chapter 7).

CHROMOSOMAL LESIONS AND AGING

Much of the research on chromosomes and aging relates to cancer. It is true that many, but not all, malignancies have chromosomal abnormalities. These and other findings raise the question of a causal role for chromosomal damage in carcinogenesis. There are many suggestive studies but no conclusive ones. What has been missing is a convincing demonstration that the chromosomal lesion preceded rather than followed the development of the malignancy. Most such studies are based on *in vitro* models.

With respect to aging in general, studies of regenerating liver in a variety of experimental animals have shown a linear increase in chromosomal abnormalities with age at a rate inversely related to life span. Human chromosomal aging data are almost entirely derived from studies of bone marrow and peripheral white blood cells, both mitotically active tissues. In general, there is an increase of hypo- and hyperdiploidy (less than 46 or more than 46 chromosomes, respectively). Hypodiploidy is more prevalent than hyperdiploidy and is found more frequently in females than in males. Studies of peripheral white cells indicate an age-associated increase in the loss of one X chromosome in women and the Y chromosome in men (Hadley, 1982). In females one X chromosome is inactivated (at random) in all cells during development. Though this might explain how females could lose an X chromosome without penalty, there is no evidence to show that the lost X is always the inactive one (the so-called Barr body). In addition to white cell studies, the bone marrow studies also show an increased loss of the Y chromosome in men. Among autosomal chromosomes, there is a suggestion of preferential loss or gain of chromosome 21 (see below under trisomy 21). The overall picture suggests a decrease in sister chromatid exchange induced by mutagenic agents with age. These exchanges represent the cellular response to DNA damage induced by various mutagens. Though the exact mechanism of these exchanges is not known, it may represent a type of DNA repair that, in this instance, also seems to decline with age. (Chromosome abnormalities in laboratory mice were described in Chapter 4.)

Chromosome loss or gain in dividing cells most likely results from errors in chromosome distribution during cell division, which in turn may result from abnormalities in the microtubules that are designed to insure regular and equal distribution of chromosomes to daughter cells. Abnormalities of chromosome structure may result from translocations, inversions, or deletions, all of which may also lead to abnormal chromosome distribution during cell division.

GENETIC DISEASE AND CELLULAR AGING

Diseases and Genes

The central role of the genes in cell replication and synthetic processes suggests that alterations in the genes may contribute to many age-related diseases and impairments in function. In this section we will focus on human diseases that have a genetic basis and mimic some aspects of senescence. We will examine some of the cellular and genetic features (where known) of these diseases. Each disease or syndrome exemplifies some, but not all the changes observed in humans with advancing years. For this reason they are sometimes called segmental progeroid syndromes, segmental since they involve only parts or segments of the process of senescence and progeroid because they tend to accelerate certain aspects of the aging process (reviewed by Martin, 1978). (Some of these diseases were briefly characterized in Chapter 3.)

Though we are not suggesting that any of these progeroid syndromes is a complete model of aging, these diseases are conditions that resemble senescence in some respects and that have an identifiable genetic defect at the level of DNA repair, chromosome abnormality, or specific mutation.

Progeria

The Hutchinson-Gilford progeria syndrome is a rare human genetic disease with many features mimicking accelerated aging (see Figure 3.7). The reported incidence is 1 per 8,000,000 live births. These individuals appear normal at birth, but age prematurely in their teens. They have normal to above average intelligence.

Progeria patients show a height decrease, decreased elasticity of the skin, and a loss of subcutaneous fat, giving prominence to superficial veins. Hair is lost and replaced with a fine down during the first year (DeBusk,

1972). During the next 10 years osteoporosis occurs. Generalized atherosclerosis and occlusion of coronary arteries occur, and strokes become
prevalent (Schneider and Bynum, 1983). The majority of progeria patients
die of heart attack at a median age of 12 years. Some features of normal
aging are lacking, such as degenerative joint disease, cataracts, diabetes,
and senile dementia. There is no obvious increase in number of cancers
(Schneider and Bynum, 1983). Nevertheless, patients look like little elderly people, and progeria may be considered as a disease model for
certain aspects of accelerated aging.

The mode of inheritance of progeria is in controversy. Since the syndrome is not associated with sex, as is baldness or color blindness, current
but conflicting reports suggest either a recessive gene carried on any of
the autosomes or rare autosomal dominant gene (DeBusk, 1972; Schneider
and Bynum, 1983).

Fibroblasts of progeria victims do not grow well in culture. Connective tissue cells may go through four to eight doublings before they cease
to divide, a situation encountered in cultures of cells derived from normal
elderly individuals. DNA repair mechanisms are reportedly deficient in
progeria patients. The incidence of this syndrome is so infrequent that
comparatively little work has been done. The results above simply indicate that some of the symptoms of the disease may be ultimately attributed to problems at the cellular level.

Werner's Syndrome

This is another collection of symptoms indicative of premature aging.
Unlike progeria, Werner's syndrome (WS) does not become manifest until
about age 20, though some signs may appear in the late teens (Epstein,
Martin, Schultz, and Motulsky, 1966).It is inherited as an autosomal recessive. The life expectancy for these individuals is 39 years.

Common in WS are calcification of soft tissues, cataracts, osteoporosis
(distal limbs), frequent sarcomas (connective tissue cancers), arterioscle-
sis, diabetes, skeletal muscle atrophy, generalized hair loss, and premature
greying of the hair. As in progeria, there is no evidence of senile dementia,
although the age pigment (lipofuscin) does appear in many tissues.

Cells of Werner's syndrome patients, like those of progeria patients,
show decreased DNA repair and rapid senescence in culture. In addition,
WS cells show an increased frequency of abnormal chromosomes.

Alzheimer's Disease and Senile Dementia

Alzheimer's disease (or presenile dementia) is a term designating a collection of conditions that includes about half of all dementias of older people
(Sinex and Merril, 1982). The diseases are sometimes collectively referred
to as senile dementia of the Alzheimer type (SDAT) regardless of the age
onset. According to the 1980 census, there are 25 million people aged 65

or older. Among these, 11 percent have mild dementia, and 4.5 percent are severely demented. Of all those over 65 showing dementia, 55 percent with clinical signs have SDAT, 15 percent have dementias relating to blood vessel blockage in the brain, and 22 percent have a combination of SDAT and dementia due to vessel blockage (Wisniewski and Kozlowski, 1982). SDAT is characterized primarily by memory loss (beginning with memory of recent events), shortened retention span, disorientation, and sometimes confabulations (the making of ready answers without regard to truth). Aphasia (inability to speak) is occasionally encountered. Death occurs 5 to 10 years after the onset of the disease from pneumonia, accidents, and sometimes respiratory arrest.

Autopsy reveals diffuse loss of neurons of the frontal cerebral cortex and the hippocampus (the associative center that converts short-term to long-term memory). Amyloid-containing plaques of degenerating neurons along with neuronal masses containing paired helical filaments appear at random throughout the cerebral cortex, usually involving the hippocampus (Bondareff, 1985). The filaments appear to be abnormal inclusions related perhaps to microfilaments of neural cells. These helical structures contain a protein called ubiquitin, a widespread polypeptide that attaches to proteins that are to be degraded, enhancing their digestibility (Mori, Kundo, and Ihara, 1987).

The hereditary form of Alzheimer's disease (familial Alzheimer's disease, or FAD) involves a single, dominant autosomal gene located on chromosome 21, near the gene coding for a protein found in the amyloid plaque, but distinct from that gene (St. George-Hyslop et al., 1987a; Goldgaber et al., 1987). In FAD the offspring would theoretically have a 50–50 chance of inheriting the disease from the afflicted parent. There are indications that FAD may be genetically heterogeneous. Analysis of autopsy-documented cases in a related group of people by Schellenberg and co-workers (1988) indicates a form of the disease that is not linked to the chromosome 21 markers utilized by St. George-Hyslop and his group. There also may be noninherited forms of the disease that are similar to FAD (Tanzi et al., 1987).

The occurrence of Alzheimer-like changes in those afflicted with trisomy 21 lead researchers to investigate dosage (duplication) of the Alzheimer locus in familial and sporadic Alzheimer's disease. Duplication is not invariably involved in either manifestation of the disease (St. George-Hyslop et al., 1987b). Neither is the disease associated with duplication of the gene for the precursor of amyloid protein associated with neuronal plaque (Podlisny, Lee, and Selkoe, 1987).

The role of amyloid proteins in normal cells is problematical. There are two forms of mRNA for the major component of amyloid (amyloid beta precursor protein). One form contains a 168–base pair insert which may be spliced out of the other mRNA. The insert codes for a protein resembling a protease inhibitor. The longer message is found in high levels in the brain of Alzheimer and trisomy 21 patients, but is also found throughout the brain of normal individuals. The role of this longer mRNA in disease states has not been established. The normal amyloid protein is highly conserved among mammals (Selkoe, Bell, Podlisny, Price, and Cork, 1987), and its structure suggests that it may normally embed in portions of the cell membrane. The amyloid-beta found in plaque is only a small fragment of the complete protein, 40 out of 695 amino acid residues. It seems reasonable, for now, to assume that the fragment may represent a degradation of the normal amyloid molecule, a result rather than a cause of pathology.

Recently, another protein (A68) has been found in the cerebrospinal fluid of SDAT patients in concentrations much higher than observed in elderly patients without SDAT. Since the disease is heritable, early diagnosis is critical for purposes of genetic counseling of families carrying the gene. The presence of this protein may provide an important diagnostic tool.

With respect to biochemical abnormalities, it has been noted that Alzheimer's disease is characterized by a deficiency in the neurons of the cerebral cortex depending on acetylcholine for synaptic transmission. An enzyme confined to these nerve fibers, choline acetyltransferase, is deficient in Alzheimer's disease, while other transmitter systems appear to be spared (Davies, 1979).

It is also known that Alzheimer patients accumulate aluminum in the brain, possibly a result rather than a cause of the disease. Aluminum induces degeneration of microfilaments of nerve cells in experimental animals. Also evident in the cerebral cortex are intracellular tangles of neurofibrils and plaque. The white blood cells of these patients show some amount of chromosomal abnormalities, though no single type of abnormality is found in all patients. Rather, it appears that the kinds of chromosomal changes are the same kinds as are observed in normally aging populations in the absence of dementia (Whalley, 1982).

There has been speculation involving a transmissible, viruslike factor in SDAT, though none has been identified. Virus vectors have been described for similar dementias such as Creutzfeld-Jakob disease and kuru.

Trisomy 21

Trisomy 21 (also known as Down's syndrome and once known as mongolism) results from having an extra autosome, specifically an extra chromosome 21. The chromosome imbalance is created at fertilization by the failure of the egg or sperm to reduce completely to half the number of chromosomes found in tissue cells. The egg or sperm retains both members of the chromosome 21 pair, so the resulting zygote has three instead of two chromosomes in the set, a hyperdiploid condition known as trisomy.

Autopsy reveals brain changes indistinguishable from Alzheimer's disease. Trisomy patients show neuronal tangles and plaques in middle age (beginning around age 40). Many develop dementia and a rapid, aggressive form of Alzheimer's disease. The A68 protein of SDAT is also present in trisomy patients in their later years. They also are characterized by degenerative vascular disease and generally seem to age faster than normal individuals with normal chromosome number (Whalley, 1982). The trisomic state of chromosome 21 in this condition focused attention on this chromosome as the possible genetic site of the lesion(s) producing Alzheimer's disease, where it was subsequently found.

Pick's Disease

This disease is difficult to distinguish from Alzheimer's disease except at autopsy. It is rarer than Alzheimer's, and women are affected more often than men. It is thought to be inherited as a rare autosomal dominant factor (Burnet, 1983).

Symptoms are similar to SDAT, but the lesions tend to be circumscribed areas of intense cortical atrophy, with heavy loss of cells. Senile plaque and neurofibrillary tangles are rare, though abnormal neurofilaments known as Pick bodies are found (see Figure 7.7).

Huntington's Chorea

Huntington's chorea (Huntington's disease) is relatively rare. Symptoms usually begin during the 40s or 50s. The characteristic brain lesions are found in specific locations in the cerebrum (Burnet, 1983) and involve specific motor neuron loss. The onset is insidious. Personality changes usually precede the appearance of jerky, involuntary movements of the face, neck, and upper extremities. Patients become obstinate and moody. Death follows the onset of symptoms in about 15 years. There is no treatment to alter the fundamental course of the disease.

The disease is controlled by an autosomal dominant gene. A marker DNA segment that encodes two genes tightly linked to the Huntington's disease locus has been identified (Gilliam et al., 1987). The sequences in question all map to the short arm of chromosome 4. The segment exhibits only rare recombination with the *HD* gene. It provides a means of preclinical screening for the disease and perhaps a means of identifying the actual *HD* gene for subsequent cloning.

Ataxia Telangiectasia

Individuals with ataxia telangiectasia seem normal at birth. Ataxic (failure of coordination) symptoms appear in late infancy. Death usually comes during adolescence. Lesions are found in the cerebellum, including loss of Purkinje cells, and are accompanied by a high incidence of malignant tumors, an immune deficiency, and deficiencies in DNA repair.

The condition is thought to be inherited as an autosomal recessive.

Amyotrophic Lateral Sclerosis, Friedreich's Ataxia, and Parkinsonism-Dementia Complex

Early loss of neurons from some segment of the brain or spinal cord is characteristic of these conditions (Burnet, 1983). In amyotrophic disease the motor nerve cells of the spinal cord are affected. The loss of motor neurons, with loss of muscle strength as a consequence, begins in early adult life, and death usually occurs two to five years after onset. In individuals experiencing normal aging, a slow loss of motor neurons might be expected to begin by age 60.

Friedreich's ataxia involves nerve cells of the cerebellum, which are lost prematurely in childhood. Symptoms include loss of control of muscle action in walking and other movements. A variant of this disease has an onset in adult life. The degeneration is progressive and always fatal. Amyotrophic disease and Friedreich's ataxia are both inherited as autosomal recessives.

The Parkinsonism-dementia complex is thought to be carried as a dominant gene with a variable expression in females (females who have the gene may or may not show symptoms), but 100 percent expression in males. The symptoms, which resemble those of amyotrophic disease, appear in the early 40s. Dementia develops in all, and death occurs about four years from onset. Autopsy indicates changes similar to both Parkinson's disease (see below) and amyotrophic disease.

Parkinson's disease is a motor disorder that appears as a chronic form of shaking palsy. Its cause is unknown (idiopathic Parkinsonism). Parkinson's disease occurred in a large proportion of survivors of the encephalitis pandemic of 1919–1926 (postencephalitic Parkinsonism), leading to a suspected viral etiology, but the virus itself remains unknown. Studies of a large number of patients with Parkinson's disease detected high levels of herpes simplex antibodies (Marttila et al., 1977); influenza virus A antigen has also been detected in six cases of postencephalitic Parkinsonism. Since Parkinson's disease is characterized by disorders in brain dopamine metabolism, it is significant that changes in brain monoamine metabolism can be induced by herpes simplex infections in experimental animals. A direct link between the disease and any virus has not been established.

A model of Parkinson's disease seems to have been attained by a strange accident. A few years ago an amateur chemist in northern California turned out a bad batch of synthetic heroin. The users who took the drug came down with parkinsonian tremors and muscular rigidity. The contaminant was a substance called MPTP (1-methyl-4-phenyl-1,2,5,6-tetrahydropyridine), a metabolic relative of dopamine (Figure 6.4; summarized by Lewin, 1986). MPTP is a neurotoxin specific for the portion of the brain (substantia nigra) involved in Parkinsonism. The complete neuropathology is generated only in older experimental animals (mice, monkeys). One (the only one found by this author) benefit of cigarette smoking is

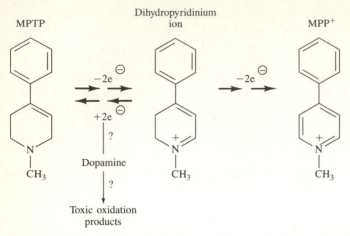

Figure 6.4 The neurotoxin MPTP and its metabolic relation to dopamine.

protection of the smoker against Parkinson's disease. The substance that seems to be involved in protection is 4-phenylpyridine (4PP); 4PP blocks the conversion of MPTP to MPP$^+$, which is the best candidate for the substance that actually kills neurons once MPTP gets into the brain. It has been proposed that MPTP may be an environmental cause of idiopathic Parkinson's disease.

Another neurotoxin associated with parkinsonian symptoms is the amino acid beta-N-methylamino-L-alanine (BMAA). It has been reported that monkeys fed repeated doses of BMAA develop corticomotor dysfunction, parkinsonian features, and degenerative changes of motor neurons of the cerebrum and spinal cord. Among the Chamorro people of Guam, the Parkinsonism-dementia complex kills an estimated 15 percent of the population. These people were known to eat large quantities of the seed of the false sago plant (*Cycas circinalis*), which contains large quantities of BMAA (Spencer et al., 1987).

The fact that some motor neuron diseases, Parkinsonism, and Alzheimer-like disease can all be triggered by the same neurotoxin implies that these diseases may be linked at some fundamental level. This does not eliminate genetic factors, but simply adds the complication that genetic diseases may somehow be triggered by external agents in persons not carrying the mutant trait. This notion is supported by the findings regarding MPTP and Parkinson's disease and has stimulated a search for other environmental chemicals that may be involved in these disease states.

Currently, potential therapy centers around transplants of dopa-producing tissues (autologous adrenal gland, fetal brain). Possession of an animal model of the disease generated by MPTP and human case studies in Sweden and Mexico allow assessment of transplant therapy. The results so far are preliminary, but promising. In mice adrenal grafts seem to enhance recovery of brain dopamine neurons through some unspecified neurotrophic action (Bohn, Cupit, Marciano, and Gash, 1987). There are indications that in humans adrenal transplants may not survive as dopamine sources, whereas in experimental animals fetal brain does. Adrenal transplants can derive from patients' own tissue, but obviously fetal brain tissue must come from abortus material, raising many ethical questions (see Lewin, 1988 for summary). Brain tissue culture may provide an alternative source of transplant material should it ultimately be shown that autologous adrenal gland is ineffective.

Xeroderma Pigmentosum

This rare disease occurs in approximately 1 in 250,000 births. Affected individuals are born without visible abnormality. The first sign that something is wrong follows exposure to sunlight; any exposed skin areas become acutely inflamed and blistered. By the time patients enter their teens, the first skin cancers begin to appear. These are of epithelial origin and can be excised, but the malignancies recur again and again. Sometimes cancers of a more serious form, malignant melanoma, appear. The malignancies are almost entirely confined to the skin, in contrast to normal aging where cancers of many types appear. The dementia observed in xeroderma patients differs in some respects from SDAT in that the brain damage appears to be congenital (found at birth).

The basic lesion, carried as a recessive gene, is related directly to a defect in the mechanisms of DNA repair. The severity of the dementia is closely related to the severity of the repair defect. Damages to DNA via the ultraviolet portion of the spectrum cannot be handled in xeroderma patients (Andrews, Barrett, and Robbins, 1972). It is estimated that normal cells are 10,000 times more efficient at DNA repair than are xeroderma cells.

Familial Amyloidosis

Amyloidosis is a family of five distinct syndromes, named for the regions of the world in which they were found. In all the syndromes there is an accumulation in various tissues of an amorphous, acellular material composed of multiple proteins related to immunoglobulins. The tissues involved are predominantly heart and nervous, though in hereditary forms of the condition the target is more usually nervous tissue. The amyloid material is the same in all cases, though the pattern of deposition is distinct. In normal individuals accumulation of amyloid occurs more frequently with advancing age, for reasons that are not understood. In familial amyloidosis accumulation begins earlier in life. Hereditary syndromes are controlled, in most instances, by an autosomal dominant gene.

Diabetes

Insulin-dependent diabetes (IDD) is associated with early years and accounts for 10 to 20 percent of all diabetes cases. About 20 autosomal recessive diseases have in common a reduced life expectancy along with an increased prevalence of diabetes. These genetic diseases include Friedreich's ataxia, trisomy 21, progeria, and Werner's syndrome. Cells of diabetes show restriction in the number of *in vitro* doublings, and cultures contain more senescent cells than do cultures of normal cells. More details on diabetes will be presented in Chapter 7 in the discussion of endocrine functions.

Autoimmune Disease

Many disease states are caused by a genetic dysfunction of the immune system in which it mistakenly attacks the tissues of the body. Ordinarily, the immune system cells know self from not-self and are restrained from attacking body tissues (Chapter 4). However, inflammations of the thyroid, certain forms of arthritis, myesthenia gravis, multiple sclerosis, and perhaps some pathologies of the heart found in the later years have been shown to be the result of attack by immune system cells on normal body tissue (Burnet, 1983). Many of these diseases can be mimicked experimentally in laboratory animals such as the guinea pig by injection of autologous tissue into the experimental animal. Autoimmunity is associated with certain genes of the histocompatibility complex (HLA loci).

Autoimmune diseases are more common in women than in men. There is no clear mechanism to account for this observed sex difference, though a study in mice indicates that male hormones may inhibit the production of certain autoantibodies (Greenberg and Yunis, 1978).

CONCLUSIONS

Cancer is a disease of old age. Cancer represents many different diseases, with many causes. Some result from environmental factors, some from oncogenes found within the genome, and still others from retroviruses integrated into the genome. Aside from childhood cancers, it seems that these malignancies arise from accumulations of effects over years and through failure in later life of the surveillance function of the immune system.

The increase in chromosmal damage with age may relate to cancer, though it is not clear that the relationship is always one of direct cause and effect. Some cancerous tissues have normal chromosome structure and number. Some abnormalities of chromosome structure may be related to impaired DNA repair mechanisms, while others may represent abnormalities of chromosome distribution during mitosis of those cells that continue to divide.

There are a number of genetic diseases that mimic certain aspects of aging, leading to the notion of a series of partial models of aging in different body tissues presumably controlled by mutant genes at specific genetic loci. Some diseases of old age may have environmental causes, including some of the so-called dementias, and some appear to be environmental in some instances and genetic in others, such as the familial and sporadic forms of Alzheimer's disease. One must not assume, however, that seemingly identical dementias of the Alzheimer type are always the same disease. Similar symptoms may have diverse and different underlying causes.

REFERENCES

Andrews, A. D., S. F. Barrett, and J. H. Robbins. Xeroderma pigmentosum neurological abnormalities correlate with colony-forming ability after ultraviolet irradiation. *Proceedings of the National Academy of Science, USA* 75:1984, 1972.

Bishop, J. M. The molecular genetics of cancer. *Science* 235:305, 1987.

Bohn, M. C., L. Cupit, F. Marciano, and D. M. Gash. Adrenal medulla grafts enhance recovery of striatal dopaminergic fibers. *Science* 237:913, 1987.

Bondareff, W. The neural basis of aging. In J. Birren and W. Schaie, eds., *Handbook of the Psychology of Aging.* Van Nostrand Reinhold, New York, 1985.

Burnet, F. M. Age-associated heredo-degenerative conditions of the central nervous system. In H. T. Blumenthal, ed., *Handbook of Diseases of Aging.* Van Nostrand, New York, 1983.

Davies, P. Neurotransmitter-related enzymes in senile dementia of the Alzheimer type. *Brain Research* 171:319–327, 1979.

DeBusk, F. L. The Hutchinson-Gilford progeria syndrome. *Journal of Pediatrics* 80:697–724, 1972.

De Vos, A. M., L. Tong, M. V. Milburn, P. M. Matias, J. Jancarik, S. Noguchi, S. Nishimura, K. Miura, E. Ohtsuka, and S.-H. Kim. Three dimensional structure of an oncogene protein: Catalytic domain of human c-H-ras p21. *Science* 239:888, 1988.

Epstein, C. J., G. M. Martin, A. L. Schultz, and A. G. Motulsky. Werner's syndrome. A review of its symptomology, natural history, pathologic features, genetics, and relationship to the natural aging process. *Medicine* 45:177, 1966.

Gilliam, T. C., M. Bucan, M. E. MacDonald, M. Zimmer, J. L. Haines, S. V. Cheng, T. M. Pohl, R. H. Meyers, W. L. Whaley, B. A. Allitto, A. Faryniarz, J. J. Wasmuth, A.-M. Frischauf, P. M. Conneally, H. Lehrach, and J. F. Gusella. A DNA segment encoding two genes very tightly linked to Huntington's disease. *Science* 238:950, 1987.

Goldgaber, D., M. I. Lerman, O. W. McBride, U. Saffiotti, and D. C. Gajdusek. Characterization and chromosomal localization of a cDNA encoding brain amyloid of Alzheimer's disease. *Science* 235:877, 1987.

Goldstein, S. The role of DNA repair in aging of cultured fibroblasts from xeroderma pigmentosum and normals. *Proceedings of the Society for Experimental Biological Medicine* 137:730–741, 1971.

Greenberg, L. J., and E. J. Yunis. Genetic control of autoimmune disease and immune responsiveness and the relationship to aging. *Birth Defects* 14:249, 1978.

Hadley, E. C. Genetic alteration and the pathology of aging. In P. C. Adelman and G. S. Roth, eds., *Testing the Theories of Aging.* CRC Press, Boca Raton, Fla.,1982.

Hirokawa, K., and T. Makinodan. Thymic involution: Effect on T cell differentiation. *Journal of Immunology* 114:1659, 1975.

Ide, T., T. Yoshiaki, S. Ishibashi, and Y. Mitsui. Reinitiation of host DNA synthesis in senescent human diploid cells by infection with simian virus 40. *Experimental Cell Research* 143:343–349, 1983.

Lewin, R. Age factors loom in Parkinsonian research. *Science* 234:1200, 1986.

Lewin, R. Cloud over Parkinson's therapy. *Science* 240:390, 1988.

Makinodan, T., and M. M. Kay. Age influence on the immune system. *Advances in Immunology* 29:287, 1980.

Martin, G. M. Genetic syndromes in man with potential relevance to the pathobiology of aging. In D. Bergsma and D. E. Harrison, eds., *Genetic Effects of Aging.* The National Foundation—March of Dimes. Alan R. Liss, New York, 1978.

Marttila, R. J., P. Arstila, J. Nikoskelainen, P. E. Halonen, and U. K. Rinne. Viral antibodies in the sera of patients with Parkinson's disease. *European Neurology* 15:25, 1977.

Mori, H., J. Kundo, and Y. Ihara. Ubiquitin is a component of paired helical filaments in Alzheimer's disease. *Science* 235:1641, 1987.

O'Brien, W., G. Stenman, and R. Sager. *Proceedings of the National Academy of Science, USA* 83:8659, 1986.

Pereira-Smith, O., and J. R. Smith. Genetic analysis of indefinite division in human cells: Identification of four complementation groups. *Proceedings of the National Academy of Science, USA* 85:6032, 1988.

Podlisny, M. B., G. Lee, and D. J. Selkoe. Gene dosage of the amyloid beta precursor protein in Alzheimer's disease. *Science* 238:669, 1987.

St. George-Hyslop, P. H., R. E. Tanzi, R. J. Polinsky, J. L. Haines, L. Nee, P. C. Watkins, R. H. Myers, R. G. Feldman, D. Pollen, D. Drachmaruni, J.-F. Foncin, D. Salmon, P. Frommelt, L. Amaducci, S. Sorbi, S. Piacentini, G. D. Stewart, W. J. Hobbs, P. M. Conneally, and J. F. Gusella. The genetic defect causing familial Alzheimer's disease maps on chromosome 21. *Science* 235:885, 1987a.

St. George-Hyslop, P. H., R. E. Tanzi, R. J. Polinsky, R. L. Neve, D. Pollen, D. Drachman, J. Growdon, L. A. Cupples, L. Nee, R. H. Myers, D. O'Sullivan, P. C. Watkins, J. A. Amos, C. K. Deutsch, J. W. Bodfish, M. Kinsbourne, R. G.

Feldman, A. Bruni, L. Amaducci, J.-F. Foncin, and J. F. Gusella. Absence of duplication on chromosome 21 genes in familial and sporadic Alzheimer's disease. *Science* 238:664, 1987b.

Schellenberg, G. D., T. D. Bird, E. M. Wijsman, D. K. Moore, M. Boehnke, E. M. Bryant, T. H. Lampe, D. Nochlin, S. Sumi, S. S. Deeb, K. Beyreuther, and G. M. Martin. Absence of linkage of chromosome 21q21 markers to familial Alzheimer's disease. *Science* 241:1507, 1988.

Schneider, E. L., and G. D. Bynum. Diseases that feature alterations resembling premature aging. In H. T. Blumenthal, ed., *Handbook of Diseases of Aging.* Van Nostrand, New York, 1983.

Selkoe, D. J., D. S. Bell, M. B. Podlisny, D. L. Price, and L. C. Cork. Conservation of brain amyloid proteins in aged mammals and humans with Alzheimer's disease. *Science* 235:873, 1987.

Sinex, F. M., and C. R. Merril, eds., Alzheimer's disease, Down's syndrome, and aging. *Annals of the New York Academy of Science* 396, 1982.

Spencer, P. S., P. B. Nunn, J. Hugon, A. C. Ludolph, S. M. Ross, D. N. Roy, and R. C. Robertson. Guam amyotrophic lateral sclerosis-Parkinsonism-dementia linked to a plant excitant neurotoxin. *Science* 237:517, 1987.

Tanzi, R. E., et al. Amyloid beta protein gene: cDNA, mRNA distribution, and genetic linkage near the Alzheimer locus. *Science* 235:880, 1987.

Varmus, H. Retroviruses. *Science* 240:1427, 1988.

Whalley, L. J. The dementia of Down's syndrome and its relevance to aetiological studies of Alzheimer's disease. In F. M. Sinex and C. R. Merril, eds., Alzheimer's disease, Down's syndrome, and aging. *Annals of the New York Academy of Science* 396, 1982.

Wisniewski, H. M., and P. B. Kozlowski. Evidence for blood-brain barrier changes in senile dementia of the Alzheimer type (SDAT). In F. M. Sinex and C. R. Merril, eds., Alzheimer's disease, Down's syndrome, and aging. *Annals of the New York Academy of Science* 396, 1982.

Chapter
7

Changes in Organ Systems I

INTRODUCTION

The discussions in previous chapters have indicated that the best available predictor of longevity is family history. Long lives tend to run in families, which is another way of saying that life span is under genetic control. Life expectancy is determined by the genetic life span as well as by prevailing living conditions and advances of medical science.

In the next two chapters we will depart from attempts to present an overall picture of senescence and describe changes in the structure and function of the human body that occur with passage of time. Our discussion deals primarily with changes due to aging and senescence alone, which occur in the absence of specific disease states. The Baltimore Longitudinal Study of Aging (Chapter 1) is an investigation of such age-related changes. The BLSA is a resource of the Gerontological Research Center of the National Institute on Aging. Its subjects are 1,000 healthy volunteers initially between the ages of 20 and 96 who return every two years for extensive medical and psychological evaluation. The study has as its objective distinguishing changes that occur with normal aging from those associated with disease.

One should keep in mind that much of the material in this chapter deals with populations of humans and that the profile of change with advancing years for each individual may diverge from the norm of the population. In this sense, we may speak of functional or physiological age versus chronological age. We are aware of young people who have early heart trouble and of older people with the vigor of those much younger. Studies of individuals remind us that humans age at different rates and that different tissues of the same individual age at different rates. To date, there is no known "potion" that will in any way reverse or even slow this process of senescence.

Though this chapter may have negative or even depressing overtones, it is nevertheless remarkable that we humans handle senescence as well as we do. The durability of the human anatomy and physiology over our comparatively long life expectancy is truly remarkable. We compensate for our gradually failing bodies in equally gradual ways that may go unnoticed until the later years. It is remarkable that the functional decline can be accommodated to the extent that many elderly people are able to live productive lives in the face of the encroachments of senescence.

The descriptions of age-related changes in particular organs (in this chapter and the next) are accompanied by brief descriptions of the normal function and anatomy of the organ. Also included is an 8-page color atlas of histology of selected aging and normal tissues (following page 132). The references most useful for general coverage of the topics to follow are Shock (1977) and Behnke et al. (1978). More detailed reference lists are to be found in Finch and Schneider (1985).

GENERALIZED CHANGES

First we will describe some general changes that occur in all of the organ systems. They are most likely a result of some underlying process of senescence and are not primary causes of aging in themselves. They are diffuse changes, difficult to pin down in a quantitative sense, but in aggregate they form the backdrop for the functional decline of each of the specific organ systems.

There are pervasive changes in the ground matrix, or connective tissues surrounding the body organs. The collagen becomes increasingly cross-linked and more rigid. The walls of blood vessels become impregnated with a plaque material possibly derived from excess dietary fat. The narrowing of the vessels results in a diminished blood supply to organs served by these vessels, including, of course, the brain.

Age pigment (lipofuscin) accumulates within many different cell types during aging in many diverse species (Figure 7.1). This pigment is seldom found in younger individuals, but as yet no specific deleterious effect is directly ascribable to it in more elderly individuals. Lipofuscin is highly insoluble and accumulates in lysosomes where it is incompletely degraded. In humans, Strehler, Mark, Mildvan, and Gee (1959) found a linear increase in lipofuscin in cardiac muscle at a rate of 0.6 percent of intracellular volume per decade. It originates as a peroxidation product of unsaturated membrane lipids and denatured proteins.

Some nondividing cells gradually atrophy and are not replaced. Aged cells of a given tissue often change appearance and vary from younger, normal cells. The altered cell appearance may also reflect changes relating to declining functional abilities.

The cause(s) of these general changes cannot be evaluated further

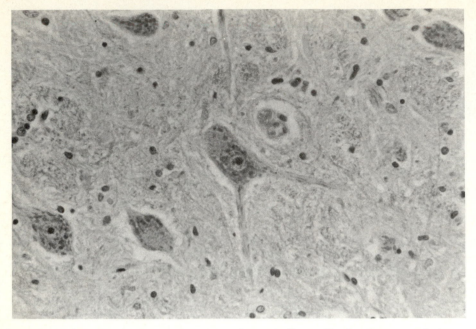

Figure 7.1 Age pigment in motor neuron. Arrow indicates lipofuscin accumulation. (Courtesy of Ballinger, M.D., University of Florida College of Medicine, Department of Pathology.)

than we have already done in Chapter 5. The development of senescence is slow and progressive. It progresses at different rates in different systems and in different individuals, leading to a loss of reserve and increasing probability of organ system failure and death.

BRAIN, SPINAL CORD, AND NERVES

The brain is the seat of identity and personality. It is the clearing house for all information gleaned from the senses, retains information as memory, and also carries out many autonomic functions. The brain interfaces with all organ systems and may influence the functioning of these organs by either conscious will or unconscious autonomic activity.

The brain is an expansion of the more simply organized spinal cord. It receives input from sense organs through the spinal cord and from nerves running directly to it from organs of special sense (nose, eyes, ears). The brain sends messages outward to effectors (muscles, endocrine glands); the effectors may also receive messages generated by reflex responses in segments of the spinal cord. There are many more sensory nerves than there are effector or motor nerves. We receive information through many sensory modes, but our motor response to stimuli is restricted to the actions of a limited number of muscles. Ultimately, sensory input must be selectively directed to converge on appropriate motor nerves.

Anatomy and Function of Nerves

All of this nerve input and output is in the form of self-propagated electrical nerve impulses, called action potentials, which are carried by long cylindrical processes (axons) of nerve cells (neurons) to the receiving fibers (dendrites) of the next neuron in the pathway leading to or from the brain or spinal cord (Figure 7.2). A large bundle of individual axons is termed a nerve.

Neurons are chemically connected at the synapse (the space between the axon of one and the dendrites of another neuron) by secretion of substances, called neurotransmitters, at the end of the axon. The transmitters bridge the gap between the end of the axon and the receiving dendritic process of the next neuron. The neurotransmitter varies with the kind of nerve, but is generally either epinephrine or acetylcholine. An action potential is a self-propagating depolarization of the nerve cell membrane brought about by direct electrical stimulation of a nerve or by the action of a neurotransmitter produced by the axon at the synapse and received by membrane-bound receptors located on the dendrites across the synapse. The neurotransmitters activate an enzyme, adenylcyclase, which converts ATP to cyclic AMP, which in turn results in ion flow and depolarization of the nerve cell membrane, generating an action potential.

In the brain two other excitatory neurotransmitters are found, dopamine and serotonin. The central nervous system also has inhibitory neurotransmitters, notably glycine and gamma-aminobutyric acid (GABA). These inhibitory substances act by hyperpolarizing the postsynaptic membrane (an action potential results from membrane depolarization). The inhibitory effects of glycine are noticeable in the spinal cord, where the activity of motor neurons of extensor muscles is inhibited by glycine during contraction of the opposing flexor muscles of the arm or leg. GABA is the most prevalent inhibitory neurotransmitter in the brain. It is also involved in motor control, and a deficiency of GABA neurons produces the uncontrolled movements seen in people with Huntington's chorea.

Sensory Information

Sensations are electrical responses to environmental events. For example, visual information from specific portions of the retina of the eye is sent as bursts of electrical activity to the brain for interpretation. The size, shape, and color of an object in view is a matter of interpretation by optical centers in the brain of the spatial pattern of neuronal activity in the retina. Similarly, the sensation of pain is basically electrical information passed to

Figure 7.2 Motor neuron from spinal cord of a cat showing origin of axon (AH), cell body (CS), axon fiber (IS), neurofibrils (nf), incoming dendrites (D). X 860. (Reprinted by permission of the publisher from L. Weiss and R. Greep, eds., *Histology*, 4th ed., Fig. 8.29. Copyright 1977 by Elsevier Science Publishing Co., Inc.)

different sections of the brain from sensory neurons in the skin. Such pain-sensitive neurons are distinct from others in the skin which are sensitive to touch or to temperature. Sensory perception is thus the transduction of environmental physical events into electrical nerve impulses which are interpreted by the various sensory centers in the brain.

The anatomical complexity of the brain and spinal cord is enormous, involving trillions of neurons and synapses. The sensory input is integrated by association neurons running between the areas of the brain and also

SELECTED SURVEY OF HISTOPATHOLOGICAL CHANGES RELATED TO AGING AND DISEASES OF AGING

The illustrations presented here were obtained from human necropsies (autopsies) and routine surgical biopsies. Some show the results of aging processes *per se* (for example, changes in the skin, age pigment deposition, and collagen deposition). Others depict changes that are characteristic of diseases common in middle and old age and represent an important aspect of aging biology as observed in the clinic (for example, atherosclerosis, osteoporosis, and some kinds of cancer). These diseases are not an inevitable consequence of aging in all individuals.

It is important to recognize that disease detectable by microscopic or chemical means may cause no overt clinical impairment. In addition, significant disease- or age-related changes can be present and not detected with even the most sophisticated tools currently in use. For example, a person may die of accidental causes and necropsy may reveal a minimal atherosclerosis of the coronary artery that is unrelated to the death of the person. On the other hand, clinically silent disease may be close to causing severe impairment or may even cause an "accident" (as when a heart attack arising from coronary atherosclerosis causes an auto accident).

Illustrations of the sort presented here are gathered from selected tissue samples in pathology files. Ideally, one would like to compare young and old tissues from the same individual and furthermore from the same location in the same individual. In practice, when dealing with human tissues, this is impossible. The histological features that characterize human aging have to be gleaned from many tissue samples from many sources. What we have here is a best effort, within the constraints of space, to show selected but representative changes related to aging and to diseases that frequently accompany the advancing years.

The color photographs and comments in the legends were provided by Sefton R. Wellings, M.D., Ph.D., professor and chairman emeritus, Department of Pathology, University of California School of Medicine, Davis. (Copyright 1988 by Dr. Wellings. Used with permission.)

PLATE I CHANGES IN GONADS

Figure 1 Cross-section of human seminiferous tubule from the testis of a 55-year-old male. Note the complete maturation sequence from spermatogonia at the periphery to spermatids and mature sperm in the central lumen. In a younger subject, and in some older men as well, more active spermatogenesis resulting in more mature sperm could be present. Hematoxylin and eosin (H&E) stain, 630×.

Figure 2 Cross-section of human seminiferous tubule showing senile atrophy of the testis in a 90-year-old man (compare with Figure 1). Note that only a few spermatogonia are present; no sperm or spermatids are observed. The maturation sequence is therefore said to be arrested or incomplete. Some of the nuclei belong to sustentacular (Sertoli) cells. A decrease of the size of the testis occurs with atrophy relating to loss of cells, decreased cell size, or both; in this case cell loss predominates. H&E, 630×.

Figure 3 Ovary of a mature human showing three primary follicles (arrows) as would be expected in premenopausal human ovaries. Note capillary (C). H&E stain, 630×.

Figure 4 Portion of a senile human ovary illustrating stromal fibrosis (increasing numbers of collagen fibers) and an atretic (degenerating) follicle at arrows. The follicle has gone through ovulation, but failed to form a corpus luteum (source of progesterone). The follicle cells (estrogen source) have disappeared. As the ovary ages, no new oocytes are added and those present gradually disappear. Oocytes and primary follicles are rare in ovaries of older women. Note the capillaries (C) in the lower portion of the figure. H&E, 630×.

PLATE II CHANGES IN THE LUNG

Figure 5 Human lung illustrating a common kind of emphysema in a 65-year-old male who smoked about half a pack of cigarettes a day for 10 years. In emphysema the walls between adjacent alveoli break down so that fewer, larger air sacs are formed. The surface per unit volume is thus decreased as is the rate of gaseous exchange across the alveolar membrane. Note the millimeter scale. The size of air sacs in the normal lung is 0.25 mm. Anything larger than this means that emphysema is present.

Figure 6 Human lung from a 70-year-old male city dweller illustrating carbon particle accumulation in white cells known as macrophages. Particles of 5 micra or less pass into alveolar spaces beyond the reach of ciliary action which ends at the level of the respiratory bronchi. The particles are insoluble and are engulfed by these white cells (at arrows). Each macrophage is so laden with carbon particles the internal cellular details are obscured. This condition is found in the lungs of virtually all city dwellers and is visible on gross examination at necropsy. In most instances no functional deficit is experienced.

Figure 7 Human lung illustrating a carcinoma arising from the bronchial tree (tip of pencil). The lumen of the bronchus is clearly visible. The white carcinoma tissue arose at the surface of the lumen of the bronchus from epithelial cells and spread into the surrounding tissues (pulmonary parenchyma) above the tip of the pencil. There are at least four lymph nodes below the tip of the pencil. Each of these is partially replaced by white, metastatic, carcinoma tissue. The noncancerous tissue is black due to carbon particle accumulation (Figure 6). Note that the alveoli are of normal size without the breakdown associated with emphysema seen in Figure 5. Neoplastic disease increases in incidence with age. Theoretically, all of us would develop some type of cancer were we to live long enough.

Figure 8 Microscopy of human bronchial carcinoma. All cells with pink (eosinophilic) cytoplasm are carcinoma cells showing squamous cell phenotype. The nuclei are large and vesicular with prominent nucleoli. The group of six cells in the center are beginning to form an epithelial "pearl," which is a spherical focus of keratin deposition. Thus, the expressed phenotype is one of skin and represents one of the pathways of differentiation of an epithelial cell. Squamous cell keratinization is also found in carcinomas of the skin and uterine cervix. H&E, 630×.

PLATE III CHANGES IN THE CARDIOVASCULAR SYSTEM

Figure 9 Atherosclerosis of the aorta from an obese, hypertensive man age 56 who died of coronary artery occlusion secondary to severe coronary artery atherosclerosis. Note essentially normal areas of the aorta (N), fatty plaque (F), fibrous, calcified plaques (C), and ulcerated plaque (U). The process of atherosclerosis is usually patchy and does not involve all arteries uniformly. In the United States essentially every necropsy of persons over the age of 12 shows at least some atherosclerosis. Age, improper diet, and genetic factors all contribute to the degree of severity at a given age. The condition is an inevitable consequence of aging in most humans.

Figure 10 Histological section of a human coronary artery occluded by a thrombus. The patient was a male age 48 who died two weeks following a "heart attack." The location of the tunica intima is indicated by the arrow. The circular profile of the lumen is filled with partially decomposed erythrocytes (orange color) and fibrin (material of the clot). Narrowing of the coronary artery is the underlying cause of thrombosis in most instances. H&E, 100×.

Figure 11 Section of human heart showing myocardial fibrosis (scarring of the muscle from collagen replacement of myofibrils), the result in this instance of an old, healed, myocardial infarction (necrosis of heart muscle cells caused by occlusion of the coronary artery, Figure 10). In this photograph the surviving myocardial fibers (M) are shown with the surrounding zones of fibrosis (F). Myocardial fibrosis much like this may appear diffusely located between myocardial fibers in the aging heart unrelated to acute coronary occlusion. In general, the relative amount of collagen in heart and other organs gradually increases during the life span. H&E, 630×.

Figure 12 Small artery (arteriole) from the kidney of a 45-year-old male with severe (malignant) essential hypertension. Note extreme hypertrophy of the vessel wall with reduced lumen. The arterioles and sometimes the small arteries are involved in this disease. Hypertension of this kind generally begins as a pathological physiological change without morphological change in the vascular system. With progression, morphological changes appear. Hypertension is common enough in our society to be considered one of the common consequences of aging. H&E, 630×.

PLATE IV CHANGES IN BONES AND JOINTS

Figure 13 Osteoporosis. Photograph of midsagittal section through a second lumbar vertebral body of a 66-year-old malnourished and debilitated woman who died of lobar pneumonia. There is a marked diminution of the number and thickness of the bony elements of the centrum with widening of the marrow spaces. The whole of the vertebra is decreased in thickness indicating a partial collapse.

Figure 14 Photomicrograph of bone without osteoporosis. A single bone element (trabecula) is shown with bone deposition by osteoblasts (arrows) on one side and bone resorption by osteoclasts on the other side (double arrow). On the deposition side the osteoblasts are lined up in a single row. On the resorption side a single multinucleate osteoclast is seen, and no osteoblasts. H&E, 630×.

Figure 15 Low power photomicrograph of the vertebral body shown in Figure 13. Note the decreased number and thinness of the trabeculae (T) with widening of the marrow spaces (M). H&E, 100×.

Figure 16 Degenerative osteoarthritis. Midsaggital section of head of femur of an older woman who complained of hip pain. Note variable thickness of the hyaline cartilage surface (arrows) which is completely lacking at some points.

PLATE V CHANGES IN BREAST AND LYMPH NODES

Figure 17 Section of lobule of mammary gland from a premenopausal woman age 48. The smallest epithelium-lined units of the lobule are called ductules (acini or alveoli; arrows). The ductules drain into a central terminal duct which then empties into progressively larger ducts. Since the lobule is an approximate sphere, this section reveals only a small portion of the structure. Compare with the atrophic postmenopausal lobule in Figure 18. H&E, 250×.

Figure 18 Photomicrograph of two atrophic lobules of a postmenopausal breast. Note the small number of ductules per lobule. Compare with Figure 17. H&E, 630×.

Figure 19 Section of a normal adult lymph node from a 22-year-old man. The edge of a large germinal center is marked by arrows. H&E, 630×.

Figure 20 Section of a lymph node from an 80-year-old man for comparison with Figure 19. Note relatively small size of the germinal center (arrow). Both T and B cell domains of lymph nodes and of other lymphatic tissues typically atrophy with age. H&E, 630×.

PLATE VI CHANGES IN THE PROSTATE GLAND AND CEREBELLUM

Figure 21 Gross photograph of the urinary bladder and prostate gland of a 63-year-old man who died of a kidney infection secondary to lower urinary tract obstruction caused by benign enlargement of the prostate gland. Benign prostate enlargement has been found to increase in a linear fashion with age until about 80 percent of men over 80 years of age are affected. In this figure the bladder and prostatic urethra have been opened from the ventral aspect (sagittal section) to reveal the interior of these structures. The interior of the prostate gland has been further exposed by an additional section in a plane perpendicular to the sagittal cut. Note hyperplastic nodules (N) within the prostatic tissue. It is these enlarging nodules that compromise the prostatic urethra and cause the obstruction. Note also the hyperplastic middle lobe (M), which acts as a ball valve to obstruct the urethra. The inner surface of the bladder (B) has prominent trabeculae representing enlarged bands of smooth muscle. This change results from the added work needed to expel urine from the bladder due to the obstruction in the urethra.

Figure 22   Low power photomicrograph of tissue from the prostate gland in Figure 21. Note part of a nodule (delimited by arrows) and the relatively empty ovoid glandular spaces (G). H&E, 250×.

Figure 23   Histological section of normal human cerebellum showing a number of Purkinje cells, five of which are visible (arrows). H&E stain, 630×.

Figure 24   Histological section of senile cerebellum with loss of Purkinje cells, one of which is visible at arrow. H&E, 630×.

PLATE VII CHANGES IN SKIN

Figure 25   Section of skin from the face of a 29-year-old human showing normal epidermis (E) and dermis (D). Compare with Figure 26. H&E, 630×.

Figure 26   Skin from the face of a 72-year-old showing loss of staining (pale areas) and clumping of dermal collagen and elastin (arrows). This is mainly a consequence of exposure to sun and relates to total dosage of sunlight over the years more than to age per se. H&E, 630×.

Figure 27   Elastin stain of skin similar to that shown in Figure 26. Note clumping, granularity, and fragmentation of the elastin fibers, which stain black in this preparation. 250×.

Figure 28   Histological preparation of malignant melanoma of the skin from an elderly man. This kind of cancer, along with basal and squamous cell carcinomas, are relatively common in elderly people and are most likely to occur in sun-exposed skin. Most of the cells in this figure are cancerous melanocytes (pigment cells). These cells show typical changes of malignancy: enlarged nuclei with increased amounts of chromatin and irregular chromatin patterns and increased numbers of mitoses over normal skin. Some of these mitotic figures are very abnormal. The DNA per nucleus of these cells is greater than the diploid amount. Chromosome counts would reveal aneuploidy with variation in chromosome number. The mode would likely be hypotetraploid. H&E, 630×.

PLATE VIII CHANGES IN THE KIDNEY

Figure 29   Gross photograph of an essentially normal kidney from a 35-year-old man. The renal capsule has been stripped away to reveal a relatively smooth cortical surface, and the kidney has been cut to show normal cortical and medullary structure. Compare with Figure 30.

Figure 30   Gross photograph of a kidney from a 62-year-old man with long history of essential hypertension involving decreased renal circulation due to arteriolar nephrosclerosis. Vessel blockage results in a loss of nephrons and the fine granular scarring of the renal surface seen here. The surface granules represent surviving renal tissues. The depressions between the granules are areas of scarring where collagen deposition has replaced the filtration units.

Figure 31   Histological preparation of a glomerulus (G) with afferent arteriole (A) showing severe arteriolosclerosis of the hyaline type. "Hyaline" refers to the pink (eosinophilic), homogeneous, refractile, protein material in the arteriolar wall (tip of arrow). The hyaline material is deposited under the vessel endothelium and probably derives from blood proteins. Hyalinization of afferent arterioles is characteristic of established hypertension of the so-called benign type, a condition frequently seen in the elderly. Some degree of hypertension and arteriosclerosis can be observed in most persons over 70. H&E, 630×.

Figure 32   Histological preparation of two occluded glomeruli (arrows) associated with a degenerating nephron. The glomerulus is being replaced with fibrous connective tissue. Fibrosis (collagen deposition) of tissues occurs to at least a minor degree in all organs as they age. H&E, 630×.

PLATE I CHANGES IN GONADS

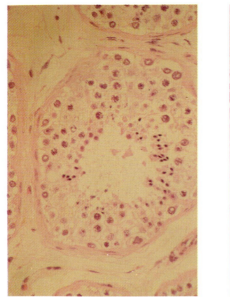

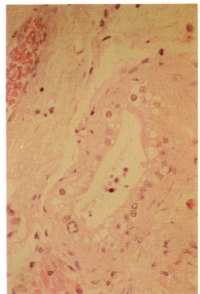

Figure 1

Figure 2

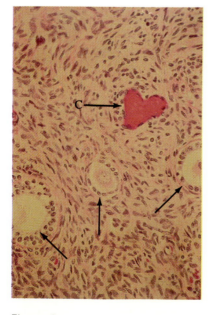

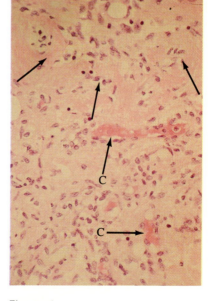

Figure 3

Figure 4

PLATE II CHANGES IN THE LUNG

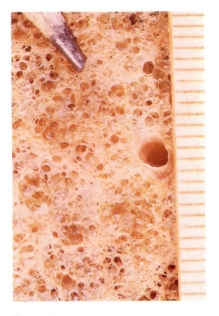

Figure 5

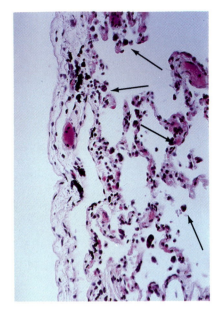

Figure 6

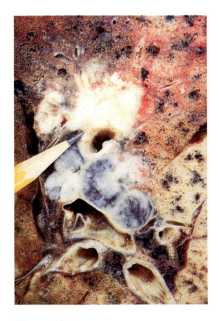

Figure 7

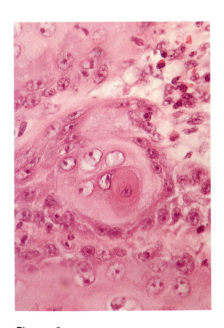

Figure 8

PLATE III CHANGES IN THE CARDIOVASCULAR SYSTEM

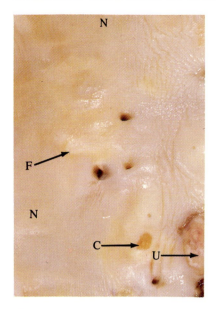

Figure 9

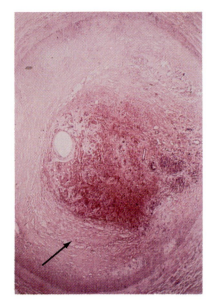

Figure 10

Figure 11

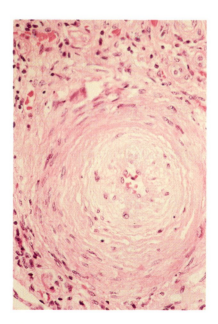

Figure 12

PLATE IV CHANGES IN BONES AND JOINTS

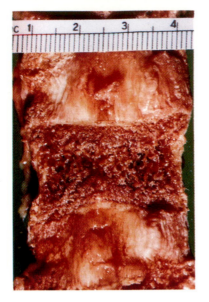

Figure 13

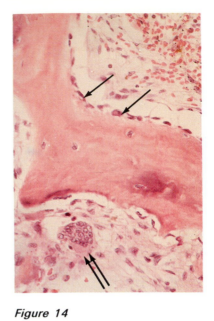

Figure 14

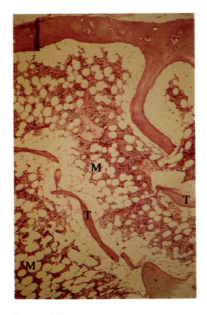

Figure 15

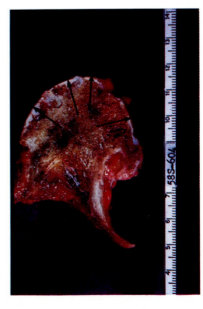

Figure 16

PLATE V CHANGES IN BREAST AND LYMPH NODES

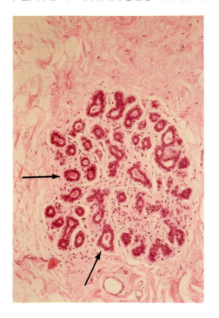

Figure 17

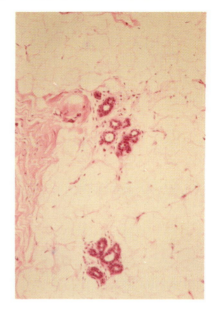

Figure 18

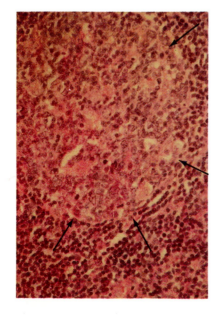

Figure 19

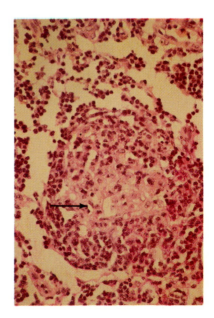

Figure 20

PLATE VI CHANGES IN THE PROSTATE GLAND AND CEREBELLUM

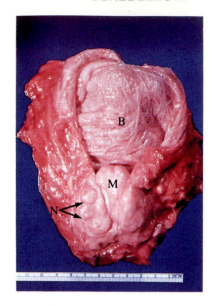

Figure 21

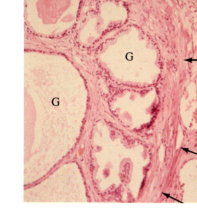

Figure 22

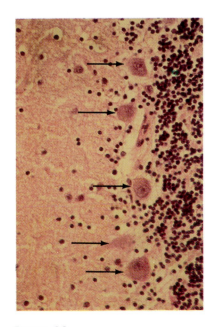

Figure 23

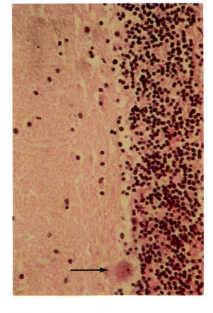

Figure 24

PLATE VII CHANGES IN SKIN

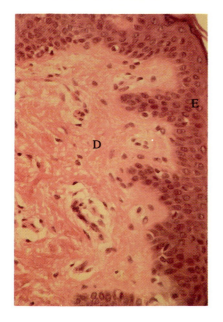

Figure 25

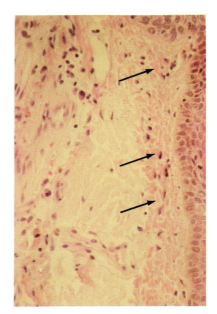

Figure 26

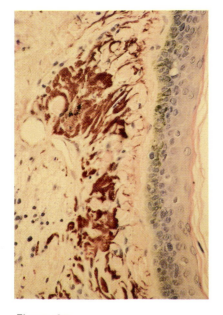

Figure 27

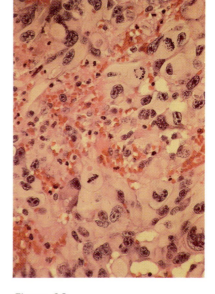

Figure 28

PLATE VIII CHANGES IN THE KIDNEY

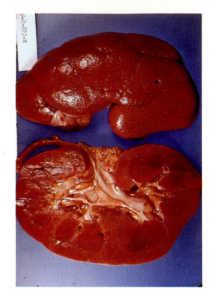

Figure 29

Figure 30

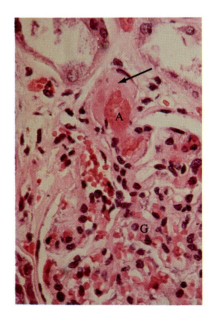

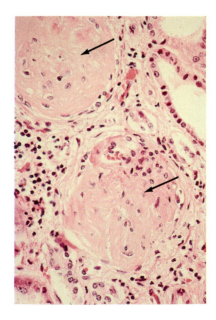

Figure 31

Figure 32

into the spinal cord. The amount of sensory information impinging on the brain in a given instant may be considerable. The brain therefore acts to suppress incoming irrelevant information.

Brain and Spinal Cord Anatomy and Function

A detailed summary of brain anatomy and function is beyond the scope of this text. What follows is a brief review of the regional specialization of the brain intended to make the ensuing discussion of age-related changes in these regions more meaningful.

External and Internal Anatomy (Figures 7.3–7.5)   The external divisions of the cerebrum according to anatomy and function are the frontal lobe, containing the areas of motor control of voluntary muscles; the olfactory bulb, containing fibers of the olfactory nerve; the parietal lobe, concerned with sensations arising in muscles, tendons, and joints; the temporal lobe, containing centers of hearing and association of vision and hearing sensations; and the occipital lobe, concerned with vision and eye movements. The two halves of the cerebral cortex are connected by the giant commissure, the corpus callosum.

The internal anatomy of the brain is more complex. The basal ganglia are masses of nerve cell bodies (termed nuclei) located deep within the white matter of the cerebrum. All of these regions are concerned with control of voluntary movements. The most prominent of the basal ganglia is the corpus striatum, which is divided into component nuclei, the caudate and the lentiform.

The brain immediately below and surrounded by the cerebrum is the diencephalon, composed of the thalamus and the hypothalamus. The thalamus acts as a relay center for all sensory information (except smell) between sensory receptors and the various areas of the cerebrum. The hypothalamus, below the thalamus, controls hunger, thirst, sleep patterns, sexual functions, and emotional reactions such as anger, fear, pain, and pleasure. In regulating emotion, the hypothalamus acts with the limbic system (see below) in evoking visceral responses to various emotional states. The posterior portion of the pituitary gland, the neurohypophysis, is found as a downpocketing of the hypothalamus. The neurohypophysis produces release hormones which are transported to the anterior pituitary gland where they regulate its hormonal secretions.

The midbrain, beneath the thalamus and hypothalamus, contains four rounded elevations (the corpora quadrigemina) just anterior to the pons. The upper two are involved in visual reflexes; the lower two relay auditory information. The floor of the midbrain also contains the red nucleus, involved in motor coordination, and the substantia nigra which, in conjunction with the basal ganglia, is also involved in motor coordination.

The cerebellum governs coordination of movement. The pons is concerned with respiratory movements. The medulla is the location of the

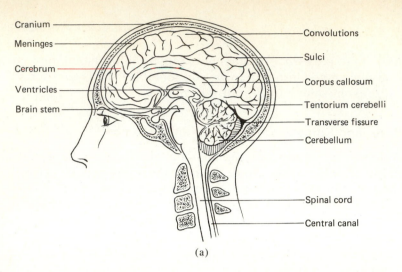

(a)

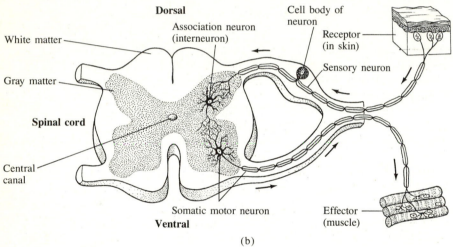

(b)

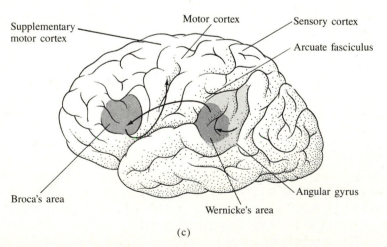

(c)

Figure 7.3 *(a)* Brain. *(b)* Spinal cord. *(c)* Surface areas of cerebral cortex.

134

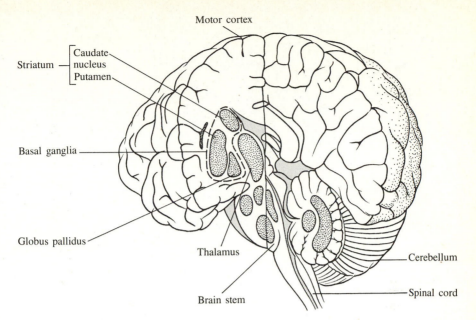

Figure 7.4 Internal brain anatomy.

crossover of fiber tracts from peripheral sensory organs on their way to the cerebral cortex, so the left side of the brain receives information from the right side of the body. The medulla is the seat of autonomic functions of breathing and cardiovascular responses through areas called vital centers. The medulla is also home to the locus ceruleus, a group of norepinephrine-producing nerve cells concerned with muscle tone and locomotion.

Limbic System   The limbic system is a group of nuclei and fiber tracts that form a ring around the brain stem (Figure 7.6) and are the neural basis of emotional states. These nuclei include the cingulate gyrus (part of the cerebral cortex), the amygdaloid nucleus (amygdala), hippocampus, and septal nuclei. There are few synaptic connections between the conscious centers of the cerebrum and the limbic system, which may help to explain why we have little conscious control over our emotions. The amygdala is associated with rage and aggression, fear, and emotional connotations of memory. The hippocampus is associated with short-term memory and with the consolidation of short-term to long-term memory. The left hippocampus is associated with verbal memory, the right hippocampus with nonverbal memory. Septal nuclei relay information between the hypothalamus and the hippocampus. The cingulate cortex (temporal lobe) is associated with maternal behavior and certain patterns of play. An evolutionarily old pathway, the median forebrain bundle, connects many limbic structures with the lateral aspects of the hypothalamus.

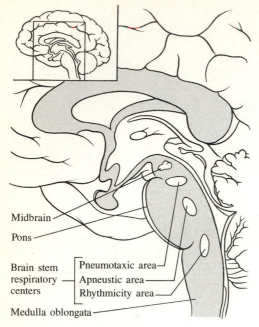

Midbrain

Pons

Brain stem
respiratory
centers
Pneumotaxic area
Apneustic area
Rhythmicity area

Medulla oblongata

Figure 7.5 Cerebral nuclei.

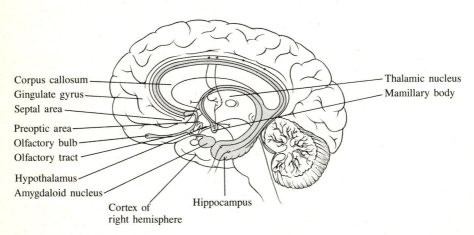

Corpus callosum
Gingulate gyrus
Septal area

Preoptic area
Olfactory bulb
Olfactory tract

Hypothalamus
Amygdaloid nucleus

Cortex of
right hemisphere

Hippocampus

Thalamic nucleus
Mamillary body

Figure 7.6 Limbic system.

Lateralization of the Cerebral Cortex Elucidated by Roger Sperry, the specialization of right and left hemispheres and consequent cerebral dominance of the left hemisphere results in the left hemisphere's containing the centers for speech, writing, calculation, while the right hemisphere contains centers for spatial relationships and simple language comprehension. The right hemisphere contains input from the left visual field of both right and left retinas, and the left hemisphere receives input from the right visual field of both retinas. The input from each ear goes to the contralateral hemisphere.

Speech Center   The speech center is located in Broca's area (see Figure 7.3) in the left hemisphere. Damage to this area produces aphasia (inability to speak) of a type where the person is reluctant to speak, and, when attempted, speech is slow and poorly articulated. Another area, in the temporal lobe, Wernicke's area, is also associated with speech. Damage to this area produces rapid speech which is without information, so-called word salad. Loss of or damage to Wernicke's area causes loss of language comprehension. It seems the concept of the words to be spoken originates in Wernicke's area and is carried to Broca's area which in turn relays the information to the motor cortex which controls the musculature of speech.

Spinal Cord   The basic anatomy of the spinal cord is indicated in Figure 7.3. The posterior sensory elements and the anterior motor elements are connected by interneurons and also by tracts leading up and down the cord to higher brain centers and to other spinal segments. The gray matter represents cell bodies, the white matter, nerve fibers.

Changes in the Brain with Age

The changes in the brain with age are manifold. There is gross atrophy of the brain, with an increase in size of the fluid-filled cavities of the brain (the ventricular system) and a parallel loss in brain weight (Figure 7.7). The normal weight loss is from 1,400 grams at age 20 to 1,334 grams at age 60. Dementia is not a consequence of this weight change. Loss of brain weight is accelerated after age 60. The loss in weight may be due to cell loss, to loss of the white matter (myelin) that surrounds the nerve fibers, and to shrinkage of dendrites. The loss in humans tends to be in specific areas of the cerebral cortex rather than a generalized loss; the visual portion of the cerebral cortex is among those areas showing decreases in neuron number with age. As the brain cavities (ventricles) enlarge, so the surface convolutions become separated by wider grooves (sulci). This is particularly pronounced in Pick's disease (see Figure 7.7). The loss of nerve cells may gradually contribute to senile dementia.

Age pigments accumulate within nerve cells in direct proportion to age. These intracellular deposits are also localized in discrete brain areas.

Neurons of aged brains may show diverse kinds of change in microanatomy, including vacuoles and viruslike particles. Extracellular plaque, including the substance amyloid, is found. The extent of this plaque is positively correlated with a number of senile psychometric changes. In aged brains and in brains of Alzheimer's disease, characteristic alterations of intracellular fibrils are noted in addition to plaque (Figure 7.8); the most extensive changes are associated with dementia.

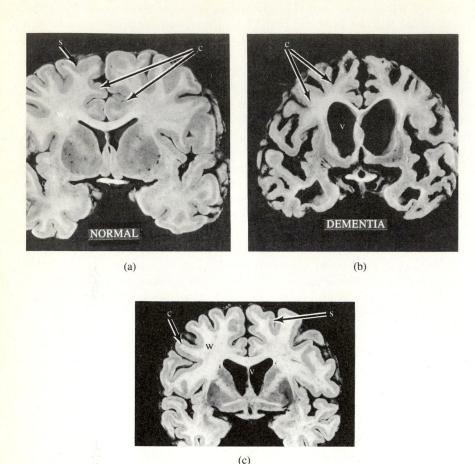

Figure 7.7 Brain ventricles. *(a)* Normal. *(b)* Pick's disease 36 years. *(c)* Normal, age 72. (Courtesy of W. Ballinger, M.D., University of Florida College of Medicine, Department of Pathology.)

Sensitive biochemical extraction techniques (Ogomori et al., 1988) reveal that the incidence of cerebral amyloid increases with normal aging. Results with brains of 66 nondemented individuals autopsied at various ages indicate that 67 percent of 9 brains from individuals in their 50s and 97 percent of 35 brains from individuals over 60 showed accumulated amyloid. The appearance of amyloid in the brain therefore seems to be an age-related phenomenon. These same studies found indications that the brains of Alzheimer patients accumulate larger amounts of amyloid than

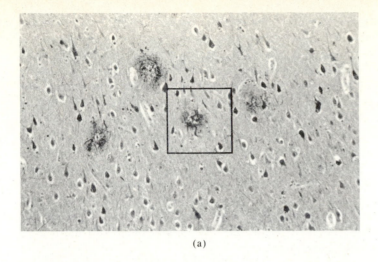

(a)

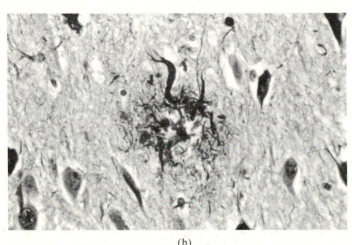

(b)

Figure 7.8 Varicosities and plaque in Alzheimer's disease. (Courtesy of W. Ballinger, M.D., University of Florida College of Medicine, Department of Pathology.) a. low power view (100 X) b. higher power showing varicosities and tangles (440 X).

the brains of "very old" nondemented patients. Even in extreme old age Alzheimer's disease is thus apparently differentiated from normal aging.

In experimental animals degenerative changes in intracellular fibrils can be induced by intracranial injection of aluminum ions. Since aluminum is found in greater than normal concentrations in brains of Alzheimer patients, it has been suggested that though this element may play some role in the development of the disease, its presence is likely a result of the disease rather than a cause.

The Cerebellum, Brain Stem, and Spinal Cord   Studies on age changes in the cerebellum in rats and mice indicate that significant decreases in synaptic density in the cerebellum occur with age. Purkinje cells are lost, along with other cerebellar elements (see Atlas section). The decline in synaptic density might be the morphological basis for the decline in integrative functions of the cerebellum that have been noted to occur with age in humans and laboratory mammals. This decline had been presumed due to synaptic delay (neurotransmitter synthesis), but may in fact reflect the loss of cellular elements in the cerebellum.

The spinal cord and brain stem show changes in neurotransmitter synthesis, covered later. Anatomically, in aging mammals the small projections from the neurons of spinal cord and brain stem nuclei seem to be lost. The dendritic surfaces appear featureless save that some dendrites appear shorter and thinner. There is relatively little anatomical information on age changes in these brain areas.

SENSE ORGANS

Normal Taste and Smell

Specific chemicals, when present in or near the appropriate receptors, give rise to the sensations of taste and smell. The two senses are superficially related, but are quite different physiologically.

The mucous membrane of the epiglottis, soft palate, and sides, root, and tip of the tongue contain specific receptor organs called taste buds. All tastes can be divided into four groups: sour, salt, bitter, and sweet. To this list some would add alkaline and metallic. Many substances give rise to mixed taste sensations, but it is possible for the subject to resolve the components, and it is virtually impossible to create an entirely new taste through combination of the basic "pure" tastes. The actual taste of a substance is as much a function of the sense of smell as it is of taste. The four taste sensations are located on different parts of the tongue. Some chemicals give rise to different sensations when applied in different places. Records from single receptor units in experimental animals (cat) indicate that there is not a distinct class of receptor for each of the four main sensations. Some receptors in the cat respond to acids, others to acids and salts, others to acids and bitter substances such as quinine, and still others to sucrose. The receptors vary in their sensitivities to the various substances, or in the amount of substance required to elicit a response (firing the nerve fiber serving the receptor).

The organs for smell are located in the upper parts of the nasal cavity. Odor-causing substances in the air in the nasal cavity dissolve in the moist nasal membrane, diffuse into the hairs of the olfactory buds, and excite the smell receptors. In contrast to taste, it is not possible to resolve each smell into components. Each substance has its own distinctive smell. Again unlike taste, the combination of two smells can produce a completely new odor which cannot be analyzed into components. One smell can normally mask another, and this masking can take place even if the two are applied to separate nostrils.

The sense of smell is characterized by rapid fatigue. A strong smell may become nearly odorless in a few minutes. This fatigue is specific for the odor causing it in the first place. The rate of fatigue is proportional to the intensity of the smell. The fatigue phenomenon is a function of the central nervous system (olfactory bulb); individual receptors are able to respond indefinitely. Some persons are deficient in the sense of smell and are incapable of detecting certain substances (hydrogen cyanide smells of bitter almonds to those who can detect it, but is odorless to others). Different odors seem to affect preferentially different groups of receptors. Discrimination of smells seems to be a function of the spatial distribution of the receptors and their projection onto the central olfactory cortex and on the timing of the response as well as on the fatigue factor.

Changes in Taste and Smell

The number of taste buds decreases as a function of age. The threshold level (the lowest concentration eliciting a taste response) for the four primary taste qualities increases in elderly individuals. The salivary secretions become thicker due to increased concentrations of mucus, contributing to the decline in taste sensitivity. The overall secretion of the salivary glands decreases, leading to dryness of the mouth as well as to a more viscous saliva.

Olfactory sensitivity declines with age. This may be related to loss of brain cells in the olfactory bulb of the brain and to long-term inhalation of toxic agents such as tobacco smoke. Sensory cells in the lining of the nasal passages are reduced in number. Most aromatic compounds tested, including camphor, show increased threshold concentrations with age. It is of some interest that elderly women may be more sensitive to the odor of domestic gas than elderly men.

Normal Vision

The eye is an optical system that focuses light from the external environment on a large number of photoreceptors in the retina. The responses of these light-sensitive cells are in turn projected via their axons in maplike manner onto the visual cortex of the cerebrum.

Acuteness of vision depends on the optical accuracy of the curved eye covering, the cornea, and the lens (Figure 7.9). The lens has high refraction in air, but it resides within the eye in fluids with refractive index close to that of the lens, so most of the resolving power of the lens is lost. The lens is concerned with the fine focus of the image on the light-sensitive cells of the retina. Before reaching the receptors in the retina, the light

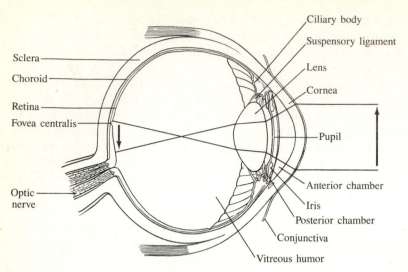

Figure 7.9 Sagittal section of human eye.

must pass through the outer (anterior) chamber behind the cornea, the inner (posterior) chamber behind the lens, and the blood vessels and nerves of the retina. The receptors are of two types, rods for night vision and cones for daylight or bright illumination. Cones are concentrated in a central depression, the fovea centralis, which is the area of the retina with greatest visual acuity (smallest distance between receptors).

Changes in Vision

In the external eye apparatus, the drooping eyelid that occurs with age (senile ptosis) is due to loss of tone in the muscle that elevates the eyelid. Tearing of the eyes appears to increase, even though tear secretions diminish with age, since the reabsorption of tears is insufficient.

Astigmatism that occurs with age is due to changes in the curvature of the cornea, which also becomes more opaque. There is a decrease in the aperture of the iris (senile miosis), which is correlated with changes in the muscles controlling pupillary dilation. Increased intraocular pressure (glaucoma) results from blockage of aqueous flow in the anterior eye chamber and is not intrinsic to aging. There is a progressive liquefaction of the vitreous body behind the lens which coincides in time with the appearance of age-related changes in the lens.

A refractive loss due to a flattening of the lens (presbyopia) moves the point of clearest vision further from the eye. Presbyopia occurs initially between the ages of 40 and 50. The lens also becomes increasingly opaque and yellowed due to increased scatter and absorption of shorter wavelengths of light (in the blue region). The increased scatter is caused by accumulation of insoluble proteins in the lens proper, perhaps related to posttranslational modifications of lens protein.

The anatomical organization of elements in the retina is disrupted with age. This is sometimes accompanied by localized retinal detachments that separate the sensory cells from the nerve cells leading to the brain. A decrease in visual acuity in bright light (glare sensitivity) increases rapidly after 40 years of age, reaching a maximum at about 65. This glare sensitivity is thought to be due to the increase in light scattering by the lens and cornea. The fidelity of color vision is diminished by 25 percent in the 50s and by 50 percent in the 70s. The loss with age may differ for each eye. These effects of age on color vision are attributed to the impaired transmission of light through the eye to the retina. As a consequence, the elderly tend to prefer bright colors. In the early 60s a decrease in visual field diameter is noted. The changes appear to be limited to the retina and may be affected by the oxygen supply to the retina. There are decreases in the number of fibers in the optic nerve and also decreases in cell number in the central visual cortex of the brain.

Changes in perception accompany the changes in the visual apparatus. There is an increase in the time required for extraction of information from visual sources. The increase in response time for form identification by older subjects could be the result of a slower central scanning process rather than changes in the visual system.

Normal Hearing and Vestibular Functions

The auditory system is concerned with detection of sound and the vestibular system with balance and orientation of the head in space.

The mechanical operation of the ear (Figure 7.10) depends on the movements of the eardrum (tympanic membrane) in response to sound vibrations. The movements of the eardrum are magnified by the ear ossicles (malleus, incus, stapes) and transmitted by the stapes to the cochlea, where movements in fluid stimulate receptor hairs throughout its coiled length. Exceedingly small vibrations can be detected by people with normal hearing. The frequency range is limited on both the high and low side, and the threshold changes with frequency. Sound localization is poorly developed in humans and is limited to within 10 degrees in the horizontal plane and slightly wider in the vertical.

Auditory fatigue occurs with prolonged stimulation at one frequency, and the fatigue is noted in both ears even when only one is being stimulated.

Deafness can reside at any point along the auditory chain. The external auditory canal (meatus) may be plugged with wax or occluded by inflammations. The eardrum may be punctured or scarred by infection, leading to loss of motion. The ear ossicles may fuse, or the stapes may be frozen into the window that connects it with the cochlea. The cochlea may show degeneration with age or in response to continued noise pollution

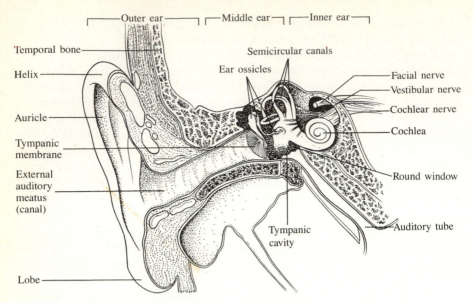

Figure 7.10 Human ear, showing auditory and vestibular apparatus.

at high amplitude (volume) at low or high registers. In addition, deafness may result from damage to the auditory nerve.

The inner ear is also the organ of balance. The portions of the inner ear involved in the vestibular system are the saccule, utricle, and semicircular canals (see Figure 7.10). The utricle and saccule contain calcareous bodies lying against receptor hair cells. They furnish information about the orientation of the head with respect to gravity. The semicircular canals are oriented in the horizontal and vertical planes and contain hair cells that are stimulated by movements of the fluid within the canals. Reflexes associated with these organs are mediated by the vestibular nerve. These reflexes control posture and the position of the eyes. Other information about the position of the body and muscle tone is derived from proprioceptors located in the muscles. These act with the vestibular system to control posture and movements and to relay information regarding muscle tension, flexion of joints, and movements of the head in space, all of which are integrated in the brain.

Changes in Hearing

In the United States hearing loss is considered to be a major medical problem. Physiological degeneration of the auditory system (presbycusis) results in bilateral loss of hearing. The threshold intensity for pure tones is elevated, with greatest sensitivity loss in the high frequency range. Impairment of discrimination between various speech sounds increases with age and may be due in part to slowing of information processing in the brain or to impaired memory.

The lesions may be located anywhere along the auditory pathway, including the eardrum, ossicles, fibers in the auditory nerve, and central brain cells. Presbycusis must be distinguished from deafness caused by noise (for example, boilermaker's disease, characterized by loss of hearing in lower frequencies), but the two sources of deafness may be additive.

Changes in Vestibular Functions

The degeneration of the vestibular system with age is considered moderate compared to hearing loss. There is cell loss both in the organs detecting position of the head and in the organs detecting motion change. There is little or no change in the number of neurons in the vestibular nerve. The elderly frequently complain of vertigo (motion sickness), which could be related to brain processing defects or to impaired detection of motion changes. Vestibular functions are also closely correlated with visual functions, and defects in balance and dizziness can also involve failure of coordination with the eyes.

Normal Perception of Pain and Touch

Pain receptors in the skin are sensitive to chemicals released by damaged tissue cells and are thus a kind of chemoreceptor. The receptors are in the form of naked (unenclosed) nerve endings (dendrites) located at discrete points throughout the integument. Touch and pressure receptors are similarly located in the skin and are found as dendrites encapsulated by layers of connective tissue (pacinian corpuscles or the more elaborate Meissner's corpuscles).

Changes in Pain and Touch Perception

The threshold for cutaneous pain caused by heat increases with age (between age 12 to over 70) by approximately 12 percent. The threshold for women is somewhat lower throughout the age range than for men. The increased threshold is interpreted as due to change in the pain receptors of the skin and to greater heat dispersion in aged skin. The touch threshold varies all over the body. When comparing equivalent skin areas, touch threshold increases with age.

CENTRAL NERVOUS SYSTEM INTEGRATIVE FUNCTIONS

Changes in Memory and Problem Solving

In humans the capacity for short-term memory declines with age. Older subjects require a longer time to recall items from primary memory than younger subjects. Recall from long-term storage is also slower with advancing years (Madden, 1985).

Elderly subjects may experience greater difficulty in solving problems and make more errors than younger subjects. If one takes into account the slower rate of processing by older people and allows extra time for problem solving, some of these differences may disappear.

Changes in Neurotransmitters

All integrative or associative functions of the brain are dependent upon the neurotransmitter substances that carry impulses from one neuron to another. The data on neurotransmitter changes with age in humans are too conflicting to permit generalizations at this time. The trend would seem to favor a decline in neurotransmitter levels in critical areas of the central nervous system with advancing age.

Acetylcholine   Acetylcholine is synthesized from choline by the enzyme choline acetyltransferase (CAT) and is broken down at the synapse by choline esterase. Acetylcholine is synthesized on the presynaptic side by CAT after reuptake of choline from the synaptic junction. Levels of acetylcholine do not appear to decline with age in experimental animals or humans (Rogers and Bloom, 1985). CAT levels and choline levels decline somewhat with age, more severely in cases of senile dementia.

Acetylcholine receptor sites do decline with age. Receptor losses in normal (nondemented) humans occur throughout the brain. The alteration is in the number of binding sites and not the affinity of the site for acteylcholine.

In Alzheimer's disease the CAT level is lower than in normal age-matched controls, but the deficit in acetylcholine receptors does not appear to be greater than in age-matched controls. This would argue that the deficit in Alzheimer's disease is on the presynaptic side of the nerve junction, not across the synapse, where receptors are located.

In experimental animals significant improvement in recall is observed on a choline-rich diet, a finding that is consistent with the central role assigned to acetylcholine in memory functions. Similar therapy has been attempted in humans, with little success. Presumably, one must begin prophylactic treatment before extensive age-related damage occurs.

Dopamine   Synthesis of dopamine requires dietary tyrosine and the enzyme tyrosine hydroxylase, which is rate limiting. The activity of this enzyme decreases with age in some areas of human and rat brains (corpus striatum and substantia nigra), but not in mice. Age-related decline in dopamine seems particularly severe in the hippocampal and hypothalamic regions. Normally, dopamine is inactivated at the synapse by reuptake into presynaptic vesicles or by action of monoamine oxidase. Monoamine oxidase levels increase in senescent humans. Dopamine receptors decline with age, most notably in the striatum. This effect holds over a wide range of mammalian species.

Norepinephrine   In the brain norepinephrine (NE) systems derive mainly from the locus ceruleus of the brain stem, spreading throughout the central nervous system, including the spinal cord. Norepinephrine is also produced by the adrenal medulla from where it is released in response to various stress situations. The release of norepinephrine in response to stress and the resting plasma level both increase with age. The synthetic pathway shares several enzymes with the dopamine system, and the age-related changes observed there carry over to norepinephrine. Norepinephrine is synthesized from dopamine via the enzyme dopamine beta-hydroxylase. Inactivation is primarily by presynaptic reuptake and by monoamine oxidase. Decreases with age in reuptake are noted in the locus ceruleus in humans. Norepinephrine receptors decrease with age in the cerebellum of humans in association with the loss of Purkinje cells. Cerebral loss has also been reported in the rat.

Serotonin   The cell bodies of origin for serotonin (5-hydroxytryptamine) are found in the pons and upper brain stem. Projections are widespread throughout the central nervous system. Synthesis of serotonin is from tryptophan using tryptophan hydroxylase.

Results on senescent alterations are mixed. Whole brain assays show a small decline to no change in mice. In one study hindbrain serotonin remains unchanged with age in humans, but in another it is said to increase. Since monoamine oxidase acts on serotonin, its increase with age may be responsible for the increase with age in catabolites from serotonin degradation, notably 5-hydroxyindoleacetic acid. However, it may be that this compound is poorly cleared in the kidneys of elderly people, which would lead to higher levels of this catabolite.

Neurotransmitters and Disease

Dopaminergic neurons are highly concentrated in the substantia nigra and in the basal ganglia, areas known to be involved in the control of voluntary movements. Degeneration of dopaminergic neurons in the substantia nigra is involved in Parkinson's disease. A deficiency of GABA neurons in the basal caudate nucleus leads to the uncontrolled movements found in Huntington's chorea. The loss of cholinergic neurons in the hippocampus and amygdala characteristic of Alzheimer's disease correlates well with the degree of dementia characteristic of this condition (Price et al., 1982). While cell loss in the amygdala and hippocampus has been well documented, the magnitude of cell loss in the cerebral cortex has been more difficult to measure in Alzheimer's disease.

Synaptic Changes

On the basis of current literature one can support almost any type of age-related change in circuitry in the CNS. In some regions dendritic spines are lost, in others they seem to increase, and in still others there is minimal change. Synaptic growth and remodeling in response to lesions occur well into old age (Schneibel, 1978).

AUTONOMIC SYSTEM

The autonomic system is implicated in many infirmities of old age, including high and low blood pressure, impaired thermoregulation, gastrointestinal dysfunctions, urinary incontinence, and impaired penile erection. Because the central relays for autonomic functions are poorly understood, it is difficult to determine whether altered autonomic responses occur at the level of autonomic ganglia or at more central levels.

The two components of the autonomic system are the sympathetic system and the parasympathetic system (Figure 7.11). The sympathetic trunk runs on either side of the spinal column with segmental connections to the viscera and to the spinal cord. The neurotransmitter produced in the viscera is norepinephrine. The parasympathetic system is represented in the main by the vagus nerve, serving the lungs, heart, and viscera, and the pudendic nerve, serving the bladder and genitalia. The visceral connections produce acetylcholine.

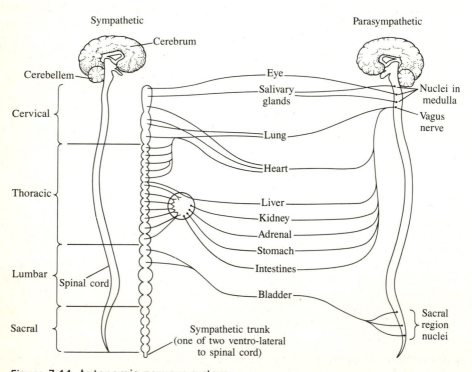

Figure 7.11 Autonomic nervous system.

Sympathetic System

It has been found that plasma norepinephrine levels deriving from the adrenal medulla are increased in aging humans in response to stimuli such as standing up and exercise, and the return to normal levels with recumbent posture is delayed. It is unclear whether the elderly release more norepinephrine or whether elimination of the substance is slowed. Age-associated sleep disturbances seem to correlate in humans with plasma level of norepinephrine. Reports of a correlation between high blood pressure and elevated plasma norepinephrine are conflicting, which is not too surprising in view of the many factors that may contribute to an elevated systolic pressure. The elevated plasma levels of norepinephrine may be associated with an increased activity of sympathetic nerves.

Some sympathetic responses are reduced with age. Cardiovascular responses to various stimuli are reduced, which may reflect diminished tissue responsiveness to norepinephrine, perhaps due in turn to diminished numbers of receptors.

Parasympathetic System

Age-correlated impairments are reported for this system, which normally opposes sympathetic activity. The acetylcholine receptors in the heart appear to decline, such that the activity of the vagus nerve in slowing heart rate declines with age in rats. Older animals may show little or no effect of vagal stimulation on heart rate. Vascular receptors for acetylcholine, on the other hand, seem to be little affected by age.

Both portions of the autonomic system are involved in thermoregulation, which is impaired with age (see Chapter 8).

COGNITIVE PERFORMANCE

Vigilance

This term refers to a central nervous system state reflecting the subject's readiness to respond to infrequent and unpredictable stimuli. In the Baltimore Longitudinal Study of Aging this was measured on 33 men using a clock face divided into 100 intervals and a pointer which moves clockwise in one- or two-interval jumps. The regular movement of one interval is interspersed with infrequent and random two-interval jumps. In a 1-hour test 23 double jumps occur at irregular intervals. Vigilance is measured by the number of double intervals noted and reported by the test subjects. A cross-sectional study showed that fewer signals were detected by an old group than by a younger group. Middle-aged individuals had the fastest reaction time to infrequent signals. The reduced proportion of stimuli detected and the slower reaction time found in the elderly test group suggest an overall reduction in reactivity of the central nervous system with age.

The 33 subjects were retested, using the same procedures, after 18 years. Those who were 70 to 88 years old during the follow-up test detected 58 percent fewer events than they had in the original test. Those aged 51 to 69 during the second test detected 1 percent more events than they had in the earlier test. The reaction time of this middle-aged group was the fastest of all groups tested. The longitudinal studies thus confirm the cross-sectional studies in indicating that vigilance reduction, though not manifest until after 70 years, is a true aging effect and is not due to cohort effects.

Problem Solving

Problem solving is divided into two categories: logical problems and concept problems. A group of 300 men from the BLSA was tested ranging in age from 24 to 87 years. Earlier cross-sectional studies showed declines with age in logical problem solving and smaller declines in concept problem solving. In the longitudinal study a decline after six years was noted only for the group that was over 70 at the first testing. Similar results were obtained for both logical and conceptual problems; declines occur only late in life.

Learning

BLSA longitudinal data on learning is perhaps the most extensive available. The design of the learning tests is complex; full details are available in Shock et al. (1984). The tests were presented to six birth cohorts beginning with the group born in 1885 and ending with those born in 1932 (age 30 years at the start of the study). These groups were measured at intervals of at least six years. The studies indicate that the largest decline occurs in the older age groups (68 to 76 years).

Visual Memory

A test of memory for designs (Benton Visual Retention Test) was administered to a sample of 857 men aged 18 to 102 years from the BLSA. The test consists of a series of geometric figures juxtaposed in various ways. Each design is shown for 10 seconds, and the subject is required to reproduce the design at his own pace. In longitudinal studies the magnitude of the change between successive tests increases. Significant increases in errors were noted only in those initially over 70 years. Vocabulary tests on the same subjects show small differences favoring increased vocabulary in older men. The evidence clearly shows that decrements in visual memory occur relatively late in life.

In all, cognitive functions seem to hold constant until the seventh decade, when decrements appear in vigilance, problem solving, learning, and visual memory.

SLEEP

Elderly individuals awaken from sleep more frequently with advancing years (65 to 95). They exhibit abrupt changes in the EEG (electroencephalogram) from a sleep pattern to wakefulness. This may correlate with nocturnal confusion and wandering seen in the elderly. Aged persons also spend a larger portion of the night with an alert EEG pattern, which may or may not correlate with behavioral arousal. Dream recall following REM (rapid eye movement) sleep is reduced. The restful quality of sleep is thus partially destroyed by advancing years. There are periods of apnea (cessation of breathing) as well as increased periodic movements in some elderly people. Those individuals with periodic movements slept significantly less than other older adults (Ancoli-Israel et al., 1985).

IMMUNITY

Cellular and Humoral Immunity

Senescence of the immune system affects cellular and humoral immunity. (The origin and function of the immune system were presented in Chapter 4.) The immune system is largely a function of the white blood cells. Cellular immunity (imparted by thymus-derived or T cells) is concerned with protection against viral diseases, tissue graft rejection, and immune surveillance against cancerous cells. The thymus gland is present on either side of the throat during the development of the T cell line; it recedes drastically in adulthood.

Humoral immunity (imparted by bone marrow–derived or B cells) is concerned with production of immune globulins (antibodies) in the blood plasma and operates to protect against bacterial toxins and other external antigens. B cells are white cells derived from parent lines found in the bone marrow of the adult. Some T cell immune functions are directed at helping the response of B cells producing immune globulins.

Involution (or regression in size) of the adult thymus and decline in T cell functions may underlie much of the decline in immune function. Observed reduction in both cell division and scavenger activity of T cells, along with the increased susceptibility to cancers found in aged subjects, all reflect T cell deficiency.

Humoral immunity is also impaired during aging, and those functions dependent on T cell help are most severely curtailed. B cell functions that do not depend on T cells are only modestly impaired in older individuals, and thus protection against bacterial infections may remain at a reasonable level, while resistance to viral disease declines.

Autoimmune Disease

During embryonic development (Chapter 4) the cells of the thymus undertake a scan of the characteristics of the body tissues, and those T cells capable of reacting against these tissues are eliminated as stem cells, leading to a condition of tolerance of self among the surviving T cells. This self tolerance becomes eroded in the later decades of life, leading to the possibility of attack on tissues once regarded as self. The loss of tolerance for some body constituents may also reflect changes in cell surface antigens as the cell membrane changes with age (Chapter 5). The phenomenon of autoimmunity, wherein T cells attack as foreign the cells of the body, is increased with age. The immune attack against autologous tissue results in various pathological conditions, including inflammations of the thyroid, joints (arthritis), nerve endings (multiple sclerosis), and testis (sterility). Autoimmunity is generally viewed as a breakdown of recognition of self by the T lymphocytes.

ENDOCRINE SYSTEM

The endocrines are a complex system of ductless glands whose secretions (hormones) are released into the bloodstream to be picked up by receptors on cells of target organs (Figure 7.12). The focal gland is the pituitary, which secretes hormones that govern the activity of other endocrine glands, including the gonads. Hormones called release hormones act to govern the secretions of the pituitary gland. Release hormones are in turn governed by nerve impulses arriving from sensory nerves that ultimately end in the base of the brain (the hypothalamus). Thus, the abnormal function of any particular gland might be related to any of a number of factors. For example, thyroid dysfunction could be due to failure of hormone-secreting cells in the thyroid gland, to loss of receptors for pituitary hormones on thyroid cells, to failure of the pituitary to secrete the thyroid-stimulating hormone, or to failure of release hormones to stimulate the pituitary. It is a most complex system intimately interwoven with the nervous system to control body function and metabolism. We will consider only those cases where some information is at hand with respect to human aging.

Release Hormones

There is little information on changes in any of the release hormones with age in humans. The hormone controlling the release of gonadal-stimulating hormones (gonadotropins) by the pituitary is reportedly elevated in

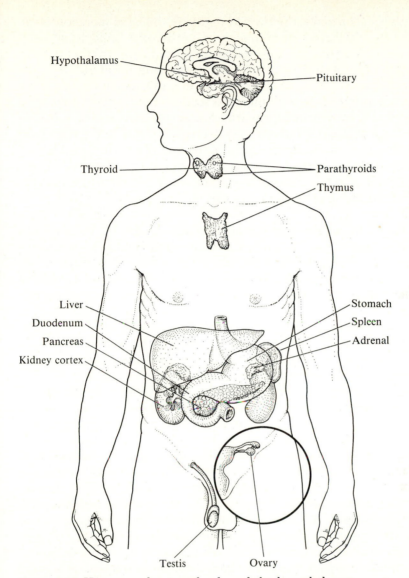

Figure 7.12 Human endocrine glands and the hypothalamus.

postmenopausal women. The effect of increased output of gonadotropins following administration of the release hormone remains unchanged in males and females.

Thyroxin

Changes are observed by some researchers in the level of thyroxin (the thyroid hormone), but other investigators hold that the amount does not change with age. Normally, the thyroid regulates the basal metabolic rate, which declines with age. A drop in activity of thyroxin could result from loss of receptors for the thyroid-stimulating hormone on thyroid cells or from a drop in the blood level of thyroid-stimulating hormone from the pituitary. Alternatively, the decline may be due to a loss of receptors for thyroxin on muscle cells or to diminished secretion of thyroxin. Since the metabolic effect of thyroxin is primarily one involving muscles, some investigators hold that, since muscle mass decreases with age, the decreases in metabolic rate with age simply parallel the loss of muscle tissue. There does not appear to be a simple answer to the question of thyroid activity with aging. Studies in rats indicate that the amount of thyroid-stimulating hormone in the pituitary is diminished in older animals.

Diabetes, Insulin Dependent and Non–Insulin Dependent   Diabetes represents a disease state and as such should really not be included in a roster of normally occuring age-dependent changes. However, it is a fairly common disease with important health implications and therefore is included in this chapter. Insulin-dependent diabetes (IDD) is associated with younger people and accounts for from 10 to 20 percent of all cases of diabetes. Non–insulin-dependent diabetes (NIDD) is associated with onset at maturity and accounts for the remainder of cases. *In vitro* studies of the growth of fibroblasts from IDD and NIDD patients show diminished life span and growth potential associated with both forms of the disease. The cells of patients recently diagnosed as diabetic performed markedly better than cells derived from patients with diabetes of greater than 10 years duration. The poorer *in vitro* performance of cells from long-term diabetics is thought to reflect less favorable *in vivo* conditions in these patients compared to normal individuals or to individuals with only recent diagnosis of diabetes (Archer and Kaye, 1989). Both IDD and NIDD are characterized by a decreased ability to tolerate (metabolize) the sugar glucose, an ability that declines gradually with age in non-diabetic individuals.

There are about 20 autosomal recessive diseases that have in common a reduced life expectancy along with an increased prevalence of diabetes. These genetic diseases include Friedreich's ataxia, Down's syndrome, progeria, and Werner's syndrome. Cells from individuals suffering from any of these diseases show diminished *in vitro* doublings along with larger fractions of senescent cells at intermediate stages of the replicative life span. Such is the case with cells of individuals suffering from diabetes of either type. The diabetic cells are less responsive to insulin in culture than are normal cells. In turn this diminished responsiveness is found to relate to an increase in the number of insulin receptors with age. These receptors may be faulty and bind insulin without effecting the cellular changes usually associated with this hormone (increased oxidation of glucose). Thus, more insulin is required to offset that which is bound to the ineffective receptors (Rosenbloom et al., 1978).

Endocrines and Immunity

The all-important immune system has endocrine connections. The data are derived from studies on inbred mice, but may have important inferences for human aging. The thymus gland is crucial for the development of the immune system as the source of T cells, cells that are active in immune surveillance and combating viral infections. The increased incidence of autoimmune disease and cancers with old age has been held to be due to thymus failure. The immune system responds to a number of hormones, including thyroxin, with increased efficiency of T cell activity. The thymus of young animals implanted in older animals increases the life span of the recipients through release of a hormone (thymosin) from the young thymus.

Though largely based on experiments with laboratory animals, research on the thymus-endocrine connection may hold considerable promise for understanding human senescence. The endocrine system is all pervasive, as is the nervous system, in addition to having effects on immune reactions. It would be well to recall the examples of autoimmune disease involving several body organs mentioned above. This information, coupled with the possible autoimmune nature of the amyloid plaque found in aging cardiac muscle, should build a strong case for the importance of an understanding of immunity and endocrines in aging. The identity of "amyloid" as found in the heart (familial amyloidosis) and brain (Alzheimer's disease) remains an open question, especially for the heart.

Sex Hormones

The gonads, both ovary and testis, are ruled by the gonadotropic hormones. The testis responds by producing testosterone in special nonreproductive cells (cells of Leydig). The ovary responds by producing either estrogen, in the cells surrounding the egg cells (follicle cells), or progesterone, in cells derived from the follicle cells after the rupture of the follicle at ovulation (luteal cells). A decline in function may be due to loss of responsive tissue in the ovaries or testes and not to loss of pituitary hormones

In the female reproductive life is rather suddenly limited at menopause. The number of egg follicles, and therefore follicle cells, then diminishes greatly, even though the amount of gonadotropin may increase. As a consequence, estrogen levels decline. This is independent of the sexual libido, which is a function of testosterone level in the female. Since the testosterone is unopposed by estrogen after menopause, the libido should theoretically increase (Eskin, 1984).

In the male testosterone production decreases gradually over the years, paralleling the loss of the Leydig cells which produce it or possibly the loss of receptors for pituitary hormone on the Leydig cells. The Leydig cells atrophy, according to some reports, and become infiltrated with age pigments. On the other hand, catabolism of testosterone also diminishes to about the same extent, leading to little if any change over the years in testosterone level in healthy men (Harman and Tsitouras, 1980). Consistent with this constant level of testosterone, males may remain relatively fertile and sexually active until well past age 70. The number of testis tubules engaged in sperm production declines with age, hence the sperm count gradually declines and may reach infertile levels.

Another effect of aging seen in male rats is the loss of testosterone receptors in the prostate gland, leading to involution of the prostate. In humans a similar involution is recorded in some men; it may be due either to testosterone deprivation or to diminished protein synthesis. This is manifest in later years by a decrease in the amount of prostatic secretions and a diminished volume of seminal fluid on ejaculation. Enlargement of the prostate is also common among older men (see also the section on kidney function in Chapter 8).

CONCLUSIONS

The brain and spinal cord show degenerative changes including cell loss and accumulation of age pigments. Formation of plaque in discrete locations in the brain may correlate with loss of memory function and dementia. Sleep functions are disturbed such that the hours spent in deep sleep are reduced in later years.

Immune functions, especially those associated with cell-based immunity (surveillance for cancer cells, protection against viral infections) diminish. Autoimmunity increases.

Endocrine function declines due to loss of hormone receptors on target organs, as well as to decreases in hormone production. Changing endocrine activity may also modify the function of the immune system.

REFERENCES

Ancoli-Israel, S., C. Crespi, M. Fusconi, L. Bonazzi, F. B. Bianchi, and E. Pisi. Sleep apnea and periodic movements in an aging sample. *Journal of Gerontology* 40:419–425, 1985.

Archer, F. J., and R. Kaye. Aging of diabetic and nondiabetic skin fibroblasts *in vitro:* Life span and sequential growth curves. *Journal of Gerontology* 44:M93, 1989.

Behnke, J. A., C. E. Finch, and G. B. Moment. *The Biology of Aging.* Plenum, New York, 1978.

Eskin, B. A. Current approaches in endocrinology. In Ficher, Fishkin, and Jacobs, eds., *Sexual Arousal: New Concepts in Basic Science, Diagnosis and Treatment.* C. C. Thomas, Springfield, Illinois, 1984.

C. E. Finch and E. L. Schneider, eds. *Handbook of the Biological Theories of Aging.* Van Nostrand Reinhold, New York, 1985.

Harman, S. M., and P. D. Tsitouras. Reproductive hormones in aging men: Measurement of sex steroids, basal leutinizing hormone and Leydig cell response to human chorionic gonadotropin. *Journal of Clinical Endocrinology and Metabolism* 51:35, 1980.

Madden, D. J. Age-related slowing in the retrieval of information from long-term memory. *Journal of Gerontology* 40:208, 1985.

Ogomori, K., T. Kitamoto, J. Tateishi, Y. Sato, and T. Tashimi. Aging and cerebral amyloid: Early detection of amyloid in the human brain using biochemical extraction and immunostain. *Journal of Gerontology* 43:B157, 1988.

Price, D. L., P. J. Whitehouse, R. G. Struble, J. T. Coyle, A. W. Clark, M. R. DeLong, L. C. Cork, and J. C. Hedreen. Alzheimer's disease and Down's syndrome. In F. M. Sinex and C. R. Merril, eds., Alzheimer's disease, Down's syndrome, and aging. *Annals of the New York Academy of Science* 396:145, 1982.

Rogers, J., and F. E. Bloom. Neurotransmitter metabolism and function in the aging central nervous system. In C. E. Finch and E. L. Schneider, eds., *Handbook of the Biology of Aging.* Van Nostrand Reinhold, New York, 1985.

Rosenbloom, A. L., S. Goldstein, and C. C. Yip. Insulin binding by cultured fibroblasts from normal and insulin-resistant subjects. *Advances in Experimental Medical Biology* 96:205, 1978.

Schneibel, A. B. Structural aspects of the aging brain: Spine systems and the dendritic arbor. In R. Katzman et al., eds., *Aging.* Vol. 1, *Alzheimer's Disease, Senile Dementia, and Related Disorders.* Raven Press, New York, 1978.

Shock, N. W. Biological theories of aging. In J. Birren and W. Schaie, eds., *Handbook of the Psychology of Aging.* Van Nostrand Reinhold, New York, 1977.

Shock, N. W., R. C. Greulich, R. Andres, D. Arenberg, P. T. Costa, Jr., E. G. Lakatta, and J. D. Tobin. *Normal Human Aging, the Baltimore Longitudinal Study.* NIH Publication No. 84–2450, U.S. Government Printing Office, Washington, D.C., 1984.

Strehler, B., D. D. Mark, A. L. Mildvan, and M. V. Gee. Rate and magnitude of age pigment accumulation in human myocardium. *Journal of Gerontology* 14:430, 1959.

Chapter
8

Changes in Organ Systems II

NUTRITIONAL INTAKE

It is clear that after the third decade all body systems begin to show the effects of senescence. Defects at the cellular level are apparently accumulating and lead eventually to diminished viability and death. Some advances in medical technology allow for correction of diminished functions, such as pacemakers for failing hearts and even organ transplants. These are stop-gap measures and of course do not alter the genetics of the biological limit imposed by the maximal life span. Chapter 9 explores the means by which the elderly can maximize the vitality of later years.

The Baltimore Study (BLSA)

This investigation of nutrition involved 180 males during three time periods: 1961–1965, 1966–1970, and 1971–1975. Seven-day dietary diaries were kept. At the time of the first diary, the age range was 35 to 74 years. The absolute nutrient intake tends to decline with age, with the exception of carbohydrate. Aging effects in the form of a significant decline were noted for four categories, namely, calories, saturated fatty acids, fat, and cholesterol. The percentage of calories derived from fat also declined with age. Over the 15-year time period there was also a slight decline in the absolute intake of protein. The intake of polyunsaturated fatty acids increased significantly over the time period.

Longitudinal changes in serum cholesterol are correlated with changes in weight over a test period of 1963–1977 on 1,011 male subjects of the BLSA aged 17 to 102 years. During the study period 1970–1972 serum cholesterol dropped by 6 percent. In an effort to explain this drop, changes in obesity, diet, and physical activity were also measured. Serum cholesterol levels were not significantly associated with body weight at the start of the study, but changes in body weight were directly correlated with changes in serum cholesterol. Still, overall the subject population did not lose weight, which means that weight alone cannot account for diminished serum cholesterol. Changes in diet were significant and were in a direction which would be expected to result in lowering of serum cholesterol, but the diet changes alone are insufficient to account for the drop. The subjects' physical activity, as measured by energy expenditure computed as calories per day, was not consistently correlated with serum cholesterol values except in the oldest group (80 to 102 years). Cross-sectional and longitudinal analysis gave essentially parallel results. The cause of the drop in serum cholesterol remains unknown and is presumed to relate to variables not measured in the study.

The Ten State Survey

The Center for Disease Control in Atlanta conducted a survey on the nutrition of low-income people in 1968–1970. The standards for adequacy of intake were developed by the World Health Organization. The recommended dietary allowances (RDA) for protein and iron were similar to the RDA recommended by the National Research Council of the National Academy of Sciences; standards for other nutrients were about 50 percent of the NRC's RDA. In all, 2,000 people were surveyed; unfortunately, all persons over 60 were studied as one group. These 2,000 subjects reported food intake over a 24-hour period, which was taken as representative of their daily diet. The most prevalent deficiences among the older subjects were iron in all men and women, vitamin A among Spanish-Americans of both sexes, riboflavin among all blacks and Spanish-Americans, and vitamin C in males of all ethnic backgrounds.

Clinical assessments performed during these studies included dental evaluations. The incidence of periodontal disease increased with age such that by age 65 to 75 over 90 percent surveyed showed evidence of this disease. No correlation between periodontal disease and serum levels of vitamins A and C was found. Neither clinical nor biochemical evaluations gave evidence of age-related nutritional deficiencies. Since the group as a whole was consuming food at 50 percent of the RDA, it may well be that the RDA is too high for this age group. The RDA was developed to meet the nutritional needs of all healthy persons and, as such, may not reflect the diminished requirements of the older population (more about this in Chapter 10).

The Health and Nutrition Examination Survey (HANES)

This survey was performed by the Department of Health, Education and Welfare in 1971–1972. The test population was a random sampling of the

U.S. population aged 1 to 74. For those over 60, the most frequent deficiencies were in dietary iron, vitamins A and C, and calcium. Clinical signs of deficiencies other than iron were found only infrequently. Many of the elderly poor (21 percent of whites and 36 percent of blacks) had caloric intakes of less than 1,000 calories. In spite of this, obesity was associated with many low-income females, specifically with 25 percent of low-income black and white women aged 45 to 74. A high percentage of elderly blacks evidenced low values for hematocrit (total red cell volume) and hemoglobin which were unrelated to dietary iron since the serum iron levels in these individuals were within normal limits.

We can define adequate nutrition as a state of physical and mental well-being that cannot be improved by adding or withholding food. Some conclusions as to an individual's state of nutrition can be drawn from mere observation, but an accurate assessment depends on collection and correlation of medical and dietary history, a physical examination, and blood chemistry. The RDAs currently in use may not be an accurate standard for good nutrition in older people.

Drug Intake and the Diet

We will deal with drug intake by elderly Americans in Chapter 9. Here, we will deal only with the effects of drugs on nutrition. Some drugs are known to alter taste perceptions. Amphetamines accent bitter taste, benzocaine intensifies sour sensitivity, and the antimetabolite-anticancer drug 5-fluorouracil alters both sour and bitter sensations. Obviously, changes in taste can alter food intake.

Amphetamines depress appetite directly, as can ingestion of bulking agents such as methyl cellulose. Bulking agents swell with imbibition of water in the stomach, giving a sensation of being full.

Any drug causing inflammation of the upper gastrointestinal tract may cause vomiting, reducing intake. Digitalis taken at high doses over long periods of time may cause severe wasting and diminished food intake reduction due to nausea. Cancer chemotherapy agents act in much this way as well.

Tranquilizers in small to moderate doses may stimulate the appetite, while large doses tend to suppress the intake of food. Appetite may be increased by insulin, some steroids, and an antihistamine (Cyproheptadine) that is used to stimulate the appetite of persons debilitated by low intake of food.

Caffeine in moderate doses is a useful drug for the elderly (especially to get going in the morning) provided there are no cardiovascular contraindications. Doses as low as 150 mg before retiring may induce altered sleep patterns. Caffeine stimulates gastric secretions in humans and thus may contribute to ulcers of the stomach. Interestingly, both decaffeinated and instant coffee are more potent stimulants of gastric secretions (including hydrochloric acid) than is caffeine alone. A patient with peptic ulcer should avoid all coffee, including decaffeinated.

Alcohol Consumption and the Diet

There is significant alcohol consumption by older Americans, and abuse of alcohol poses a threat to health at all ages. We will deal with alcohol as a drug in Chapter 9 and consider here only its effect on nutritional intake.

Alcohol provides essentially empty calories and its consumption can and frequently does lead to weight loss and malnutrition. Alcohol impairs liver and pancreas function (both important for maintenance of normal blood levels of sugar) and interferes with the absorption of amino acids and fat from the intestinal tract.

Small amounts of alcohol before meals act to stimulate gastric secretions and thereby to improve appetite and digestion.

GASTROINTESTINAL SYSTEM

Mouth and Teeth

The surface epithelium of the mouth (oral mucosa) atrophies, and the underlying connective tissue degenerates with age.

The tooth enamel becomes harder, and the formation of reparative dentin increases with age. The teeth increase in translucency. In old humans approximately 90 percent of tooth pulp is calcified. Resorption of bone in the jaws increases in some individuals after age 30, leading to loosening of the teeth and pockets between gum and teeth. Secondary infections and irritation from dental plaque cause severe gum inflammation (periodontitis) and degeneration in some individuals before 50 years. All these changes may lead to loss of teeth. In primitive humans this loss shortened lives.

After age 50 there is a reduction in the amount of salivary secretion and a reduction in the amount of ptyalin, the enzyme that breaks down starch. This slows the initial digestion of complex carbohydrates.

Esophagus

Swallowing begins with the relaxation of the upper esophageal sphincter. A traveling peristaltic wave down the esophagus moves the food being swallowed to the lower sphincter, which relaxes to allow passage to the stomach. In older people the peristaltic wave may not be initiated with every swallow, and the lower sphincter may fail to relax. The result of these changes is the delayed entry of food into the stomach, which is perceived as a fullness beneath the breastbone. For many older people this reduces the pleasure of a meal.

Stomach

In the stomach aging may result in chronic gastritis associated with atrophy of the gastric mucosal lining. This condition results in decreased absorption of vitamin B12 and iron through the stomach. In 16 percent of subjects over 60 years, an autoantibody directed against the factor responsible for B12 transport is found. There is also a decrease in acidity of stomach digestive juices, which causes a diminished rate of digestion by enzymes such as pepsin.

Small Intestine

In individuals without gastrointestinal disorders the small intestine may show age-related impairment of digestive capacity. Between the ages of 34 and 71 years, one study indicates a diminished capacity to digest or absorb large amounts of dietary protein; other studies find no change in young and old individuals in their ability to digest gelatin.

Liver

The liver undergoes a substantial weight loss between the ages of 60 and 90, and liver functions also decline. There is a decline in the number of hepatocytes per unit volume of liver. The result is a diminished capacity for metabolism of drugs and hormones.

This diminished capacity is extremely important clinically, since it means that some medications spend a much longer time in the body in elderly patients as compared to younger patients. The implications of this for prescribed drug doses are obvious. Dosage data based on clinical trials of a drug in young or middle-aged patients may not apply to the elderly population. Tolerance for alcohol, which is metabolized in the liver, decreases markedly with age.

Colon

The large bowel (colon) succumbs to decreased motor function and decreased smooth muscle tone, leading to more frequent constipation in later years. Bulges (diverticula) of the colon increase to 50 percent in subjects over 70 years. The diverticula can become inflamed and may be painful, requiring surgery. There is also an increase in colorectal cancer with age. Recently, colorectal cancer has been associated with elevated serum cholesterol levels in men and women. The association is not inverse, as stated in earlier reports, but a small but significant positive association (Mannes et al., 1986).

SKELETAL MUSCLE

The changes associated with aging in striated muscle are similar to those observed following denervation of the muscle or long-term muscle inactivity. The degree of atrophy is more prominent in the lower half of the body than in the upper half. In some human muscle (particularly the abdominal muscles), there is a decrease in the size and number of muscle fibers with advancing age. The atrophy is in some measure the result of disuse, so called "hypokinetic disease."

The maximal tension developed by a particular muscle declines steadily after 30 years of age with an increased rate of loss after 50. This may also correlate with a significant loss of neurons in both sensory and motor elements of the spinal nerve serving a particular muscle. A loss of cells in the spinal cord is recorded in humans over 80 and may be due to the loss of muscle fiber units served by these nerve cells as much as to the degeneration of motor and sensory cells in the cord. The time between the sensing of a stimulus and the muscle response (reaction time) is increased with age.

BONE

Turnover and Remodeling of Bone Substance

Bone represents the deposition of calcium phosphate and calcium carbonate in extracellular space by cells known as osteoblasts. Bone is continually being deposited by osteoblasts and resorbed by cells known as osteoclasts. Osteoclasts, apart from striated muscle fibers, are the largest cells in the body. They may exceed 100 Mm in diameter and may have as many as 100 nuclei. A state of turnover of bone substance persists throughout life. When a fracture occurs, repair is by means of deposition of new bone by osteoblasts.

From 18 to 20 years of age, when bone density is at a maximum, there is a uniform compact appearance to the shafts of the long bones in x-rays. With aging, porosity increases in the basic elements of bone, the Haversian systems (Figure 8.1). Those bone elements nearest the marrow cavity become converted into spongy, trabecular bone. The loss occurs more rapidly in females than in males.

Bone is continually remodeled by resorption of older or damaged sections and secretion of new bone by osteoblasts. In early adult life about 10 percent of the bone is remodeled annually. With age the activity of osteoclasts increases and that of osteoblasts decreases, leading to an overall increase in resorption of bone. This reduction in bone substance is universal in humans, but, as we might expect, it varies in severity.

Extreme thinning of bone brings about a condition known as osteoporosis, wherein the bones become exceedingly fragile and brittle. This condition is especially prevalent in postmenopausal white women and may be slowed by estrogen and calcium therapy. The substances believed to be involved are parathyroid hormone, estrogen, vitamin D, and calcitonin. Estrogen deficiency may accelerate bone loss in postmenopausal women by increasing the sensitivity of bone to the resorbing action of parathyroid hormone. The cutoff point between normal and pathological

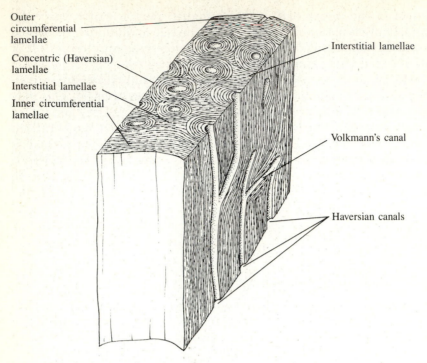

Outer circumferential lamellae

Concentric (Haversian) lamellae

Interstitial lamellae

Inner circumferential lamellae

Interstitial lamellae

Volkmann's canal

Haversian canals

Figure 8.1 Structure of compact bone.

bone loss is arbitrarily taken to be the point at which spontaneous fractures occur. The gradations between normal and osteoporotic individuals are continuous, so one cannot identify separate and distinct populations of each.

Bone loss as a function of age is a universal phenomenon among humans with one notable exception. Men over 80, as opposed to those aged 75, manifest a reversal of bone loss and actually show an increase in bone mass. This has been interpreted as a phenomenon peculiar to a biologically select group. Those males surviving to age 80 also exhibit better health and physical vigor, which have allowed them to outlive their former contemporaries (Exton-Smith, 1977).

The resorption of bone is related to muscle use and bone stress as well as to age. In zero gravity situations, as with prolonged space flight, resorption of bone is accelerated and calcium is lost through the urine.

Ligaments, Tendons, and Joints

Bones are held in position at joints by ligaments. Tendons of muscles insert on bones, and the muscles span the joints. Ligaments and tendons are composed largely of collagen, which becomes increasingly cross-linked and more rigid with age, leading to a loss of joint flexibility. Joint surfaces are also collagenous and are lubricated by enclosure in fluid-filled sacs. Inflammation of the joints (arthritis) may arise if the joint surfaces and the surrounding sac become the targets for an autoimmune reaction. Joint surfaces may be damaged even to the point of fusion of the joint.

The BLSA studied changes in the osteoarthritic grades of the left hands of 478 male subjects between 21 and 97 years of age. The joints were inspected radiographically at intervals of 12 to 16 years. The x-rays were graded 0 to 4 for degree of involvement in osteoarthritis, with 0 signifying none and 4 severe. The maximum rate of degeneration is seen in the distal interphalangeal joints where the increase is about 1 grade per individual in a 12- to 16-year interval. The rate of degeneration of the proximal interphalangeal joints is much lower than that of the distal joints.

The progress of degeneration in the distal interphalangeal joints of an individual, measured longitudinally, follows closely the changes observed in the population viewed cross-sectionally. The youngest age group (less than 40 years) initially showed approximately 5 percent of subjects with some indication of osteoarthritis greater than that observed on the first visit. The results are summarized in Figure 8.2. The rate of change in the osteoarthritic grade of the hand closely agrees with the changes observed in the distal interphalangeal joints. The data support the idea that osteoarthritis of the hand is a slowly progressing disease, with the highest rates of joint degeneration in the group which was 70 years and older at the first visit.

INTEGUMENT

Skin and Sweat Glands

Changes in the skin with age largely involve changes in connective tissue and fat in the tissue just below the epidermis (the dermis). The collagen of connective tissue becomes cross-linked and stiff with age. This reduces the elasticity of the skin. At the same time subcutaneous fat accumulates up to a given age and then decreases. The increased fat is evidenced by the increased thickness of skin folds throughout the body, but especially in the abdomen and chest. The loss of elasticity is often said to lead to permanent furrowing or wrinkling of the skin, but there are few if any histological changes in the areas involved. The areas of epidermis not exposed to sunlight become thinner with age. The layer of cells at the base of the epidermis (the Malpighian layer) are mitotically active in wound healing, but are slower to respond in elderly people leading to longer healing time.

The leathery quality of the skin of older humans may also result from continual exposure to sunlight and a consequent increase in thickness of the outer epidermis in those places exposed to sun (for example, the back of the neck). There is an increase in skin cancers with age.

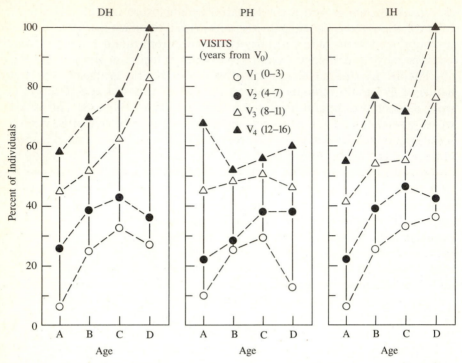

Figure 8.2 Osteoarthritis of the hand. Frequency of patients whose osteoarthritic grade in distal (DH), proximal (PH), and all hand joints (IH) was higher in subsequent visits (V_1–V_4) than it was in the first visit (V_0). The age groups are A, less than 40 years; B, 40 to 54; C, 55 to 69; D, 70 and over. Broken lines show differences between age groups within visits; solid lines show differences between visits within the same age group. From C. C. Plato & A. H. Norns. American Journal of Epidemiology 110:740 1979. CR. Johns Hopkins Univ. School of Hygiene & Public Health. Used with permission.

Sweat glands also show diminished function with age; there are fewer active glands and they produce less secretion.

Hair

Hair is lost, especially in men, from the head and body. The loss of hair is the result of the death of hair-forming cells in the hair follicles. Hair that is not lost tends toward gray due to loss of the pigment-forming cells of the hair follicle. The graying of axillary (armpit) hair is one of the most predictable age changes occuring in the body. Some men past 40 develop hairiness of the ears; women may sprout hairs on the lip or chin. Obvious loss of pubic hair is seen in 20 percent of males and 30 percent of females. Decreased growth of facial hair in elderly males responds to administration of testosterone, indicating continued responsiveness of the follicles.

BLOOD

Red Blood Cells

Changes in number of red cells with age and in amount of hemoglobin per cell may be related to smoking. Some studies indicate a decline in erythrocytes and in hemoglobin levels in smokers over 50 years but not in nonsmokers. Other studies claim that the mean hemoglobin content of red cells does not change with age or increases only slightly. No age-related changes in the volume occupied by red blood cells (hematocrit) have been observed in humans, but the hematocrit is the only parameter of red cells to decline in mice. Old mice and rats respond to bleeding by producing more red cells, but their responses are slower than in young animals. The rate of red cell formation (hematopoesis) seems to be unchanged in elderly humans.

White Cells and Platelets

There is no change in number of white cells per unit of blood with age. Macrophage numbers remain the same with age, as do B lymphocytes. There appears to be no change in the distribution of white cells among the various subclasses. The T lymphocyte population declines somewhat, with changes in the various classes of T cell (Figure 8.3).

No age-related changes are found in the population of the clotting elements of blood, the blood platelets. Clotting time of the blood is little affected by age.

Serum Cholesterol

The elevation of plasma levels of triglycerides (fats) and cholesterol begins at an early age (as early as 20) and continues steadily with advancing age. The causal connection between dietary fats and cholesterol, serum cholesterol concentrations, and diseases of the arteries and heart is complex. Lowered intake of saturated fats is indicated for most people, especially those with a family history of hypertension or heart disease. Diet and heredity are both involved in changes in the heart and blood vessels which occur with age.

Obesity plays a critical role in elevation of triglycerides and cholesterol in plasma. Curves for triglyceride and cholesterol increases with age are superimposible on the obesity curve in populations. Primitive people who remain thin throughout adulthood do not show an increase in plasma lipids with age. Thus, the more overweight a person is, the greater the rate of production of both triglycerides and cholesterol, and the greater the risk of coronary occlusion and generalized atherosclerosis.

The Framingham study has served, among many other things, to focus the attention of the physician on serum cholesterol levels as they correlate

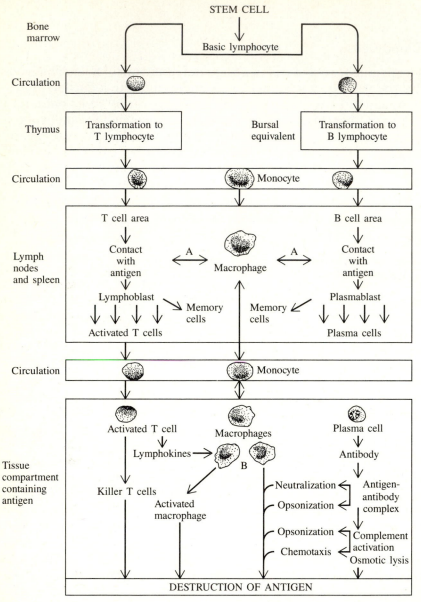

Figure 8.3 Classes of WBC. From M. H. Ross & E. J. Reith. Histology. Copyright 1985 by Harper & Row, Publishers, Inc., New York.

with cardiovascular disease. The Framingham study shows a distinct correlation between elevated cholesterol and risk of cardiac disease and atherosclerosis. Two articles have recently appeared dealing with analyses of data relating cardiovascular disease (CVD), cholesterol, smoking, and blood pressure (Taylor, Pass, Shepard, and Komaroff, 1987; Anderson, Castelli, and Levy, 1987).

Taylor and coworkers pose the question: Should every person undertake and maintain a dietary program to reduce serum cholesterol levels? Up to now a majority of authorities have maintained that such a reduction is recommended and prudent. A minority view holds that most people need not concern themselves with programs for lipid modification. Taylor and associates addressed themselves to the magnitude of the benefits to be expected from reduced serum cholesterol. The benefits were calculated in terms of increased life expectancy for a person overtly free of ischemic (diminished cardiac blood supply) heart disease (IHD) and are expressed as a function of age, sex, and risk factors for IHD. The risk categories include smoking, serum cholesterol level, high density lipoprotein (HDL) level, and blood pressure. Incorporated into the predictive model were two assumptions: (1) Lowering serum cholesterol level has the effect of imparting the lower risk factor associated with the lower cholesterol level. (2) Lowering serum cholesterol level does not increase mortality for conditions other than IHD.

The results of this study are presented for 12 representative groups: women or men, aged 20, 40, or 60 years, at low or high risk for IHD due to risk factors other than cholesterol level. High risk is defined as being in the ninetieth percentile of age and sex stratum for mortality from smoking or high blood pressure and having HDL levels in the tenth percentile (low). HDL is the serum carrier molecule for cholesterol, and higher values imply less tissue deposition of cholesterol as arterial plaque. Low risk is just the converse: tenth percentile for blood pressure (90 percent of the sample is higher) and smoking habit and ninetieth percentile for HDL (90 percent of the sample has lower serum HDL).

The life expectancy gains for people at high risk who control dietary cholesterol range between 18 days and 12 months. For persons at low risk the benefit is correspondingly less, between 3 days and 3 months. Both high- and low-risk ranges are dependent on age, sex, and initial cholesterol level. The benefits of lower cholesterol intake are concentrated in those who begin such a program before age 50; beyond that age there is insufficient time for the benefits of cholesterol reduction to become manifest.

These authors also compare gains from cholesterol reduction with smoking and blood pressure control. Whereas cholesterol control produces gains of weeks or months in life expectancy, cessation of cigarette smoking or control of elevated blood pressure yields increases in life expectancy of months or years for many persons. Thus, cessation of smoking or blood pressure control has a much greater effect on the level of risk for cardiovascular disease than does lowering cholesterol level. It is well to recall that we are dealing with the concept of life expectancy on a population basis and that predictions regarding the mortality of individuals cannot be made. On an individual basis, a person may give up smoking and die a year later of IHD or other cause. To complicate matters, there is some evidence that lowered cholesterol levels may be correlated with mortality from causes other than IHD.

The Anderson, Castelli, and Levy study (1987) summarizes 30 years of follow-up from the Framingham study. From 1951 to 1955 serum cholesterol levels were measured in 1,959 men and 2,415 women between 31 and 65 years of age, all of whom were ostensibly free of cardiovascular disease and cancer. Under 50 years of age overall death and CVD-associated death increase by 5 percent and 9 percent, respectively, for each 10 mg/dL of serum cholesterol. After age 50 there is no increased overall mortality with either high or low serum cholesterol levels. There is a direct association over age 50 between falling cholesterol levels over the first 14 years and mortality over the next 18 years (that is, between ages 50 and 64 and between ages 50 and 68, respectively). An 11 percent increase in overall mortality and 14 percent increase in CVD death per 1 mg/dL drop in serum cholesterol levels is noted in this age bracket. So, under 50 lower cholesterol increases life expectancy. After age 50 the data are confounded by the presence in the sample of people whose cholesterol is falling, perhaps due to the presence of diseases other than CVD that predispose to death.

The lack of association between mortality and serum cholesterol after 50 does not mean that cholesterol levels should be ignored. But, considering these findings in conjunction with the findings of Taylor and associates, physicians might perhaps give patients the options in terms of expected gains in life expectancy. The gains are much greater before 50 than after. Better yet, it would seem that quitting cigarettes and lowering elevated systolic pressure are a more efficient life-saving option. In any event, counseling with a physician is the only reliable way to approach the problem for individuals.

CARDIOVASCULAR SYSTEM

Normal Structure and Function

The heart is divided longitudinally into the right and left heart, each with an atrium and ventricle. The right heart serves the pulmonary circulation, the left the systemic circulation. The capacity of each ventricle when relaxed is about 140 to 200 mL. The wall of the heart is composed of the heart muscle (myocardium), which is lined by the endocardium and covered by the epicardium. The heart muscle layer is relatively thin over the atria compared with the ventricles, which develop greater tension during contraction. Heart muscle is striated, with the mononucleate myocardial cells connected end to end by intercellular junctions called intercalated discs. The myocardial cells also branch laterally and anastomose with neighboring cells. The myocardium of the atrium of each side is continuous with the ventricular muscle on that side. Heart muscle cells of the right atrium near the junction of the superior vena cava are modified to form the sinoatrial (pacemaker) node. Conduction from the atria to the ventricles is via the atrioventricular node of tissue, which in turn connects with the bundle of His, which serves both ventricles.

The cardiac cycle begins with the contraction of both atria, followed by both ventricles. As the ventricles empty, the blood enters the pulmonary arteries from the right heart and the aorta from the left. The heart rate is governed by the autonomic system acting on the pacemaker node, with adrenergic nerve fibers accelerating the beat and cholinergic fibers depressing the rate. The cardiac output can be calculated, using oxygen and carbon dioxide exchange, to be approximately 4.8 L/min at rest in humans. During strenuous exercise the heart output can reach 20 to 30 L/min. The heart rate is sensitive to the carbon dioxide content of the blood which is monitored by receptors at the base of the carotid arteries. Heart rate is also sensitive to venous return rate, monitored by pressure receptors in the inferior vena cava, and to pressures in the aorta, carotid artery, and other arteries, monitored by baroreceptors in the artery walls. These receptors modify the tone or contraction state of the walls of the arterioles and thus influence blood pressure.

The arteries are lined with an endothelium, the tunica intima, continuous with the arterioles and capillaries on the one hand and the endocardium on the other. The walls of arteries have a muscular layer, the tunica media, and an outer layer, the tunica adventitia, containing connective tissues and nerves (Figure 8.4). The muscle layers are smooth muscle and

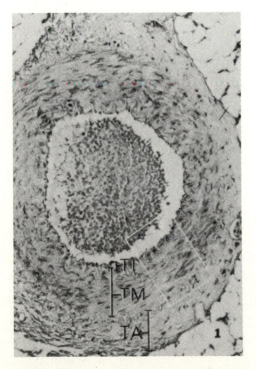

Figure 8.4 Cross-section of artery. TI, tunica intima; TM, tunica media; TA, tunica adventitia. From M. H. Ross and E. J. Reith. *Histology.* Copyright © 1985 by Harper & Row, Publishers, Inc., New York.

can contract or relax on stimulation. The state of constriction or dilation of the small arteries (arterioles) determines the amount of blood flow to any particular organ. The pressure in the arteries varies with each heart beat and has a maximal (systolic) and minimal (diastolic) value. The difference between the systolic and diastolic pressures is known as the pulse pressure. The pulse pressure relates directly to the volume of blood expelled at each systole (stroke volume). Increased cardiac output raises systolic, diastolic, and pulse pressures, while increased peripheral resistance increases the diastolic more than systolic pressure thus decreasing the pulse pressure. Loss of elasticity or decrease in diameter of the aorta and connecting arteries leads to loss of the damping of the thrust of ventricular contractions and to elevated pressure.

The heart itself is supplied with blood through the coronary arteries which leave the aorta just outside the heart; the blood returns to the right heart via a series of veins. The coronary circulation has flow rates of 150 mL/min at rest to 1 L/min during exercise. Coronary occlusion results in starvation of some of the heart muscle for oxygen and, ultimately, the death of that muscle sector.

Changes in Heart and Vessel Structure

The Heart   Longitudinal studies on aged men reveal that heart muscle mass is diminished and fibrous tissue is increased. In hypertensive individuals, there may be left ventricular hypertrophy. The right and left atrial volume increases in older men free of heart disease.

A study of 7000 human hearts at autopsy concluded that, in spite of altered proportions of heart muscle and fibrous tissue mentioned above, there is no evidence that the heart truly atrophies (diminishes in size) with advancing years. A small (1.5%) portion of hearts examined showed deposition of amyloid in the heart muscle. The origin of the amyloid substance is unknown. Lipofuscin pigment in heart muscle cells increases with age. Degenerative calcification of the aortic valve leading from the heart is observed in the absence of additional pathology in later years (age 70–90).

Genetic Factors and Early Coronary Heart Disease   The early appearance of coronary heart disease (in the 40's or 50's) is strongly influenced by genetic factors. These men and women may have normal systolic blood pressure, but are predisposed to what is called "coronary insufficiency", meaning an inadequate blood supply to the heart muscle. As a consequence of inadequate blood supply, sections of myocardium may suddenly be deprived of oxygen, leading to a "heart attack". Exercise (Chapter 9) may be beneficial for those suspecting this condition because of early parental mortality associated with heart disease.

Arteries   The major change that occurs in arteries with age, including the coronary arteries, is a continuous symmetrical increase in the intimal layer, resulting from an accumulation of smooth muscle cells migrating from the intimal layer. The lipid content of the arterial wall may also increase with age, resulting ultimately in patches of arterial plaque and atherosclerosis, or hardening of the arteries. Arteriolosclerosis, a narrowing of the arterioles due to proliferation of the intimal layer and smooth muscle migration from the media to the intima and also to accumulated plaque, must be distinguished from atherosclerosis of the larger arteries (Figure 8.4). Arteriolosclerosis is associated with hypertension and hypertrophy of the left ventricle.

Atherosclerosis, the most prevalent form of arteriosclerosis, occurs so commonly in industrialized populations that the disorder has been mistaken for a natural consequence of aging. Environmental factors (e.g., diet) operate over years in concert with intrinsic factors (genetic) to produce the condition. The condition may be preventable through altered diet and exercise programs if begun early enough in life.

Changes in Cardiac Function

Cardiac Output   In terms of cardiac output, heart function at rest diminishes in normal men in supine position from age 20–90. In the sitting position, no change in resting cardiac output with age is observed. The differences may reflect the functioning of reflexes which increase cardiac output when the heart must pump against gravity, as when the subject is sitting erect. Also evident with aging are decreased maximal heart rate and slower myocardial relaxation.

Heart Work Load in Response to Stress   In response to stress, the work load performed by the heart in standard tests is diminished. Peripheral vascular resistance, both at rest and under work load, increases with age. The maximum heart rate with exercise is diminished with advancing age (30–83 years) in normal men. Maximum consumption of oxygen both at rest and during exercise is diminished in both men and women with advancing years. This difference between younger and older subjects persists even after physical conditioning.

Blood Pressure Changes

Age Related Changes   Arterial blood pressure (Table 8.1) is divided into two components: systolic pressure during the contraction of the heart ventricle and diastolic during the filling of the ventricle, the difference between these two pressure readings is called the pulse pressure, which provides the driving pressure pushing the blood towards the capillaries.

With age, the systolic pressure shows moderate increases while the diastolic pressure remains relatively constant or increases slightly, and pulse pressure increases. The increases in systolic pressure are attributed

Table 8.1 EFFECT OF AGE ON BLOOD
PRESSURE, WHITE MALES
AND FEMALES

Age (yr)	Blood pressure (mm Hg)	
	Systolic	Diastolic
Females		
25–34	117	75
35–44	124	80
45–54	133	84
55–64	144	87
65–74	153	86
Males		
25–34	126	81
35–44	128	85
45–54	135	88
55–64	140	87
65–74	147	85

Source: National Center for Health Statistics, U.S.
Public Health Service, Washington D.C., 1976.

to a progressive loss of elasticity of the large arteries. Peripheral resistance
due to arteriolosclerosis leads to more of an increase in diastolic pressure
than in systolic pressure, and thus also leads to a decrease in the pulse
pressure. In some countries of the world, there is no correlation between
age and increased systolic blood pressure (Ethiopia, Delhi (India), Kenyan
frontier). Perhaps diet and stress levels are different from those of Western
countries. It does not follow that elevated systolic or diastolic pressure is
a *normal* consequence of aging.

Hypertensive Disease Hypertension, or increased blood pressure, is classified in a number of different ways. For our purpose, we will define primary
(essential) hypertension (90% of cases) as that derived from unknown
sources (idiopathic). The remaining 10% of cases are called secondary
hypertension and follow as a result of a known disease state involving the
kidney, adrenal tumors producing nor-epinephrine, or blockage of the
renal artery. Hypertension is frequently encountered among the elderly
population, but as a pathology of later years and not as a natural consequence of aging per se. Some kinds of hypertension are curable surgically,
while others require medications.

The kidney figures prominently in blood pressure changes, as does the
sympathetic nervous system. High salt intake leading to water retention,

stress leading to sympathetic nerve activity (nor-epinephrine) and vaso-constriction (increased peripheral resistance) seem to interact synergistically in the development of hypertension, in that one begets the other in hypertensive people. Hypertrophy of the left ventricle, increased peripheral resistance, increased blood volume (sodium retention), and increased cardiac rate as well as progressive atherosclerosis of the arteries and arterioles all may contribute to both primary and secondary hypertension. Increases in cardiac rate and peripheral resistance affect the diastolic more than the systolic pressure. The increases in stroke volume (hypertrophy of the left ventricle) and blood volume found in some cases have a greater affect on systolic pressure. The interactions between salt intake, sympathetic nerve activity, cardiovascular responses to increases in nor-epinephrine, kidney function (including the renin, aldosterone, angiotensin complex), and genetics make it most difficult to sort out cause and effect in essential hypertension. It has been suggested that there is no single cause and effect, but rather a web of causes and effects.

Some cases of hypertension are the result of a genetic predisposition to the condition, and may manifest as a rapidly developing disease with *diastolic* pressures exceeding 130 mm Hg. This particularly rapid and severe form of hypertensive disease is known as malignant hypertension. If untreated, the malignant form is fatal within 2 years.

URINARY SYSTEM

Normal Structure and Function

A section through a mammalian kidney is shown in Figure 8.5. The functional unit of the kidney is the nephron, which starts at one end with a filtration device, the glomerulus and Bowman's capsule. The glomerular capillary under pressure from the heart squeezes a filtrate of plasma into the capsule. Remaining behind in the capillary are the blood cells and plasma proteins. The proximal tubules connect to the loop of Henle, which extends into the renal medulla and is primarily concerned with water reabsorption. The loop of Henle passes into the distal convoluted tubules, and they in turn empty into collecting ducts that pass down to the renal calyces, the renal pelvis, ureter, and finally into the urinary bladder. Functionally, urine is formed by reabsorption or secretion of sodium, reabsorption of sugars, retention of urea and sulfates.

The function of the kidney is to remove waste and to govern the osmoregulatory functions of the body. The kidney performs these functions using mechanical energy from the heart and chemical energy from cellular metabolism for the performance of osmotic work (secretion against a gradient).

The antidiuretic hormone of the pituitary acts to increase tubular permeability and reabsorption of water. A kidney enzyme, renin, acts on the adrenal cortex, which in turn initiates a cascade of reactions to pro-

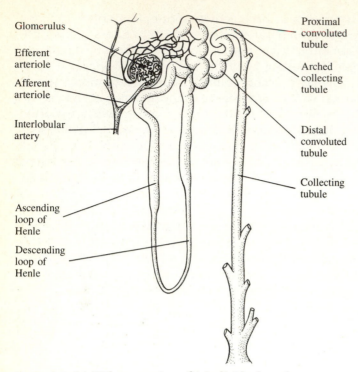

Figure 8.5 *(a)* Kidney section. *(b)* Individual nephron.

duce the protein angiotensin and the steroid hormone aldosterone. Angiotensin causes constriction of the arterioles, leading to elevation of blood pressure, primarily the diastolic pressure. Aldosterone elevates systolic and pulse pressure, since it causes retention of both sodium and water leading to increased blood volume and excretion of potassium.

Changes in Kidney Function

The weight and volume of the kidney decrease by 20 to 30 percent during adult life. The decrease is mainly in the outer portion of the kidney, where entire nephrons disappear and are replaced by scar tissue. The number of scarred glomeruli (which are spherical balls of collagen) increases with age (5 percent at 40 or less; 37 percent at 90). The associated kidney tubules likewise atrophy and are replaced by scar tissue. The filtration rate accordingly declines at an accelerated rate after age 40, amounting to a decrease of about 1 percent per year. The filtration units in the outer cortical area are reduced by constriction of the arterioles (nephrosclerosis) that supply them. This leads to a scarred, granular appearance of the kidney surface. There is also a decrease in the fraction of total cardiac output received by the kidney between 20 and 90 years. Elimination of nitrogenous waste is thus increasingly impaired with age.

Glomerular filtration rate is measured by the appearance in the urine of materials in the plasma that are not reabsorbed by the kidney tubules. The materials usually used for such measurements are inulin, urea, and creatinine. Inulin is a polysaccharide that is injected into the blood and does not occur naturally in the body. The other substances are metabolites present in the glomerular filtrate and secreted into the urine by kidney tubules. These substances are not reabsorbed and are thus said to "clear the kidney." Creatinine is filtered through the glomeruli and is also secreted by the kidney tubules, so its clearance or excretion rate is a combination of filtration and, to a lesser extent, secretion. Creatinine clearance is used as a measure of glomerular filtration rate. The units are standardized as milligrams per minute per square meter of body surface.

Creatinine clearance was studied in 884 BLSA subjects, males aged 17 to 96 years. Studies were both cross-sectional and longitudinal and were carried out over a 10-year period, 1961 to 1971. The men spent two to three days in testing at 12- to 18-month intervals. A highly significant reduction in creatinine clearance with advancing age was found in these normal subjects. The data suggest that clearance remains constant until age 34 and declines thereafter (Figure 8.6). The rate of decline increases

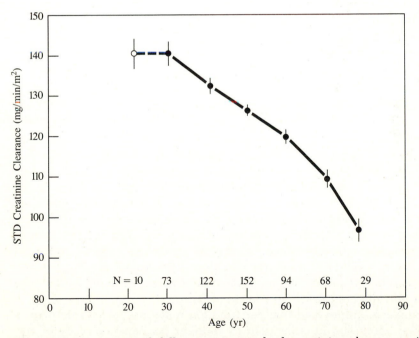

Figure 8.6 Cross-sectional differences in standard creatinine clearance with age. The number of subjects in each age group is listed above the abscissa. Values are plotted $\pm$ standard error of the mean. From J.W. Rowl et al. *Journal of Gerontology* 31:158 1976. CR The Gerontological Society of America. Used with permission.

after age 65. The clearance data are associated with a less striking increase in serum creatinine, which is also age-related.

Changes in creatinine clearance do not represent changes in kidney tubule secretion of creatinine. Inulin, which is not secreted by tubules in the kidney, and creatinine clearances have been measured simultaneously in some of these subjects and it was found that renal handling of creatinine relative to inulin does not change with age. The decline in creatinine clearance is therefore due to a decline in glomerular filtration rate. It is independent of blood pressure, and is not influenced by prostatic enlargement.

Renin and aldosterone levels decline throughout life in inverse relation to blood pressure increases with advancing age. The low renin values of elderly patients can still stimulate the adrenal cortex to produce angiotensin and aldosterone. The contributions of the renin system to elevated blood pressure in elderly individuals are not understood. However, ingestion of large amounts of salt causes elevation of blood pressure by increasing blood volume. An interesting account indicates that both delays and changes in amplitude of observed circadian rhythms in the renin-angiotensin-aldosterone system are observed in essential hypertension among the elderly population (Cugini et al., 1987).

Changes in Bladder Function

Changes in the bladder with age include lower capacity and a higher volume of residual urine after voiding. These changes lead to frequent filling, increased frequency of urination, and sometimes incontinence. Incontinence is also often associated with age-related abnormalities of the central nervous system. However, it is not necessarily a consequence of aging and may occur from one or another cause relatively early in life.

In men voiding is influenced by the prostate gland which surrounds the urethra at the base of the bladder. In most men the glandular tissue of the prostate enlarges as a benign overgrowth called benign nodular hyperplasia (BNP). In extreme cases the urethra is occluded. In most cases the obstruction is partial and leads to retention of urine. The presence of a functioning testis is required for development of glandular hyperplasia, leading to speculation on the role of androgens (testosterone) in this condition. Treatment is effected by removing a section of the prostate from within through the urethra wall (a surgical procedure called a transurethral resection). The effects on the bladder of prolonged blockage of the urethra can be extremely damaging, leading to functional failure to store and periodically void urine and to renal failure.

Changes in kidney and bladder function make nocturnal micturition much more common in older than in younger people. In a study of 140 persons over 65 (Barker and Mitteness, 1988), 72 percent reported the need to get up and urinate at night, sometimes two or three times. A few of the subjects experienced sleep deprivation because of these nocturnal interruptions. In addition to sleep disturbances, feelings of fatigue and falls are linked to this voiding pattern. The phenomenon is frequently dismissed as unimportant, whereas in reality this behavior has consequences that definitely color the quality of life during the daytime. Investigations on means to alter this pattern are clearly needed.

REPRODUCTIVE SYSTEM AND SEXUAL ACTIVITY

Sexual Activity and Menopause

As seen above, there is decline in the anatomy and function of most bodily systems with age, though no system is shut down completely. An exception might seem to be the reproductive system in the human female, which terminates function rather dramatically at menopause. But one must make a distinction between reproductive function and sexual activity. Even though reproductive functions are ended, the postmenopausal female may experience increased sexual arousal and capacity for orgasm. The female libido is dependent on female testosterone, the levels of which are essentially unchanged by the menopause. In short, sexuality and the capacity to experience sexual pleasure are lifetime attributes of many females (Hite, 1981).

Responsiveness of the Male

In males a parallel situation exists as to the capability for sexual activity (Masters and Johnson, 1966). Penile erection may take longer at ages over 50 as compared with the rapid (3 to 5 seconds) erection in younger men. If the erection is lost, the refractory period before erection can be reattained is much longer for older men than for younger men. Periods of impotence (failure of erection) are often experienced without apparent physical cause and may disappear as abruptly as they appeared. Once achieved, erection may be and frequently is maintained for extended periods of time without ejaculation. The increased control over ejaculation in older men seems to be a phenomenon of age and not of technique. It is indeed fortunate that in these respects the sexuality of elderly men seems to be adapted to the increased libido frequently encountered in the female. It is unfortunate that male mortality is higher, leaving fewer men than women alive in later years, especially in view of the social barriers encountered when older women seek sexual outlets with younger males.

RESPIRATORY SYSTEM

Structure and Function

The organs of respiration have the form of an inverted, branched tree (the respiratory tree) with the trachea as its trunk and branching bronchi and bronchioles terminating in tiny air sacs known as alveoli (Figure 8.7).

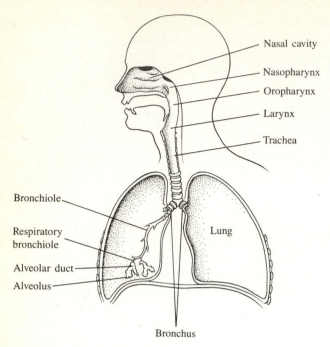

Figure 8.7 Respiratory system.

The number of alveoli in the lung increases from 24 million at birth to about 300 million at 8 years and then remains constant through young adulthood. The maximum number of pulmonary capillary segments is also reached at 8 years. The surface area of the alveoli increases rapidly to 8 years, then more gradually, until the adult value of 70 to 80 m^2 is reached. Increases between age 8 and adult life are due to expansion of existing air sacs.

Respiration is under voluntary and autonomic control. Cholinergic nerves cause constriction of the bronchi, while adrenergic nerves cause dilation. Breathing rate is closely governed by the amount of carbon dioxide in the blood through the carotid reflex mentioned in connection with the circulation. Rapid breathing leads to loss of blood carbon dioxide and slower respiratory rate.

Changes in Respiratory Function

During aging (40 years onward), the ducts leading to the alveoli increase in volume at the expense of alveolar volume, so the surface area for exchange of respiratory gases decreases. The alveoli lose elasticity, beginning at about 50 years. The thickness of the bronchial mucous gland layer increases.

The vital (respiratory) capacity of the lungs reaches a maximum at 20 to 25 years (earlier in females), then decreases throughout life. The reduction in vital capacity is related to loss of chest wall mobility, thus restricting the tidal flow of air. The amount of dead space, or nonrespiratory space, increases with age. The flow rate during forced expiration reaches a peak at the time of highest vital capacity and thereafter declines, more rapidly in males than in females.

In terms of gas exchange, the above alterations in lung function result in diminished diffusion capacity for oxygen (inward) with age, again more rapidly in males than in females. This results in lower amounts of oxygen in the arterial circulation with advancing years and involves both the transfer of oxygen into the blood from the alveoli and the loading of oxygen onto hemoglobin in the red cells. Transfer of carbon dioxide out of the plasma into the alveoli is slowed in older subjects. Respiration simply becomes progressively more difficult from the age of 40 on. At the same time, the consumption of oxygen by body tissues decreases at rest or with exercise.

The BLSA reports a longitudinal study of 408 healthy male subjects ranging in age from 20 to 102 years. In general, in older subjects vital capacity is reduced and there is a complementary increase in residual volume such that maximal breathing capacity decreases. Even in the aged, however, available ventilation of the lungs is adequate for the metabolic demands of almost all ordinary activities. Aging alone may not account for all the observed decline in maximal breathing capacity. Long-time inhalation of noxious agents may also relate to lung impairment.

BODY COMPOSITION AND METABOLISM

Changes in Muscle and Fat

Lean body mass (a measure of muscle mass) falls with age in longitudinal studies of the U.S. population during young adulthood and middle age. Concurrently, the basal (at rest) metabolic rate decreases, possibly the result of loss of muscle tissue. The rate of decline increases in later years and is greater in men than in women. Total body water declines with age as does intracellular water. Cell mass also decreases between 25 and 80 years of age, with the rate of decrease accelerating in the later years.

In a cross-sectional and longitudinal study of the BLSA involving 699 males aged 25 to 84 years, the following information was gathered. The weight of total body fat remains fairly constant in the cross-sectional study, but fat-free weight falls markedly with age. Data from soft-tissue radiographs reveal that in the lower trunk (upper thighs) subcutaneous fat increases through middle age. Abdominal diameter increases during this period, indicating enlargement or sagging of the contents of the abdomen. In the extremities the diameter of the calf and arm decline while fat is relatively stable, indicating loss of lean (muscle) tissue with age.

The longitudinal study is composed of a smaller sample (35). Yearly increments are reported. Longitudinally, weight increases in the first three age groups (30 to 55) and declines between 55 and 74. The oldest individuals show the most marked decrease in weight. Height decreases in each age group to an increasingly greater degree. Fat-free weight declines in all age groups except the 55 to 74 group. Fat in the extremities remains stable in cross-sectional studies, but longitudinally it is seen to decline through adulthood. The middle trunk undergoes a net loss throughout this period, and the lower trunk seems to be a site of gain in fat stored around organs and tissues.

Energy Metabolism and Thermoregulation

Reserve capacity for physical exercise is reduced in elderly subjects. The loss is due in part to the loss of functioning elements in organs and tissues. Energy metabolism is reduced as a consequence of tissue loss and reduced activity.

There is a decline in heat storage between age 15 and 70. During exposure to a cold environment (15°C), the decline in skin temperature is more rapid in older individuals. During exposure to a hot environment (35° to 49°C), the internal body temperature rises significantly with age, while evaporative heat loss is not significantly affected between ages 20 and 67 years. There is a significant increase in the threshold temperature for the start of sweating between 20 and 89 years. The overall result of age is the reduction of adjustment to thermal stress, either heat or cold.

CONCLUSIONS

Intestinal motility and absorption are diminished. The colon may develop diverticula and obstructions. Rectal and colon cancers increase.

Skeletal muscle strength decreases; muscle fiber number may be decreased. Bone resorption increases over bone deposition, especially in postmenopausal women.

Collagen under the skin becomes rigid. Subcutaneous fat increases in some regions. The epidermis in general (sun exposed or not) thins. In sun-exposed areas, focal thickening (senile keratosis) and several kinds of cancers (squamous cell carcinoma, basal cell carcinoma, and malignant melanoma) may form.

Red blood cell formation continues relatively unimpaired in later years, with the exception of smokers. The heart and major blood vessels are altered by changes in the proportions of elastic and fibrous connective tissue. Systolic blood pressure increases with age.

Kidney filtration efficiency is decreased correlated with a loss of functioning nephrons. Bladder functions are altered to favor increased urinary frequency.

Reproductive functions cease in the female at menopause, but continue with reduced fertility in the male until the 70s or 80s. Sex drive and libido may be increased in the postmenopausal female, while persisting in somewhat diminished form in the male. The capacity for sexual pleasure is a lifetime attribute.

Overall, the body loses muscle and gains fat. The metabolic rate declines, as does the ability to regulate body temperature.

The Baltimore study attempted to measure biological age apart from chronological age using 24 physiological tests (Borkan and Norris, 1980). When the results were analyzed, it became evident that within the same individual some tissues are older than others and organs do not age at the same rate. No single aging clock seems to be functioning for all tissues. Chronological age by itself is not a reliable predictor of functional age in individual adults. This same study also attempted to make visual estimates of chronological age. Men judged to look older than their years turned out to be physiologically older in 19 of the 24 tests. Surprisingly, subjective visual assessments seem to be fairly reliable indicators of biological or functional age.

REFERENCES

Anderson, K. M., W. P. Castelli, and D. Levy. Cholesterol and mortality. 30 years of follow-up from the Framingham Study. *JAMA* 257:2176, 1987.

Barker, J. C., and L. S. Mitteness. Nocturia in the elderly. *The Gerontologist* 28:99, 1988.

Borkan, G. A., and A. H. Norris. Assessment of biological age using a profile of physical parameters. *Journal of Gerontology* 35:177, 1980.

Cugini, P., G. Murano, P. Lucia, C. Letizia, D. Scavo, F. Halberg, and H. Schramm. The gerontological decline of the renin-aldosterone system: A chronobiological approach extended to essential hypertension. *Journal of Gerontology* 42:-461, 1987.

Exton-Smith, A. N. Functional consequences of aging: Clinical manifestations. In A. N. Exton-Smith and X. Evans, eds., *Care of the Elderly: Meeting the Challenge of Dependency.* Grune & Stratton, New York, 1977.

Hite, S. *The Hite Report.* Dell, New York, 1981.

Mannes, G. A., A. Maier, C. Thieme, B. Wiebeuke, and G. Paumgartner. Relation between the frequency of colorectal adenoma and the serum cholesterol level. *New England Journal of Medicine* 315:1634, 1986.

Masters, W. H., and V. E. Johnson. *Human Sexual Response.* Little, Brown, New York 1966.

Taylor, W. C., T. M. Pass, D. S. Shepard, and A. L. Komaroff. Cholesterol reduction and life expectancy. *Annals of Internal Medicine* 106:605, 1987.

Chapter
9

Life Style, Health, and Aging

OVERVIEW OF LIFE DURING SENESCENCE

Turning from the generally depressing picture of decline and senescence encountered in Chapters 7 and 8, there are some heartening things to be said about health, life style, and old age in the present chapter. First, many active older people demonstrate physical fitness and aerobic capacities far in excess of their sedentary counterparts and superior to sedentary younger adults as well. Reaction and movement times for active older people are often faster than those exhibited by nonactive young or old individuals.

Second, some physiological processes known to decline with age can be modified by exercise and physical conditioning. A few improvable areas are cardiac efficiency (decreased resting pulse rate), arterial distensibility (lower systolic blood pressure), increased lung function, and decreased loss of bone calcium. The first step is for the individual to know his or her medical condition and limitations and the next is to start on the proper conditioning program as early in life as possible.

INCREASING LIFE EXPECTANCY

Life expectancy has been increasing and is approaching 85 years; 85 has been postulated to be a limit for human life expectancy. It has been argued that as one age-related mortality factor is controlled, another will take its place to negate any increase in survivorship. Actuarial data do not bear out this contention. The most rapidly growing population in the United States is the group aged 85 and above. Cardiovascular mortality has declined 12 percent in individuals over 65 since 1965. In the same period deaths from cancer have shown a modest 1 percent increase. There has not been an increase in other diseases to offset the decrease in cardiovascular disease. The absolute number of deaths after ages 65, 75, and 85 is declining.

The life span still remains constant at about 113-114 years. Transplantation studies (Chapter 5) show that some body tissues can survive *in vivo* beyond the life span of the donor. Cells *in vitro* have a finite life, but the relationship between number of doublings and life span of the organism providing the cultured cells is not at all clear. The life span of the individual may be a limit that cannot be exceeded without genetic change, but there might be ways to extend life expectancy or even to extend life span beyond the present limits. In Chapter 3 we reviewed some claims to longer life spans among more primitive societies. These claims were found wanting, the results of distortions or perhaps just errors in recording true age. Nonetheless, life expectancy appears to be greater in these societies than in the Western democracies.

Advances in medical control of infectious diseases in the form of antibiotics and vaccines have led to optimism for a similar breakthrough in aging—a "magic potion" to extend life. As we have seen, many theories of aging have focused on a single mechanism (for example, the free radical theory) and have seemed to encourage research to find a single remedy for growing old. On the other hand, medical research points to multiple causes for various diseases of old age, necessitating multiple interventions to prevent or cure these maladies. It also seems increasingly probable that we are dealing with multiple mechanisms underlying aging per se and increasingly unlikely that a single "potion" will be found to reverse or delay aging.

The existence of multiple causes and mechanisms of aging and mortality should not deter researchers from using an approach that attacks one cause at a time. For example, if the decline of the immune system with age could be stalled, a reduction in infections and perhaps even malignancies might be attained, with concomitant gains in life expectancy and quality of life. There are, of course, risks in this particular approach or any approach that focuses exclusively on a single problem. Enhancing the function of the immune system might give rise to more autoimmune disease among older people, if indeed autoimmunity derives in some measure from alterations of body constituents with age (see Chapter 5). Conceivably, this sort of consequence is testable in experimental animals. The single-cause approach may raise as many problems as are solved, but is still more likely to improve life expectancy and the quality of later years than is the panacea approach.

A caution: Early in the text we mentioned the consequences of the rectangularization of the human survival curve. Additional years provided by increased life expectancy would have drastic consequences for social relations, economic structure, and political institutions. No facet of society

would be left untouched. Enough preamble. We will now examine some
measures that may make for a longer life—keeping in mind the consequences for society that success would bring along with the benefits of an
increase in life span or life expectancy.

PROGRAMS TO REVERSE OR RETARD AGING EFFECTS

Diet

The nutritional needs of older people and younger people are substantially the same, with the notable exception that elderly people need fewer
calories per day. Recall that body muscle decreases with age, and fat tends
to increase. The activity level also tends to decrease regardless of conditioning programs, as does the rate of body metabolism. Fewer calories are
needed for maintenance of the lean body weight, and as a consequence,
any excess calories go to increase the amount of body fat.

Nutritional balance remains important, especially adequate intake of
essential vitamins and minerals. High protein diets can be particularly
dangerous in that elimination of large amounts of nitrogenous waste can
place a strain on the kidneys (Wurtman, 1979). Saturated fats, as found in
animal products (especially dairy products and red meat) and certain
vegetable oils (such as coconut oil), should be minimized. Recommended
daily dietary allowances for various nutrients and vitamins for people over
50 are given in Table 9.1.

The obesity that often accompanies old age should be avoided. It
increases the difficulty of bending over, getting into and out of chairs,

Table 9.1   RECOMMENDED DAILY DIETARY
ALLOWANCES FOR PERSONS OVER
50 YEARS (NRC-1980)

	Women	Men
Calories (kcal)	1,800	2,400
Protein (gm)	46	56
Vitamin A (IU)	4,000	5,000
Vitamin E (IU)	12	15
Vitamin C (mg)	45	45
Niacin (mg)	12	16
Riboflavin (mg)	1.1	1.5
Thiamin (mg)	1.0	1.2
Calcium (mg)*	800	800
Iron (mg)	10	10

*Intake of over 1,000 mg provides maximum absorption.

Source: Recommended Dietary Allowances, 9th Rev. ed.
National Academy of Sciences, Washington, D.C., 1980.

walking up and down stairs, and engaging in any kind of movement, activity, or exercise program. Health risks are associated with obesity at any age. These include hypertension, heart stress, adult-onset diabetes, increased serum fats, respiratory difficulties, and pain from overstressed joints. Weight gain usually occurs gradually and may not be perceived as a problem. In conjunction with a reasonable diet, exercise is the best way to produce weight loss, but reluctance to try new daily routines and fear of doing themselves physical damage deter many elderly people from beginning an exercise program.

According to the Metropolitan Life Insurance Company, 68 percent of women and 57 percent of men between ages 60 and 69 are between 10 and 20 percent overweight. The solution to the problem of overeating and snacking on high calorie foods depends on changing habits acquired over a lifetime; supportive group discussion sessions along with a system of telephone "buddies" may prove helpful.

Caloric Restriction   The effect on life span of caloric restriction in experimental mammals has been discussed. The life span of rats on a nutritionally adequate diet with severe caloric restrictions was extended. Even the life span of germ-free rats of long-lived strains was increased by caloric restriction, a result which, among other things, bears out the reality of survival of transplanted tissues beyond the life span of the donor.

The effect of a low protein diet tends to parallel the effect of caloric restriction, though some of the protein effect appears to be due at least in part to the caloric restriction of some low protein diets. The protein effect may be due to the amino acid tryptophan. Rats raised on a diet low in this amino acid show effects similar to the effects of caloric restriction conditions. Deficits in thermoregulation that appear in controls are absent from the tryptophan-deficient rats, indicating a possible link with age-related changes in the central nervous system. Tryptophan is the precursor of the neurotransmitter serotonin.

Severe caloric restriction administered immediately after weaning creates developmental abnormalities, mainly retarded growth. However, mild caloric restriction begun in mid-life seems to extend the life span of laboratory animals. In rats fed on a self-serve basis (*ad libitum*), the incidence of tumors parallels the caloric intake. In calorie-restricted mice, there is a diminished frequency of tumors over their life span, though the number of tumors may equal the control group over the latter's shorter life course. A number of chronic diseases of aging (for example, atherosclerosis) are also decreased in incidence in calorie-restricted animals. Calorie-restricted rats do not show the same increase in serum triglyceride levels, serum insulin levels, or abnormalities of the islet of Langerhans cells as do controls.

The tumor effect may be mediated through the immune system, since caloric restriction begun after weaning results in improved B and T cell responses compared to unrestricted, age-matched controls. Caloric restriction in mid-life leads to decreased occurrence of autoantibodies. These effects on the immune response are impressive, even though the mechanisms of the effects on life span are obscure.

The relationship between body weight and survivorship in humans does not follow the calorie-restriction picture. The heaviest and thinnest humans have the shortest survivals, while those slightly over the "ideal body weight" have greatest survival (Andres, 1981). We must be sure of what we mean by "ideal" weight, but it is of interest that insurance companies' ideal body weight figures have been revised upward. Even so, most people are over the ideal limit. Perhaps food restriction has some merit.

Antioxidants   The free radical theory of aging (Chapter 4) states that free radicals produced during normal metabolism may react with critical biological molecules with destructive consequences, and the accumulated damage from such activities would result over time in age-related changes in cell and body function. Some free radicals, such as superoxide (O_2^{-}), are extremely short-lived in the body, whereas others, created by the action of superoxides on cell constituents or by ionizing radiation, may be macromolecular and long-lived. Many of these compounds and their derivatives are potent oxidants.

Among the harmful reactions that occur are those involved in the peroxidation of lipids, which has been proposed as a major avenue of damage to the integrity of the cell membrane. The results include generation of compounds resembling age pigments (from cell lipids and proteins), cross-links in DNA and proteins, and generation of many other intermediate and generally harmful compounds.

There are few convincing demonstrations of the protective value of antioxidants, many depending on decreases in lipofuscin as evidence of a positive effect. For various reasons some vitamins and other compounds have come to be regarded as promoting longevity. Examples are vitamins A, C, and E and ribonucleic acid (RNA). It is generally true that serum levels of vitamins A and E are highest in long-lived species. It is also true that RNA from yeast is degraded in the human body to uric acid (urate), another powerful free radical scavenger. Vitamins A and C are implicated as effective anticancer agents. Both are antioxidants and as such would be effective in removing free radicals. While correlations exist between life spans of various species and levels of these various "geroprotectors," it remains to be seen whether large doses, in excess of the recommended daily allowance, of any of these substances have any effect on the life span of the individual ingesting them. There is also a danger of accumulation in the body of excess fat-soluble vitamins (A and E). Excess vitamin A (in patients receiving more than 100,000 units daily) may cause drying and cracking of the skin, headache, joint pain, and internal bleeding. The effects of excess vitamin E are less well established.

An enzyme, superoxide dismutase (SOD), exists in cells for the sole purpose of destroying free radicals. The enzyme catalyzes the reaction between superoxide and hydrogen ions to produce hydrogen peroxide, which then decomposes into water and oxygen gas, both harmless products, through the activity of another enzyme, catalase. SOD occurs in two forms, one in the liquid phase of the cytoplasm and the other associated with mitochondria. Most studies deal with the soluble cytoplasmic form of the enzyme. SOD is present in large amounts in cells, thus ensuring the rapid removal of superoxide molecules. There are conflicting reports, but most agree that SOD activity remains at a high level in most mammalian tissues when measured as a function of age.

Comparative aging studies show that SOD has higher activities in animals with longer life spans, lower in mutant (vestigial wings) *Drosophila* than in wild type, with highest activities in human tissues. Unfortunately, the amount of mitochondrial SOD was not quantitated in these studies, and the fraction of SOD in mitochondria varies with the species (8 percent in the rat, 50 percent in the human). There also exist other means for maintaining the cells in proper oxidation-reduction balance. Catalase, glutathione, vitamin E, vitamin C all may act in this area. It is tempting, but probably unwarranted at this time to assign a pivotal role in longevity to SOD, though its importance as one efficient antioxidant is unquestioned.

Exercise

In a speech delivered in the year A.D. 44, Cicero, at the age of 61, asserts that "it is possible for a man by exercise and self-control, even in old age, to preserve some of his original vigor." From ancient Roman times exercise and moderation in food and drink have been prescribed as a means of preserving vigor in advancing years. The value of exercise for maintaining health has certainly been accepted in the present century (if only in a limited way for geriatric individuals), so an old idea has been given new life in our time.

In the late nineteenth century the popular belief was that vigorous exercise damaged the body and so decreased life expectancy. In England many studies centered on the crews of Oxford and Cambridge throughout their postgraduate lives. When compared with the mortality of the population as a whole, the oarsmen showed decreased life expectancy. But when compared with their nonrowing classmates, there was no difference in survival. Similar studies of college athletes and their not so vigorous classmates have been performed in the United States, with similar results: no difference between the athletic and nonathletic students. These studies neglect to take into account exercise or lack of exercise among athletes after their college years. Finnish cross-country skiers who remain active into their later years have significantly greater life expectancy than the male population matched for age. This does not measure other aspects in the life styles of the skiers versus the sedentary population; the nonskiers may smoke more, be under more stress, and so forth, so that the difference may not be due to continued exercise but to other life-style factors.

The Framingham study (Chapter 1) reveals that within the generally sedentary group, the level of cardiovascular mortality is inversely correlated with physical activity. It is not the incidence of myocardial infarction that is changed, but the mortality from such an event. Apparently, exercise may not prevent cardiovascular disease, but may increase the ability of heart muscle to withstand the circulatory loss associated with coronary artery occlusion.

Beginning in 1950 cardiologists began to depart from advising complete bed rest for heart patients and began leaning toward greater and earlier activity. Interest in sports medicine began in the United States in the early 1960s with recognition of the fact that persons who are physically active, even in later years, are healthier than sedentary persons. Exercise relaxes some people better than drugs. Optimal relaxation following exercise appears immediately and lasts up to an hour. In one study involving a group of tense, elderly males, a 15-minute walk at a pace brisk enough to raise the pulse rate to about 120 beats per minute produced more muscle relaxation than a single dose of meprobamate (Miltown). (However, even though general muscle relaxation is enhanced, it is ill advised to exercise immediately before retiring for sleep, because the stimulation of exercise activity may prevent drowsiness for some time.) According to cardiologist Paul Dudley White, rapid walking and other forms of exercise, carried to the point of fatigue, are ideal antidotes against emotional stress. The advisability of exercise for people in their 70s and 80s is no longer a serious question, provided proper medical precautions are taken (Harris et al., 1977).

Ideally, physical conditioning should begin in childhood and continue throughout life. This is not usually what happens. Conditioning in the younger years frequently gives way to the inactivity of a sedentary job, followed by retirement, with at best only sporadic attention to the exercise needs of the body. Elderly people express interest in and may engage in some physical activity, but less than 20 percent of those in their 60s exercise with the intensity required to improve cardiovascular function.

It is possible to begin some form of conditioning at any age. Almost any age-related "handicap" can be circumvented for the purposes of conditioning the cardiovascular, pulmonary, and neuromuscular systems; there are exercise regimens for those who cannot walk. After a thorough checkup by a physician, which should include an electrocardiogram, a program of conditioning can be begun. Usually, mild exercise such as walking is followed by short-distance jogging, swimming, aerobic exercises, or other exercise until the desired level of activity is reached. It is best to be noncompetitive and to work well within the heart rate limit specified by the physician. These comments actually hold true for any age.

The benefits from an exercise program are good physical fitness, pleasure and recreation, preservation of vigor, weight control, and an overall feeling of well-being. Elderly individuals who are in good physical condition perform better than inactive people on a number of tests designed to measure the behavioral slowdown that accompanies advancing years.

Aerobic Training   The maximum possible heart rate under stress (MHR) decreases with age (Table 9.2). MHR is a convenient reference for aging, and various formulas for conditioning utilize it. The object of aerobic exercise is to work at a rate at which the heart is able to supply oxygen to the tissues without incurring an oxygen debt (anoxia). As the heart-lung system becomes stronger, the heart rate reached for a given task (say, running 3 miles in 36 minutes) drops. The training effect, or improvement in heart-lung efficiency, is manifest only after a certain level of exertion (measured by a percentage of MHR) has been maintained for a specified time, which varies with each individual's age and physical condition. A percentage of MHR may be used as an indicator of what level of exercise is required to maintain a given level of fitness.

   There is no substitute for starting early, but available data suggest that older people are just as trainable as younger individuals. After the initial training period, the maintenance of an achieved level is dependent on continued, regular exercise. The remarkable results of such aerobic training for individuals suffering from various heart, lung, diabetic, and arthritic conditions are described in Kenneth Cooper's book (1968) on aerobic exercise.

Rhythmic Versus Isometric Activity   Exercise patterns for older people should maximize rhythmic activity of large muscle masses and minimize static (isometric) muscle contractions and should provide the aerobic conditioning mentioned above. This translates to mean that natural activities

Table 9.2   MAXIMAL HEART RATES AND RATES AFTER EXERCISE FOR
UNCONDITIONED AND WELL-CONDITIONED SUBJECTS OF DIFFERENT AGES

	Age						
	25	35	45	55	65	75	85
Maximal rate (untrained)	197	193	189	184	180	176	172
Heart rate of unconditioned subjects following 3 minutes of step test*	180	168	156	150	144		
Heart rate of well-conditioned subjects following 9-minutes of step test	144	138	132	126	120		

*Step test consists of going up and down two standard risers at a pace comparable to a fast walk.

Source: Data adapted from R. J. Shephard. Physical Activity and Aging, Second Edition. Year Book Medical Publications, Chicago, 1987.

such as jogging, swimming, walking, and dancing are recommended; weight-lifting is not.

Rhythmic contraction and relaxation of larger muscles ensures that unresisted blood flow is provided to the muscle during the relaxation phase. This in turn minimizes the increase in blood pressure required to serve the contracting muscle, which resists blood flow by squeezing the capillaries during the tight contractions needed for isometric exercise. Underused muscles often become sore during the initial phases of conditioning because they do not completely relax. The partially contracted state results in poor blood supply, which causes pain. The cycle is most easily broken by doing stretching exercises designed to relax the muscles both before and after the rhythmic and aerobic exercises.

Experimental Intervention

Centrophenoxine   The drug centrophenoxine (dimethylaminoethyl p-chlorophenoxyacetate) has been called an "aging reversal" drug since it purportedly removes lipofuscin deposits from neurons and heart muscle. There is a lack of information regarding the pharmacology of this compound. It is related to dimethylaminoethanol, a precursor of choline. It reportedly reverses the accumulation of water-insoluble proteins in brain and liver tissue of some text animals, a finding that may relate to the helical filaments observed in Alzheimer's disease and some otherwise normal aging brains. It also seems to extend the maximum doublings of cultured human neuroglial cells. In many test mammals and in human patients, centrophenoxine was associated with increased metabolic rate and weight loss. If the weight loss is due to the presence of centrophenoxine, the effects attributed to the action of the drug may in fact instead be the result of caloric restriction.

Centrophenoxine has proved effective in reducing the accumulation of lipofuscin deposits in guinea pig brain, myocardium, and liver and in some tissues of rats and mice, but there is little evidence that the presence of lipofuscin is damaging to the function of cells (Chapter 4). Some human brain nuclei (inferior olivary nucleus of the medulla) accumulate so much lipofuscin that their cell nuclei are displaced, yet no neuronal loss is detected even into the ninth decade. Apart from the lack of evidence for any role of age pigments in the aging process itself, recent studies of the effects of centrophenoxine on lipofuscin content of rat brain and retinal cells have been equivocal at best. These studies failed to show any reversal of pigment accumulation in the presence of the drug (Katz and Robison, 1983).

DHEA   Serum levels of dehydroepiandrosterone (DHEA), a steroid, also correlate well with life span, and serum levels decline with age in humans. The high concentration in the blood of young adults and its subsequent decline have led to speculation that DHEA may play a role in the aging process. In addition, this compound administered orally to mice and rats increases resistance to cancer induction and extends life span (Schneider and Reed, 1985). The onset of autoimmunity in mice prone to this condition is delayed by DHEA.

The biological role of DHEA in normal animal function is unknown at present. The anticancer effect may be due to its antioxidant properties. Some studies report weight loss in experimental animals (mice), leading to speculation that it may act in a manner similar to caloric restriction. Use of DHEA with human subjects is understandably limited until its role and the effects of its administration are better understood.

L-Dopa   Studies of neurotransmitters (Chapter 7) indicate a loss of some of these substances with age, including dopamine. Administered over the life span of male, Swiss, albino mice in near toxic level doses, L-dopa produced increased survivorship. Again, the mice experienced weight loss compared with controls. Parkinson's disease patients receiving L-dopa live longer than untreated patients, but the longevity of the treated Parkinson's patients is less than that of the population at large. Using L-dopa at a lower dosage to prevent side effects, such as undesirable weight loss, removes its life-extending properties. It is difficult to conclude that the substance has any direct effect on life span.

Gerovital-H$_3$ This product has been promoted for the past 30 years for treatment of a variety of age-related disorders and age changes. It is a solution of procaine (an anesthetic), stabilized with benzoic acid and metabisulfite. It has the properties of a mild antidepressant. Studies of its effect on life span are equivocal. Most of its effects, if not all, relate to its antidepressant properties, which induce a feeling of well-being in human subjects.

Immunological Intervention   This approach involves transplants of immune cells or tissue from young donors to older recipients (Chapter 5). Bone marrow, spleen, and thymus transplants have been utilized. Young thymus cells may decrease the appearance of autoantibodies in old mice. Lymph node lymphocytes have been reported to prolong the life of a progeroid strain of mouse. Spleen cells confer immunity to *Salmonella* in old mice if the donor was previously immunized against this bacterium. Converse experiments wherein old spleen cells were placed into young mice resulted in increased autoimmunity in the young recipients. In a strain of mice prone to autoimmune disease, transplants of young thymus glands extended life expectancy. Combined bone marrow and thymus grafts improve the clonal response of the older recipient to stimulants to cell division. Thymus grafts restore T cell activity (allograft rejection) of thymectomized mice. Since T cell activity is the main target of aging in the immune system, thymus implants would seem to be a natural choice for prolonging life expectancy.

An interesting finding involves a factor called coenzyme Q_{10}, a substance involved in electron transport in mitochondria. This factor declines with age in several organs, most notably the thymus. Administration of Q_{10} to old mice restores a deficit in B cell function and enhances immune surveillance against a particular virus-induced leukemia.

These effects are the product of a single laboratory and require confirmation before any conclusions are drawn.

Pituitary Gland   Acting on the supposition that the pituitary gland produces "aging hormones," a number of experiments involving hypophysectomy followed with trophic hormone replacement therapy have been performed. The experimental animals so treated displayed retardation of a number of age-related changes in body structure and function. These changes were accompanied by weight loss. A number of the observed changes in the pattern of aging strongly resemble the effects of calorie restriction, which incidentally leads to pituitary atrophy in intact animals. Experiments exploring the relationship between diet restriction and hypophysectomy may, if nothing else, lead to a better understanding of the mechanism by which reduction of food intake affects aging, along with information on the role of the pituitary gland in aging.

HAZARDOUS HABITS

Tobacco

The long-term effects of tobacco are all bad. These effects are due to nicotine, tars, and the irritating property of any form of smoke to the trachea and lungs. The effects of tobacco are altered somewhat if it is chewed rather than smoked; the irritating effects are localized in the mouth, but the systemic effects remain the same. Use of tobacco has been widespread for centuries; it may be one of the most difficult substance habits to break.

Nicotine is one of a group of plant-derived substances known as alkaloids. In addition to nicotine, the group includes strychnine, caffeine, morphine, quinine, and atropine, all very biologically active compounds. Nicotine can cause tachycardia (racing of the heart) and premature ventricular contractions. It causes constriction of the small arterioles of peripheral circulation and thus may increase blood pressure. Its use is addictive and withdrawal produces a variety of uncomfortable symptoms.

Tobacco tars are a complex mix of molecules that are known to be carcinogenic, producing lung and mouth cancers in tobacco users. Chewing rather than smoking tobacco may reduce the possibility of lung cancers, but it does not rule out the possibility of mouth cancers.

Tars and smoke particulates are also irritants and can cause permanent loss of elasticity in the alveoli of the lungs and inability to expel trapped air. The condition is known as emphysema. The onset of emphysema is slow, especially in sedentary people and may go unnoted until 60 to 70 percent of the tidal capacity of the lung is lost. In extreme cases the lung ruptures, allowing air to escape into the chest cavity (pneumothorax), and collapses. Both lung cancer and emphysema are irreversible and usually fatal.

In addition, combustion of tobacco produces definite amounts of both carbon monoxide and cyanide. These chemicals combine with hemoglobin in the lungs and block the loading of oxygen in red blood cells. The impairment is significant for all aerobic functions, especially for people whose lung capacity is already diminished by age, emphysema, or other lung disease.

In spite of knowledge of these deleterious effects, smokers persist in smoking, possibly because the biological effects do not lead to objectionable behavioral changes such as are encountered with chronic intake of alcohol. The effects of moderate smoking are probably worse for elderly people than the effects of moderate drinking.

Alcohol

We are not discussing here the habit of the occasional cocktail before dinner. Alcohol in moderate amounts has been used for centuries as a social instrument of relaxation and, as such, may promote a longer, happier life than complete abstinence. We are concerned with the effects of the intake of harmful amounts of alcohol (ethanol), realizing that what constitutes a harmful amount varies somewhat from individual to individual. Alcohol abuse is a problem that affects the aged. Until recently, little research or clinical attention has been focused on the area; chronic alcoholism was thought to be primarily a self-limiting disease whose victims by and large failed to reach advanced years.

Alcohol Consumption by the Elderly A number of studies reported from the general population and from clinical settings put the drinking rate (those consuming any amount) at greater than 75 percent for males and 62 percent for females over 60 years, compared with 90 percent and 83 percent respectively for males and females in their 50s. The over-60 group classified as heavier drinkers (more than 1 ounce of absolute, or 200 proof, alcohol per day) includes 14 percent of males and 7 percent of females over 60 (Barnes, 1982). This kind of reporting masks some kinds of drinking behavior, such as periodic binges, and thus the figures probably represent minimum percentages. Also, the biological effects of alcohol, which is metabolized primarily in the liver, are greater for older than for younger individuals. Even the relatively modest amount of 1 ounce of 200 proof alcohol per day may be a hazard for some elderly people. One must also keep in mind that the reporting of amounts of alcohol consumed by alcohol abusers is notoriously unreliable and almost always underestimated. Drinking by elderly persons results in problems in approximately 9 percent of cases. The problems range from simply being intoxicated to criticism by peers and family members to serious accidents and death. Serious accidents and deaths related to drinking often are misreported as being due to other causes or are deliberately covered up to protect the drinker.

Attempts have been made to relate heavier drinking (more than 1 oz. 200 proof daily) among the elderly to various stresses of old age. The following is a list of situations in which no correlation with alcohol use can be detected in men or women: death of a spouse, retirement, degree of satisfaction with life, degree of social activity, and state of health. A recent study of the relationship between alcohol behavior and life events (La Greca, Akers, and Dwyer, 1988) showed, in a large sample (1,410), that significant life events, if anything, tended to decrease alcohol consumption. As will be seen below, some of these life event situations may correlate with alcoholism, if not with the use or nonuse of alcohol. Among the nonalcoholic elderly population, it appears that some people simply find alcohol pleasant while others do not.

Elderly Alcoholics Data on the number of alcoholics (as opposed to heavier drinkers) among the elderly are few and vary according to whether "alcoholic" is defined in terms of amount of liquor consumed or medical damage. Best estimates of the number of elderly in the population as a whole with alcohol problems vary between 2 and 10 percent. It has been estimated that 10 percent of alcoholics in treatment are over age 60. There is a general feeling that elderly alcoholics may not be a homogeneous group. It seems that a large proportion of elderly alcoholics who live to age 65 have given up their drinking pattern of younger years.

The majority of actively drinking elderly alcoholics began having alcohol problems in their 40s and 50s (late-onset alcoholism). This late-onset group differs from the survivors who began alcohol abuse early in life and continued drinking into their later years. The differences include poorer health among the early-onset drinkers and association of late-onset alcoholism with depression, bereavement, retirement, loneliness, marital stress, physical illness, or simply stress of growing old.

Most people undergoing stress do not develop alcohol or drug problems. However, those who do abuse alcohol suffer from intensified depressions, various bodily complaints (from pancreatitis to hangovers), isolation, and loss of status with peers and family. The exact cause of alcoholism is unknown, but there is evidence of a genetic component. Some feel that alcoholism is a symptom of underlying emotional problems. However, the coexistence of emotional problems and alcohol or drug abuse in the same individual is no proof that one caused the other (Schuckit, 1977). Regardless of the cause, it remains that in addition to the primary effects of alcohol, alcoholism masks or mimics a number of physical and emotional disease states and makes medical diagnosis of a patient's true condition difficult.

Males and females do not differ in the effects of excessive alcohol intake. There do seem to be sex differences in age of onset of heavy drinking (later in females) and drinking patterns (females are more apt than males to drink alone, as closet drinkers, or with one or two friends in someone's home).

Though some losses of cognitive functions are reversible, older alcoholics who are not currently drinking perform less well than nonalcoholic age cohorts when compared to a similar test group of "recovered" younger alcoholics and their age cohorts. The tests included verbal ability, visual-spatial ability, and sensory-motor function. Thus, aging has profound effects on the ability of the alcoholic to recover cognitive functions following alcohol damage. From extensive studies on animal models (rats and mice), ethanol is known to have toxic effects on the central nervous system. These effects on animals are noted in humans, in the absence of nutritional deficiency. There may be no intake threshold below which no effect is observed. Cognitive impairment, as assessed by multiple performance tests of different brain pathways, is evident in alcoholic mice and rats. The damage to the cerebral cortex, as revealed at autopsy, can be correlated with cognitive impairment. It would seem from such studies that alcohol is a potent drug at any age and especially potent in large doses for the elderly.

Treatment of alcoholism among the elderly should focus on medical detoxification supervised by a physician. This should be followed by group support such as is offered by Alcoholics Anonymous, where other recovering people, sometimes of the same age, can be found. Alcoholism at any age is a lonely disease until the sufferer realizes that he or she is not the only person around with the problem.

DRUG ABUSE AND POLYPHARMACY

Persons over age 55 are the largest consumers of legal drugs, receiving annually over 225 million prescriptions, which includes over 180 million for mood-altering drugs. Drug abuse in the broad sense may be due to self-administration of a drug or overprescription of a drug by medical personnel. Polypharmacy refers to the simultaneous administration of a number of drugs whose interactions and individual effects may prove harmful to the patient.

Inadvertant abusers are those who are not intentionally seeking drug effects, but who through accident, misinformation, or confusion do not take medications as prescribed (Schuckit, 1977). Also, older individuals sometimes gather together and in close living situations may tend to share drugs with each other. The medications so abused may be inappropriate for some users, out of date, and unsafe. An additional problem comes from the tendency of some elderly individuals to mix over-the-counter drugs with prescribed medications and alcohol, thus increasing the chance of adverse reactions.

Some older individuals are deliberate abusers. They seek out drugs to take, getting them from a variety of medical sources. The most frequently abused drugs are barbiturates, laxatives, codeine preparations (pain killers and cough suppressants), and aspirin compounds.

Adverse Reactions and Polypharmacy

Change with age in ability to handle drugs via the liver was mentioned in Chapter 6. This reduced rate of drug elimination by the liver is coupled with decreased plasma volume and decreased extracellular fluid, both of which act to maintain an elevated level of a given drug in the blood. Some drugs are eliminated in active, unmodified form through the kidney, an avenue that is diminished in elderly people. With drugs remaining in the body longer and at higher concentrations, it is obvious that adjustment in dosage for the elderly must be made to avoid overdose.

Over-the-counter antihistamines, Dramamine, and preparations containing scopolamine are dangerous and may cause a variety of physical and psychological symptoms in the elderly (Schuckit, 1977). Other drugs that may cause adverse drug reactions include barbiturates, benzodiazepines (Valium and Librium), antidepressants (Elavil), and major tranquilizers (Thorazine). Many of these are potentiated to dangerous levels in the presence of alcohol—itself a potent drug.

Some combinations of drugs interact to produce significant and perhaps unexpected side effects (Caranasos, 1982). Combinations such as Valium for nerves and barbiturates for sleep will produce additive and possibly fatal effects at any age. In the presence of barbiturates, higher doses of anticoagulants (heparin, for example) are needed in stroke and heart disease patients to inhibit clot formation and blockage of blood vessels supplying the heart or brain. The presence of barbiturates stimulates the breakdown of the anticoagulants by the liver. Withdrawal of the barbiturates after the heparin dose has been increased to compensate for their presence may then create an overdose situation for heparin, with subsequent bleeding and prolonged clotting time. A parallel situation is found when barbiturates are given with digitalis, a drug used in cases of congestive heart failure. The presence of barbiturates (anticonvulsant and antihistamine drugs act in a similar manner) leads to an increased rate of excretion of both drugs and consequent increase in dosage requirements for digitalis. Use of diuretics or laxatives may cause dehydration and may deplete potassium ions from the body, and this loss may in turn cause paralysis, changes in the electrocardiogram, and exaggeration of the effects of digitalis. Antacids given with tetracycline antibiotics effectively neutralize the absorption of the antibiotic.

The list of such drug interactions is a long one; these are simply representative examples to illustrate the phenomenon. Complex situations are encountered when a list of drugs is prescribed and added to over long periods of time, without adequate review, as during residence in a nursing home. This situation constitutes one of the most critical problems in medical care for the elderly.

Drug Mimicry of Dementias and Other Disorders

When some drugs accumulate in the body, symptoms that mimic a variety of disorders, including dementia and organic brain syndrome, may result. In about 10 percent of patients with dementia or significant cognitive impairment, the condition is reversible. The most commonly encountered causes of such reversible conditions are reactions to medication, alcohol abuse, malnutrition, and endocrine abnormalities. Complaints of forgetfulness, confusion, loss of appetite, weakness, tremor, or anxiety may be accepted by both patient and physician as signs of aging. However, a review of the patient's medication, physical condition, and habits may reveal that the signs have other causes, and changes in these factors may make the "dementia" disappear.

Many examples of such drug effects can be given. Vitamin B12 deficiency may show up as dementia or depression before any anemia (another symptom of the deficiency) is observed. Propanolol, an antihypertensive drug, has been reported to mimic Alzheimer's disease. Organic brain syndrome (OBS) is defined as impairment due to loss of brain cell function with consequent disorientation, memory impairment, and impairment of intellectual function. Valium and barbituates are often used in long-term care facilities as a means of behavior modification and are notorious for mimicry of OBS. Symptoms disappear after the drugs are discontinued. We have already mentioned the effects of alcohol on cognitive abilities. Thyroid dysfunctions are sometimes associated with cognitive impairment. Replacement therapy (thyroxin) may prevent such damage from becoming permanent. Obviously, a thorough medical examination including tests for thyroid function, vitamin deficiency, and overall neurological function and evaluation of drugs being taken must be done before the cause and possible treatment of "dementia" are decided.

Elimination of Unnecessary Medication

It may be possible on occasion to eliminate entirely or greatly reduce the dosage of a seemingly essential drug. Digitalis intoxication, caused by excessive blood levels of digitalis, leads to a wide variety of side effects including fatigue, weakness, psychic disturbances (anxiety, bad dreams, listlessness, delirium), loss of appetite and nausea, abdominal pain, and visual complaints (hazy vision, altered colors). Many elderly patients have been treated with digitalis for congestive heart failure without adequate demonstration of heart disease. In one study (Dall, 1970) the drug was stopped in three-quarters of elderly patients receiving it without detrimental effect.

It is abundantly clear that the elderly patient is at considerable risk from overprescription of drugs without adequate review of the total number of drugs being taken, of the appropriateness of the dosages, and of the need for the drugs. It is also clear that elderly persons may abuse drugs, both prescription and over-the-counter varieties. The chances of drug-related illness and misdiagnosis of the patient's medical condition are especially high in older people (Chapter 10).

PROSTHETIC DEVICES

Prosthetic devices, allowing for complete or partial replacement of body parts and more recently of body functions, are of particular importance to older people. Some simple devices such as crutches, false teeth, artificial limbs, and eyeglasses have been with us for some time. Innovations in materials and design are being made to supplement and replace physiological functions, to increase compatibility with tissues of the body, and to improve effectiveness of physical devices. Some of these developments are far from clinically usable, but progress is being made.

Synthetic Prostheses

Examples of some replacement parts made from new synthetic materials are individual teeth that are actually incorporated into the jaw structure, corneas, and vitreous bodies to replace the inner gelatinous material of the eye that becomes opaque in patients with advanced diabetes. Total hip replacement is now a common operation.

The most common neuroprosthesis is the artificial pacemaker to correct irregular heart beat. More recent developments include electrical devices for control of bladder function, control of reflex breathing to replace defective control centers in the brain stem, control of epilepsy, and stimulation of denervated muscles using electrical activity of undamaged muscles.

Under development are prostheses designed to aid those who have lost sight and hearing. These senses are difficult to duplicate because of their natural complexity, though some progress has been made on devices designed to stimulate directly either the retina or the optical cortex of the brain to provide some sensations of vision in the blind (Dawson, 1978). Some auditory functions can be replaced by direct stimulation of the inner ear.

It has been found that skeletal muscle can be conditioned for continuous work by long-term, low frequency stimulation. Fatigue is greatly reduced. Experiments with dogs utilizing the latissimus dorsi muscle beneath the shoulder show that skeletal muscle can be conditioned to aid the heart ventricle. In these experiments skeletal muscle ventricles (SMVs) were constructed by wrapping the muscle around a hollow Teflon cone of about 20-ml volume. After a period of adaptation the Teflon cones were removed, a circulation bladder and an electronic pacemaker were implanted in each SMV, and the devices were connected to the arterial circulation. After two weeks the SMVs were generating systolic pressures comparable to the dogs' normal heart and were pumping about 20 percent of the normal cardiac output. It was suggested that SMVs could be used as auxiliary pumps to aid weakened human hearts (Acker et al., 1987).

Organ Transplants

Natural prostheses, meaning organ transplants, are possible, provided a proper donor is found and the condition of the recipient is stable enough to undergo surgery. Transplantable organs and tissues include the heart, lung, heart-lung combined, kidney, liver, pancreas, cornea, and bone marrow. Kidney transplants are unique in that the organs are paired, opening the possibility of live donors as opposed to use of cadaver material.

Organ transplantation gives the terminally ill patient a choice between life and death. Also, the life of the heart or kidney transplant patient, though limited by the possibility of graft rejection and infection, may be more acceptable than the life of the patient maintained by an artificial heart or dialysis on a kidney machine. Publicity surrounding the human recipients of artificial hearts has dramatized the many limitations of this approach. Increased successes with organ transplants are due in part to the availability of drugs that minimize graft rejection without impairing the ability of the patient to fight infection. Even so, the survival rate after five years is around one in four for most kinds of transplants.

Aside from surgical risks and rejection problems, two major problems confront potential transplant recipients. The first is availability of suitable organs. It is estimated that perhaps 2,000 Americans are potential heart transplant candidates, and some 8,000 are awaiting kidney transplants. There simply aren't enough organs to go around. The second problem is expense. A heart or liver transplant costs about $55,000. Kidney or pancreas transplants cost about $25,000. One must weigh the possibility of life extension for a period of years against the expense and other hardships of transplantation. Obviously, the drawbacks are worth it for many people.

CONCLUSIONS

In spite of the "ravages of time" and the decline of body systems with age, it is possible to preserve a degree of physical fitness through exercise. If the body remains in condition, the mind may retain much of the sharpness of younger years. Coupled with the richness of experience and wisdom that are the natural rewards of longevity, life after 60 can be enjoyable and fulfilling. Most elderly do not finish out their lives in institutions for the frail. Many older people enjoy active lives which, incidentally, contain sexual activity and romance as major factors.

Many effects of aging are minimized with regular exercise. Nutritional needs of the elderly are similar to the needs of younger adults, but fewer calories are required per day.

The so-called geroprotectors, such as vitamin E, vitamin A, vitamin C, superoxide dismustase, and urate, are found in highest concentrations in the body fluids of long-lived organisms. There is little evidence that intake of these substances beyond the minimum daily requirement increases life expectancy in humans.

Tobacco and alcohol both have harmful effects. Alcoholism is known to exist as a problem in 2 to 10 percent of those over 60 who drink.

Drug abuse and adverse reactions, which are prevalent among the elderly, may be traced to deliberate or inadvertent self-administration, unnecessary prescribed medication, incorrect dosages in prescribed medication, and harmful drug interactions.

A number of artificial prostheses that are compatible with body tissues have been developed. Organ transplants are also possible and may provide some advantages over artificial organs.

REFERENCES

Acker, M. A., R. L. Hammond, J. D. Mannion, S. Salmons, and L. W. Stephenson. Skeletal muscle as the potential power source for a cardio-vascular pump: Assessment in vivo. *Science* 236:324, 1987.

Andres, R. Aging, diabetes, and obesity: Standards of normality. *Mount Sinai Journal of Medicine* 48:489, 1981.

Barnes, G. M. Patterns of alcohol use and abuse among older persons in a household population. In W. G. Wood and M. F. Elias, eds., *Alcoholism and Aging*. CRC Press, Boca Raton, Fla., 1982.

Caranasos, G. J. Drug use in the elderly. *Journal of the Florida Medical Association* 69:294, 1982.

Cooper, K. H. *Aerobics*. Evans, New York, 1968.

Dall, J. L. C. Maintenance digoxin in elderly patients. *British Medical Journal* 2:705, 1970.

Dawson, W. W. Biocompatible prosthetic devices. In J. W. Brookbank, ed., *Improving the Quality of Health Care for the Elderly*. University of Florida Press, Gainesville, 1978.

Harris, R., et al. *Guide to Fitness After Fifty*. Plenum, New York, 1977.

Katz, M. L., and Robison, G., Jr. Lipofuscin response to the "age reversing" drug centrophenoxine in rat pigment epithelium and frontal cortex. *Journal of Gerontology* 38:525, 1983.

La Greca, A. J., R. L. Akers and J. W. Dwyer. Life events and alcohol behavior among older adults. *The Gerontologist* 28:552 1988.

Schneider, E. L., and J. D. Reed. Modulations of the aging process. In C. E. Finch and E. L. Schneider, eds., *Handbook of the Biology of Aging.* Van Nostrand Reinhold, New York, 1985.

Schuckit, M. A. Geriatric alcoholism and drug abuse. *The Gerontologist* 17:168, 1977.

Wurtman, J. J. *Eating Your Way Through Life.* Raven Press, New York, 1979.

Chapter
10

Clinical Aspects of Aging

INTRODUCTION

Years of study, both longitudinal and cross-sectional, have shown more clearly than anything else that the older people become, the more dissimilar they become. These dissimilarities are due to differences in aging rate, disease history, response to illness, and response to health care and health care professionals. The degree of disability, or lack thereof, also depends strongly on psychological and sociological factors (Besdine, 1980). It should be recognized that most elderly people enjoy relatively good health, though they may have financial or other living problems.

AGE CHANGES AND DISEASE

Factors That Do Not Change with Age

Clinically, the most important type of change may be a change in a physiological measure that is generally not affected by age. For example, the hemotocrit (Chapter 8) generally remains constant throughout life. If an elderly person is found to have a low hematocrit volume, a physician may be tempted to categorize the finding as evidence of natural aging, or "anemia of old age," and may fail to pursue the cause. The cause is most likely to be nutritional iron deficiency, vitamin B12 deficiency, or iron deficiency due to internal blood loss. The last may indicate a malignancy of the lower bowel.

Some factors that do change with age balance one another and combine to appear as no change at all. For example, testosterone level appears not to decline in healthy elderly men (Chapter 7). This results from both a drop in testosterone production and a drop in rate of destruction of testosterone. Similar phenomena may also exist for insulin.

Some changes relate to the longer time the elderly have been alive and not to any aging process per se. For example, older people have encountered a wider variety of infectious diseases which may be reflected in their antibody levels for these diseases. Cutaneous cancers may result from accumulated exposure to sunlight over the years. Since the ability to repair DNA damage due to radiation may not change with age (Chapter 5), the increased likelihood of skin cancer may relate more to passage of time than to aging (Gilchrest, Blog, and Szabo, 1979). Similarly, those who smoke cigarettes require time to accumulate a carcinogenic dose from tobacco (cigarette smoke has a low dose-response curve), pushing the appearance of pulmonary cancer into later life (Doll and Petro, 1976).

Age Changes That May Affect the Course of Disease

Some age changes diminish the severity or likelihood of some diseases. Carcinoma of the breast runs a less virulent course in postmenopausal than premenopausal women. Further, the response to hormone treatment of breast carcinoma increases with the number of years after menopause. Elderly women might be expected to enjoy a more favorable clinical course of this disease than younger women.

It is speculative, but some diseases with autoimmune bases may be less likely in old age due to the decline in T cell activity (Chapter 7). Autoimmune diseases that occur more frequently in younger individuals include systemic lupus erythematosis, myasthenia gravis, and multiple sclerosis. Alternatively, early autoimmune disease may simply be an expression of early, segmental aging in individuals genetically predisposed to it (Chapter 6).

Some aging changes enhance disease symptoms. Normal aging is accompanied by reduced pulmonary function (Chapter 8). Therefore, acute respiratory diseases, such as bacterial pneumonia, are likely to run a more severe course in elderly people. Renal impairment in later years means that loss of a kidney due to trauma, obstruction, or vascular occlusion results in more severe loss of filtration since the remaining kidney is likely to be operating at a deficit. A reduced capacity for thermoregulation makes accidental hypothermia more frequent among the elderly population. Not only may the symptoms appear under conditions of insufficient heat, but reduced body temperature may develop spontaneously without apparent cause.

Some age changes alter disease symptoms in the sense that they change the course of a disease, not just the severity of the symptoms. A prime example is the hyperglycemia of diabetes. Young diabetic subjects develop overpowering thirst to compensate for increased urine production; they may become comatose and often develop acetone bodies (ketoacidosis) as a consequence of accumulation of products of beta-oxidation of fatty acids. Elderly people in diabetic crisis may also become comatose, but they show no acetone bodies and show a strikingly elevated blood sugar due to the higher renal threshold for glucose in older people. The coma is termed hyperosmolar nonketotic. The absence of acetone bodies, which normally can be smelled on the breath, can be initially misleading.

Age Changes That Mimic Disease Symptoms

Some changes with age produce conditions that an earlier age would be symptoms of some disorder. These changes must be taken into account in order to arrive at an accurate clinical evaluation of an elderly person. For example, the increased renal threshold for glucose referred to above leads to higher blood sugar and poor performance on oral glucose tolerance tests measuring efficiency of glucose metabolism. The changes in glucose tolerance with age are so dramatic that 50 percent of individuals over 60 years would be diagnosed as diabetic if age-adjusted criteria were not employed (Davidson, 1979).

Age Changes with Direct Clinical Consequence

Some disorders seem to result from bodily changes associated with aging processes. Menopause is a natural outgrowth of aging, but leads to increased incidence of osteoporosis (Chapter 8). Cataracts of the eye lens with loss of flexibility and increasing opacity are possibly the result of posttranslational modifications of lens protein (Chapter 4). Hypertrophy of the prostate (Chapter 6) may result from accumulation of by-products of testosterone metabolism in the prostate (Geller and Albert, 1982). Among these dihydrotestosterone (DHT) accumulates as a result of decreased breakdown of DHT to other androgens; DHT is a growth factor for prostatic tissue. Enlargement of the prostate may interfere with urinary function to the point of damaging the kidneys. Most cases are treated surgically before renal involvement occurs. The problem is largely an age-related phenomenon.

Incontinence affects 5 to 15 percent of community-dwelling elderly people and 50 to 60 percent of those in nursing homes. The condition creates a doubling of required nursing time and is a major reason for the institutionalization of older people by their families. The condition is frequently treatable, but requires a thorough examination to determine cause and temporary or long-term nature. Remedies may include surgery for an enlarged prostate, drugs, or perhaps psychotherapy or behavior modification.

Age Changes That Affect Medical Assessment

There are barriers to communication with elderly people. There is a high prevalence of hearing disorders (22 percent), visual deficits (15 percent), and communication difficulties associated with mental and nervous disorders (10 percent) (Rowe and Minaker, 1985). Care during history-taking and reliance on family or friends to put the complaints in perspective may be of critical importance in assessment. Awareness of the effects of age changes on symptomology and incidence of disorders that were mentioned above and awareness of changes in overall strength and ability to move are required.

Failure to report illness in its early stages is a characteristic of many geriatric patients. A medical system that assumes that symptoms will provoke entry into it seems to be inadequate in caring for the elderly. The reasons are multiple. It is a prevalent notion in society as a whole and among the elderly in particular that old age is a time for pain and suffering and that the elderly must expect and accept disabilities. The incidence of depression is high (15 to 30 percent) among the elderly (Blazer and Williams, 1980), and a state of depression reduces interest in regaining health. The memory may also be failing to some degree in those so depressed, and the combination makes for cloudy judgment on health matters. Many older people suffer some degree of cognitive impairment and are unable to act on their own to identify symptoms and request help. The consequence of these delays is that illness is more advanced and less treatable if and when medical aid is sought.

Diagnosis and treatment are further complicated by the phenomenon of multiple illness or pathology which increases with advancing years.

LONG-TERM CARE

In spite of the fact that many elderly people are in reasonably good health, they all face the possibility of needing day-to-day care in chronic or acute phases of aging changes or disease. Some have families and the financial means to provide care in their own homes or their children's homes; many are not so fortunate. Long-term care may be continuous or intermittent, but in either case it can be very expensive. The cost of long-term care has risen in the United States from $0.5 billion in 1960 to an expected $76 billion by 1990.

Percentage at Home and in Institutions

Most elderly people in the United States live at home. Since 1966 there does not seem to have been an increase in the percentage of people aged 65 or older living in long-term care facilities (nursing homes, mental hospitals, jails, institutions for the mentally retarded); the figure stands at 5 percent. (For those over 80, 25 percent are in long-term care facilities.) In 1960, prior to health insurance legislation, about 4 percent of all older people were living in institutions (Shanas, 1978). After health legislation the percentage rose to 5 percent in 1970. The actual number of people in extended care institutions increased substantially between 1960 and 1970, but the total number of older people also increased, so the percentage stayed approximately the same. The percentages given may be somewhat misleading, since life expectancy in extended care is shorter than in the elderly population as a whole, and turnover of nursing home residents is therefore rather high. The proportion of people who are likely to spend some time in an extended care institution may be as high as 10 percent.

Medicare and Health Needs of the Aged

Medicare has not increased in any substantial way the numbers of older people in institutions nor has it had any impact on the numbers of elderly who are either bedfast or housebound. It seems to have had little effect on the overall health of the elderly segment of the population (Shanas, 1978). This is not surprising when one considers that medicare provides very limited protection against the cost of long-term illness, focusing instead on acute illness requiring immediate treatment. Medicare also has a strong bias toward providing care in hospital settings, though for the aged population home care and nursing home services are often preferable.

The Caretakers

Who are the caretakers of the elderly population? In large measure, it is their families. Data indicate that the helper in most cases is either a spouse (among those who are married) or an adult offspring or relative. These data suggest that the elderly living at home are in general a relatively healthy group and point to an area in which health services for the elderly might be expanded. Those older people who do become ill at home and their caretakers would benefit greatly from programs providing visiting nurses and family physicians.

Movement from State Hospitals

There is an increasing trend toward "deinstitutionalization" of health care for the elderly who require long-term medical supervision. First, there have been efforts to remove persons who are "only senile" from state mental hospitals to nursing care facilities or bed and board living groups. Secondly, there have been efforts to improve domiciliary care facilities in terms of medical care offered, nutrition, and physical surroundings. Finally, there are efforts to keep more elderly at home with family members, with medical care provided in the home. Much of this has become possible because of the advent of tranquilizing drugs, which have emptied mental hospitals of many chronic patients of all ages.

Quality of Nursing Home Care

Surveys of nursing home facilities have predictably revealed many substandard operations as well as many model institutions.Facilities for recreation and physical therapy are essential, as are supervisory therapists who understand the needs and limitations of older people. The problems of drug abuse and polypharmacy addressed in Chapter 8 must be assessed. The use of medication to induce tractability in residents and the "warehousing" of tranquilized patients must be eliminated. Facilities run by unscrupulous operators who provide inferior and inadequate medical treatment and supervisory care while charging maximal fees must be shut down.

Nursing homes may be classified as skilled nursing facilities, intermediate care facilities, or residential care homes. Each type has a role in caring for a specific type of geriatric patient. Discussions of areas of health care will do well to emphasize that the older population is not a homogeneous group. Those at 75 have considerably different sets of problems than those at 85 or 65. The type of care required varies accordingly. At the skilled nursing facility one would have a right to expect stringent supervision of medical problems; high standards of medical care ought to be provided at the intermediate care facility, though round-the-clock attendance by registered nurses and in-house physicians may not be required. Even though only 5 percent of elderly people find themselves permanently in such institutional situations, it is incumbent on those in authority to provide a high standard of care for them.

Residential care homes are an alternative. They can satisfy the needs of those who require daily supervision without extensive medical care and are much less expensive than nursing facilities. They vary from small, foster family arrangements to nonmedical facilities housing hundreds of people. The smaller care homes have lower staffing costs, though they may have higher food costs. Nevertheless, these smaller homes commit more resources to resident care than their larger counterparts (Mor, Gutkin, and Sherwood, 1985).

Day care centers, which can meet the needs of elderly people who require even less supervision, are beginning to appear. They are most useful for working caretakers of the older population.

In the mid 1970s a federal government survey of domiciliary care facilities (Glasscote et al., 1976) painted a grim picture of the quality of care available. Although some institutions surveyed were exemplary, others suffered to varying degrees the deficiencies listed below:

Lack of human dignity

Lack of activities

Untrained staff

Insufficient numbers of staff

Lack of control of drugs

Profiteering

Unsanitary conditions

Poor nutrition

Poor fire protection

Unnecessary use of physical and medical restraints

Negligence leading to injury or death

Lack of psychiatric care

Untrained administrators

Reprisals against complaints

Lack of dental care

One of the best ways to ensure better treatment in any facility is through frequent visits by the family of the resident. Not only does the visit cheer up the person restricted to the institution, it also makes the staff aware that someone from the outside is judging the care provided. Some institutions invite participation by family and friends of clients in monthly meetings. Since public awareness of the problems existing in some of our extended care facilities has been heightened, we might aspire to changes and improvements in the future. No item on the list of deficiences should apply to any facility.

RETIREMENT, SOME BIOMEDICAL CONSEQUENCES

The effect of retirement on life style and health is discussed here as an example of the relationship between psychosocial and biomedical factors. Though retirement is not a biological matter, it is important to consider environmental changes that have biomedical consequences.

Leisure

Among retired individuals life may suddenly seem to be composed of nothing but leisure. Assuming normal health and vigor, this may be a blessing for some. For others, whose work has been their life, such an unstructured existence may be viewed as a vacuum. It is not at all clear that a career of leisure, in the absence of work, has a positive influence on the quality of life in later years.

The 1983 amendments to the social security act are designed both to restrain growth in social security expenditures by reducing the amount of lifetime benefits to be paid to future beneficiaries and to encourage continued work by removing the work disincentives (reduced benefits in the face of a given level of earnings). The reduction in benefits is certain, but continued work is unlikely in most cases; the trend to early retirement continues. Therefore, legislated reductions in lifetime benefits may cause financial hardships among the beneficiaries who depend on social security for support, mostly surviving wives of retired workers (Boaz, 1987). Income reduction is inevitable for most retired people.

Health Problems

Retirement at any age is accompanied by an abrupt change in life style and a reduced income. This can cause severe emotional stress (Streib, 1984). This level of stress may be associated with serious physical illness and even premature death. The highest mortality rate for retired workers turns out to be the first year following retirement. This does not mean that retirement per se caused illness or death. To some extent the statistics reflect the fact that those in ill health tend to retire when the health problem affects their work. This tendency will bias the data in favor of more illness and higher mortality among retirees. Nevertheless, changes in social role do have strong health implications.

The void that sometimes accompanies unlimited leisure may lead to changes in smoking and alcohol consumption, physical fitness, dietary habits, mental activities, and participation in community activities. These changes, where they occur, may be associated with loss of a regular routine and, more importantly, with a loss of feeling useful. Many circumvent these negative impacts by doing volunteer work, continuing their education, finding hobbies, or sometimes finding new employment and new careers.

There is a growing trend for individual flexibility for retirement at early and later ages. Suggestions include retirement as a transitional process with employees allowed to diminish responsibilities before and after any regular retirement age. Another approach involves the option of temporary retirement, coupled with training, followed by a return to work in a new capacity. Perhaps the best option would be that of no retirement at all for those judged to be physically and mentally capable of continued employment; retirement would be reserved for the time when age-related decline in ability to perform in a satisfactory manner is encountered. This of course relates to the concept of functional versus chronological age.

The profound effect of life style on health status and life expectancy is now widely recognized. Continued longitudinal studies will be required to relate critical events such as retirement, death of a spouse, and changes in living arrangements and surroundings to the onset of disease states.

Because of their changing role in society and longer life span, studies on women will be of special importance. Above all, longitudinal studies emphasize the individuality of aging and the difficulty in projecting the future course of aging in a particular person.

CONCLUSIONS

Interactions between diseases and normal aging show that some age changes alter disease states, mimic disease states, diminish the impact of disease, or intensify disease symptoms.

There are changes that make diagnosis of disease in the elderly segment of the population difficult, including multiple pathologies and impaired communication with the elderly patient. Some of these same changes may lead to delays in seeking medical help.

Retirement serves as an example of the interchange between social environment, psychological well-being, and biomedical status. There are hazards to extended, unstructured leisure which may be compounded by the diminished income of retirees. Changes in habits and life style such as drinking, smoking, exercise regimen, and social role may have profound impacts on health. More flexibility is necessary to allow those who are functionally capable to work, despite their years, to remain on the job in some capacity.

Longitudinal studies have pointed out the distinctly individual patterns of aging. Extension of these studies should provide more data on the impacts of retirement on mortality and health, especially in women, whose life expectancy exceeds that of men.

We are some distance from understanding the basic nature of aging, being reasonably certain only that it seems to result from more than a single cause, that it is primarily a genetic phenomenon, and that at present we can do little about it. Chapters 9 and 10 are included to give some clues as to what can be done to improve the quality of our lives while the mystery of senescence is being unraveled.

REFERENCES

Besdine, R. Geriatric medicine. *Annual Review of Gerontology and Geriatrics* 1:135, 1980.

Blazer, J. T., and C. D. Williams. Epidemiology of dysphoria and depression in the elderly population. *American Journal of Psychiatry* 137:439, 1980.

Boaz, R. F. The 1983 amendments to the Social Security Act: Will they delay retirement? A summary of the evidence. *The Gerontologist* 27:151, 1987.

Davidson, M. B. The effect of aging on carbohydrate metabolism: A review of the English literature and a practical approach to the diagnosis of diabetes mellitus in the elderly. *Metabolism* 28:688, 1979.

Doll, R., and R. Petro. Mortality in relation to smoking: 20 years' observations on male British doctors. *British Journal of Medicine* 2:1525, 1976.

Geller, J., and J. Albert. The effect of aging on the prostate. In S. G. Korenman, ed., *Endocrine Aspects of Aging.* Elsevier Biomedical, New York, Amsterdam, 1982.

Gilchrest, B. A., F. B. Blog, and G. Szabo. Effect of aging and chronic sun exposure on melanocytes in human skin. *Journal of Investigative Dermatology* 73:219, 1979.

Glasscote, R. M., et al. *Old Folks at Homes.* Joint Information Service, APA and NIMH, Washington D.C., 1976.

Mor, V., C. E. Gutkin, and S. Sherwood. The cost of residential care homes serving elderly adults. *Journal of Gerontology* 40:164–171, 1985.

Rowe, J. W., and K. L. Minaker. Geriatric medicine. In C. E. Finch and E. L. Schneider, eds., *Handbook of the Biology of Aging.* Van Nostrand Reinhold, New York, 1985.

Shanas, E. New directions in health care for the elderly. In J. W. Brookbank, ed., *Improving the Quality of Health Care for the Elderly.* University of Florida Press, Gainesville, 1978.

Streib, G. F. Retirement: Implications for clinical practice. *American Family Physician* 29:239, 1984.

Glossary

Acetone bodies Products of fatty acid metabolism that accumulate when glucose oxidation is blocked by low insulin levels.

Adenoma A benign epithelial tumor with a glandular-like appearance.

Aldosterone A steroid hormone secreted by the adrenal cortex that stimulates sodium retention by the kidneys.

Alkaloid Any of a group of water- and alcohol-soluble derivatives of aromatic nitrogen containing bases mainly of plant origin. Many are active pharmacologically, e.g., atropine, caffeine, nicotine, belladonna.

Allele One of the possible forms of a gene found at a particular locus on a chromosome (e.g., allelic genes controlling eye color).

Amphetamine A compound related to adrenaline having activity similar to that compound, that is, stimulation of the sympathetic nervous system.

Amyloid An extracellular protein related to portions of the immunoglobulin molecule; found in plaque deposits in diverse tissues such as heart, blood vessels, brain.

Angiotensin A compound which in active form causes increases in blood pressure by constriction of the walls of arteries and arterioles; created by the action of the enzyme renin (from kidney cells) on angiotensinogen of the plasma.

Anticodon The triplet of bases in transfer RNA that matches the code on messenger RNA thus setting a particular amino acid in the synthetic sequence. Each tRNA has its specific anticodon and carries a particular amino acid.

Arteriosclerosis The general term for sclerification (hardening) of artery walls and the consequent narrowing of the lumen, both of which lead to elevated systolic pressure.

Atherosclerosis The most common form of arteriosclerosis, caused by deposition of plaque in the artery or arteriole wall.

Autoimmunity The production of humoral antibody or cellular (T cell) antibody against normal body tissues of the same individual; immunity against self.

Autonomic system That portion of the nervous system that regulates smooth muscle, cardiac muscle, and glands and operates without conscious control; composed of the sympathetic and parasympathetic divisions.

B cell A cell of the white cell series producing serum antibody and derived from bone marrow.

Baroreceptor A receptor stimulated by pressure, as in the baroreceptors in the arteries that are sensitive to systolic blood pressure.

Basal ganglia Collections of nerve cell bodies within the cerebral hemispheres involved in the control of voluntary movements.

Bowman's capsule The end of the kidney tubule reflected around the capillary knot or glomerulus.

Broca's area An area of the cerebral cortex concerned with the mechanics of speech.

Cambium Stem cells of plants located between the vascular tissues and giving rise to xylem and phloem cells.

Cancer An abnormal tissue, or tumor, derived from normal tissue and possessing enhanced growth potential; usually refers to malignant tumors, that is, growths that are invasive and usually lethal.

Cancer virus A virus capable of transforming normal cells into malignant cells.

Carcinogen A chemical capable of transforming normal cells into malignant cells.

Cardiac cycle The cycle of contraction and relaxation of the heart chambers involved in pulmonary and systemic circulation of the blood.

Cardiac output The volume of blood per minute pumped by either the right or left ventricle.

Catecholamines A group of molecules, including epinephrine, norepinephrine, and L-dopa, having effects similar to those produced by stimulation of the sympathetic nervous system

Cell fusion More properly, somatic cell fusion. The formation of hybrid somatic cells by fusion of two distinct cell lines, usually using inactivated Sendai virus particles which form bridges between adjacent cell membranes, leading to membrane fusion and cytoplasmic confluence. *See* Complementation.

Chimera A mosaic tissue or individual composed of cells derived from two or more diverse genetic backgrounds.

Cholesterol A 27-carbon steroid serving as a precursor to elements in membranes and hormones.

Chromatin The material in chromsomes including DNA, basic proteins (histones), and nonhistone chromosomal proteins; the extended form of chromosomes in mitotic interphase.

Chromosome Structures occurring in pairs in the cell nucleus carrying the genes and composed of DNA, various proteins, and nascent RNA. Each species has a characteristic number of chromosome pairs.

Clone A population of cells all derived from the same parent stem cell.

Codon One of the triplets of bases in DNA, which, when transcribed into messenger RNA, specifies a particular amino acid in the sequence coding for a polypeptide; receives the anticodon on transfer RNA bearing the specific amino acid.

Collagen A glycoprotein forming the major component of fibrous connective tissue.

Complementation The formation of a cell hybrid between parent cell lines, each of which is deficient in some cell function controlled by a gene on homologous chromosomes, such that the recessive deficiencies are corrected by the presence of the reciprocal dominant alleles.

Conjugation Cellular mating.

Contact inhibition That property of normal tissue culture cells which signals cessation of cell division when cells' membranes abut one another.

Creutzfeld-Jakob disease A transmissible disease with a virus vector which affects the central nervous system causing dementia.

Cytoplast The cytoplasm of a cell that has been enucleated.

Demography The science of vital and social statistics.

Dependency ratio The number of retired elderly divided by the number of unretired persons in the work force.

Diabetes A disease characterized by a lack of insulin and consequent inability to metabolize glucose.

Diastolic pressure The pressure in arteries during the relaxation phase of the left ventricle.

Digitalis An alkaloid derived from the foxglove causing elevation of the blood pressure through strengthening of the ventricular systole and contraction of the arterioles.

DNA Deoxyribonucleic acid, a substance found in the nucleus of the cells composed of nucleotide bases that contain the sugar deoxyribose; contains the genetic code.

DNA, reiterated DNA sequences represented by more than a single copy, including ribosomal DNA, histone gene sequences, and other sequences of unknown function which are interspersed with single-copy DNA.

DNA, single-copy Unique sequence DNA, or sequences represented only once in the genome; includes structural genes.

Dopamine A central nervous system neurotransmitter.

Down's syndrome Trisomy 21.

Elastin The major component of elastic connective tissue, as found in elastic ligaments and artery walls.

Elongation factor A factor operating on the polyribosome involved in elongation of the growing (nascent) polypeptide chain.

Endoplasmic reticulum A system of membranes within the cytoplasm of the cell. Those membranes associated with ribosomes and participating in protein synthesis are called rough endoplasmic reticulum. Those without ribosomes are smooth endoplasmic reticulum.

Eosinophyllic Having an affinity for the red dye eosin. Eosin stains primarily protein in the cell cytoplasm.

Epinephrine Also known as adrenalin. A hormone from the adrenal medulla causing, with norepinephrine from sympathetic nerve endings, increased blood pressure and pulse rate to prepare the animal for "flight or fight."

Estrogen The female sex hormone produced by cells of the ovarian follicles.

Fibroblast A cell of fibrous connective tissue.

Fibrosis Deposition of fibrous (collagen) connective tissue.

Follicle cell A cell forming the wall of the ovarian follicle (Graafian follicle) which produces estrogen.

Gene amplification The recopying or reiteration of a gene sequence in DNA, beyond the level normally encountered in somatic cells.

Germ cells Those cells set aside to become the gametes of the adult, as distinct from somatic cell lines.

Glaucoma A disease of the eye marked by intense intraocular pressure resulting in atrophy of the retina and blindness.

Glomerulus The capillary knot found within the Bowman's capsule of the kidney filtration unit.

Glycation (glycosylation) The non-enzymatic addition of glucose residues to proteins and DNA.

Hematocrit The volume of packed red blood cells in a given volume of plasma.

Heterosis Hybrid vigor, or the enhanced vitality or survival of offspring of genetic crosses between species or between inbred lines of the same species.

Histones Basic proteins found associated with DNA in chromatin.

HnRNA Heterogeneous nuclear RNA. Large molecules of RNA found as transcripts of DNA in the nucleus, some of which are processed and transported to the cytoplasm as messenger RNA and the remainder of which are turned over in the nucleus.

Hyaline Clear, transparent. A translucent nitrogenous substance found around cells.

Hydrocortisone The principal corticosteroid hormone secreted by the adrenal cortex.

Hyperglycemia Elevated blood sugar.

Hypertension Elevated blood pressure.

Hypokinetic Lower than normal level of physical activity or movement.

Hypothermia Lower than normal body temperature.

Immune globulin A protein produced by the B cells of the immune system in response to a foreign substance, or antigen; antibody.

Immune surveillance The monitoring of the body for foreign tissue (e.g., neoplasms) by the T cell series of white blood cells, specifically killer cells of the T series.

Immune tolerance The tolerance of foreign tissue or substances by an animal leading to failure to reject foreign grafts or to failure to produce antibody to the specific antigen in question.

Indeterminate growth Growth without limit.

Insulin The polypeptide hormone produced by the islets of Langerhans of the pancreas. Insulin accelerates the transport of glucose from the blood into cells, thus lowering plasma sugar levels.

Interleukin 2 A lymphotrophic hormone produced by T cells that stimulates the proliferation of both T and B cells.

Ischemic disease Disease caused by a diminishing blood supply.

Isogenic The condition of genetic identity between members of an inbred strain after many generations of brother-sister matings.

Killer cells T cells involved in immune surveillance which attack and kill neoplastic cells.

Leukemia A cancer of the white blood cells.

Leydig cell Also called interstitial cell. A cell located in clusters between the testis tubules which produces testosterone.

Ligament A mass of parallel collagen fibers that spans and strengthens a joint or supports an organ.

Lipofuscin Also called age pigment. A product of membrane oxidation.

Loop of Henle A portion of the kidney tubule of the mammalian kidney that functions to resorb water from urinary secretions.

Lysosome A membrane-bound organelle of the cytoplasm containing enzymes that is the site of intracellular digestion.

Macrophage A phagocytic white blood cell found in circulation and within tissues that also facilitates stimulus of antibody-producing cells by antigen.

Meiosis The cell divisions involved in reduction of chromosome number during the production of gametes (eggs and sperm).

Menopause The cessation of ovulation and menstruation in primate females.

Miosis Excessive contraction of the pupil of the eye.

Mitosis Cell division.

Morbidity The rate of sickness or proportion of disease to health in a community.

mRNA Messenger RNA. The transcription product of DNA that travels to the ribosome and serves as a template for the manufacture of a protein.

Mutation A change in genetic sequence, leading to an altered form of the gene at a given locus.

Necropsy Also called autopsy. A postmortem examination.

Neoblast A reserve cell or stem cell of flatworms that forms new tissues during regeneration of lost parts.

Neurofibril Intracellular microfilament found in nerve cells.

Neurohypophysis *See* Pituitary gland.

Nuclear equivalence With reference to the cells of the early embryo, the undifferentiated and interchangeable nature of the nuclei.

Nuclear transplants The introduction of a nucleus from a cell of a late embryonic stage or adult tissue into an enucleate egg. Transplantation of nuclei between two single-celled individuals.

Nucleoplast A nucleus with a halo of cytoplasm which has been isolated from the bulk of its cytoplasm.

Oncogene A gene sequence that, when activated in the adult, causes the cell containing it to become malignant, or cancerous.

Osteoblast A cell that builds bone.

Osteoclast A cell that resorbs bone.

Osteoporosis Excessive loss of bone substance leading to extremely fragile bone structure.

Parasympathetic system That portion of the autonomic nervous system utilizing acetylcholine as the neurotransmitter; antagonistic to the sympathetic system.

Parenchyma The functional elements of an organ, as distinct from the connective tissue.

Periodontal disease A disease of the mouth and jaws characterized by bone loss in tooth sockets (with consequent loosening and loss of teeth) and inflammation and necrosis of gum tissue.

Peristalsis Waves of smooth muscle contraction along the digestive tract serving to propel the contents of the intestines in one direction.

Pituitary An endocrine gland at the base of the brain consisting of two lobes: the anterior pituitary, or adenohypophysis, which secretes hormones that regulate a wide range of bodily activities, and the posterior pituitary, or neurohypophysis, which controls the release of hormones secreted by neurons in the hypothalamus.

Plaque In arteries, raised lesions composed of extracellular lipid and cell debris covered by a cap containing large numbers of smooth muscle cells, white cells, and collagen; lesions of atherosclerosis. In the brain, "senile plaque" composed of degenerating neuronal processes and amyloid.

Plasma The fluid portion of unclotted blood minus the formed, or cellular elements.

Polyadenylation The addition of adenylphosphate residues to messenger RNA.

Polysome Polyribosome. A chain of ribosomes along a molecule of messenger RNA.

Polyunsaturated fat Fat containing numerous unsaturated (double C—C) bonds.

Position effect Alteration of gene expression due to the repositioning of the gene within the genome.

Postmitotic cell A cell that has ceased to divide and is in phase G0 of the mitotic cycle.

Posttranslational modification A modification of protein molecules made after translation of messenger RNA on the polyribosome that does not involve changes in the primary sequence of amino acids in the protein.

Presbycusis Lessening of the acuteness of hearing that occurs with age.

Presbyopia Farsightedness that occurs with age due to the decreasing ability of the eye lens to accommodate to nearby objects causing the near point of distinct vision to be moved farther from the eye.

Progeria Hutchinson-Gilford syndrome. A condition characterized by the appearance of many features of old age in the early (teens) years.

Ptosis The sagging of an organ or part, especially the drooping of the eyelid.

Ptyalin A salivary enzyme involved in starch digestion.

Pulse pressure The arithmetic difference between the systolic and diastolic blood pressures.

rDNA Ribosomal DNA. A type of DNA associated with the nucleolus, coding for the RNA subunits of ribosomes.

Release hormone A hormone produced in the hypothalamus and transported to the anterior pituitary gland where it regulates the secretion of hormones by the gland.

Renin An enzyme produced by the kidney that converts angiotensinogen of the plasma to angiotensin, which acts to cause a rise in blood pressure and an increased secretion of aldosterone from the adrenal cortex.

Retina The photosensitive element of the eye, containing the rod and cone cells concerned with night and day vision respectively.

Retrovirus An RNA-containing virus that uses the host cell and the enzyme reverse transcriptase to make a DNA copy of itself. It may integrate into host genome and become a carcinogenic virus, in effect, an oncogene.

Reverse transcriptase An enzyme catalyzing the synthesis of DNA using an RNA template.

Ribosome A cytoplasmic granule of protein and ribosomal RNA which is the site for the translation of messenger RNA during protein synthesis.

RNA Ribonucleic acid, a substance found in the nucleus of cells composed of nucleotide bases that contain the sugar ribose.

RNA, heterogeneous nuclear *See* HnRNA.

RNA, messenger *See* mRNA.

RNA, ribosomal *See* rRNA.

RNA, transfer *See* tRNA.

rRNA RNA produced by the ribosomal DNA of the cell nucleolus which forms the nucleic acid portion of the ribosome.

Saturated fat Fat that has been hydrogenated so that it contains no unsaturated (double C—C) bonds.

Serotonin A molecule related to catecholamines (dopa, epinephrine), reputedly active as a neurotransmitter in the central nervous system.

Stroma The connective tissue that forms the ground substance of an organ.

Sympathetic system That portion of the autonomic system utilizing epinephrine/norepinephrine as the neurotransmitter; antagonistic to the parasympathetic system.

Synapse The junction between the axon of one neuron and the dendrite of another across which impulses are carried by neurotransmitter molecules.

Systolic pressure The pressure in the artery during the contraction phase of the left ventricle.

T cell A cell of the white blood cell series producing cellular immunity and derived during development from the thymus.

Tendon A dense connective tissue that connects a muscle to the bones of its origin and insertion.

Teratocarcinoma A malignant tumor of the primary germ cells.

Testosterone A male sex hormone (androgen) produced by the Leydig cells of the testis.

Thymus A bilobed gland that atrophies by adulthood, serves as the source of T cells, and produces hormones that stimulate T cells after they leave the thymus.

Trabecula A septum or ingrowth from the enclosing wall into the interior of a structure or organ.

Transcript processing Alterations (excision of internal and terminal sequences) made to nuclear transcripts (portions of heterogeneous nuclear RNA) before they are exported to the cytoplasm.

Transcription The synthesis of RNA from a DNA template.

Translation Protein synthesis, utilizing the sequence information found in messenger RNA.

Triglyceride A fat composed of glycerol esterified with fatty acids.

tRNA Transfer RNA. RNA that transports activated amino acids to the specific site on the polyribosome messenger RNA designated by the anticodon of the transfer RNA.

X chromosome The sex chromosome. Female determining in the absence of a Y chromosome in humans.

Y chromosome The heteromorphic male sex chromosome; the chromosome that determines maleness in mammals.

Zygote The cell formed by the fusion of two gametes.

Index

ISBN 0-06-041019-1

90000

9 780060 410193